BASIC English Grammar

FOURTH EDITION

VOLUME A with Audio

Betty S. Azar
Stacy A. Hagen

Basic English Grammar, Fourth Edition
Volume A with Audio

Azar Associates: Shelley Hartle, Editor, and Sue Van Etten, Manager

Pearson Education, 10 Bank Street, White Plains, NY 10606

Staff credits: The people who made up the ***Basic English Grammar, Fourth Edition, Volume A*** team, representing editorial, production, design, and manufacturing, are, Dave Dickey, Nancy Flaggman, Amy McCormick, Robert Ruvo, and Marian Wassner.

Text composition: S4Carlisle Publishing Services

Illustrations: Don Martinetti—pages 5, 6, 8, 9, 17, 18, 19, 21, 22, 26, 29, 31, 33, 34, 36, 40, 41, 45, 46, 47, 48, 50, 51, 52, 53, 54, 59, 61, 63, 64, 69, 71, 74, 77, 78, 79, 81, 85, 89, 90, 91, 99, 101, 103, 106, 112, 114, 117, 125, 126, 129, 130, 133, 135, 139, 142, 143, 144, 146, 147, 153, 154, 155, 156, 162, 164, 171, 172, 173, 180, 184, 187, 188, 191, 192, 193, 197, 200, 202, 203, 204, 206, 207, 208, 210, 211, 212, 213, 214, 216, 217, 219, 220, 221, 222, 223, 228, 229, 230, 234, 237, 256, 258, 260, 262

Chris Pavely—pages 1, 3, 13, 14, 15, 16, 21, 32, 35, 38, 39, 43, 44, 49, 52, 62, 67, 68, 75, 79, 81, 88, 92, 95, 96, 98, 102, 103, 104, 105, 107, 108, 109, 120, 124, 148, 149, 151, 158, 161, 169, 173, 174, 175, 178, 181, 185, 189, 216, 236, 241, 247, 250, 252, 255, 259

Printed in the United States of America

ISBN 10: 0-13-294229-1
ISBN 13: 978-0-13-294229-4

1 2 3 4 5 6 7 8 9 10—V057—19 18 17 16 15 14

To Shelley Hartle

For her watchful eye, her vast expertise, her indefatigable good cheer

Contents

Preface to the Fourth Edition

Basic English Grammar is a developmental skills text for beginning English language learners. It uses a grammar-based approach integrated with communicative methodologies to promote the development of all language skills in a variety of ways. Starting from a foundation of understanding form and meaning, students engage in meaningful communication about real actions, real things, and their own lives in the classroom context. Grammar tasks are designed to encourage both fluency and accuracy.

The eclectic approach and abundant variety of exercise material remain the same as in the earlier editions, but this fourth edition incorporates new ways and means. In particular:

- **CORPUS-INFORMED CONTENT**
  Based on corpus research, grammar content has been added, deleted, or modified to reflect discourse patterns. New information highlighting differences between spoken and written English has been added to the charts, and students practice more frequently used structures. We have been careful to keep the information manageable for beginning students.

- **PRESENTATION OF KEY GRAMMAR**
  Chapter 15 (in earlier editions of *BEG*) has been moved to Chapter 6 of this edition in order to teach possessive forms earlier and present all pronouns together.

- **WARM-UP EXERCISES FOR THE GRAMMAR CHARTS**
  Newly created for the fourth edition, these innovative exercises precede the grammar charts and introduce the point(s) to be taught. They have been carefully crafted to help students *discover* the target grammar as they progress through each warm-up exercise. The warm-up exercises can help the teacher assess how much explanation and practice students will need.

- **MICRO-PRACTICE**
  At the beginning level, a single grammar structure (e.g. basic pronouns and possessives) sometimes needs to be presented in several steps. Additional exercises have been created to give students more incremental practice.

- **LISTENING PRACTICE**
  Recent research highlights the importance of helping students at all levels understand authentic spoken English. New as well as revised exercises introduce students to relaxed, reduced speech. An audio CD accompanies the student text, and a full audio script can be found in the back of the book.

- **READINGS**
  This fourth edition now has a wide selection of readings for students to read and respond to. The content is carefully controlled so that the vocabulary is accessible to beginning students and the grammar structures appropriate to the chapter(s) studied.

- **WRITING TASKS**
  New writing tasks help students naturally produce the target grammar structures in extended discourse. These end-of-chapter activities include writing models for students to follow. Editing checklists draw students' attention to the grammar focus and help them develop proofreading skills.

Basic English Grammar is accompanied by

- A comprehensive ***Workbook,*** consisting of self-study exercises for independent work.
- An all-new ***Teacher's Guide,*** with step-by-step teaching suggestions for each chart, notes to the teacher on key grammar structures, vocabulary lists, and expansion activities.
- An expanded ***Test Bank,*** with additional quizzes, chapter tests, mid-terms, and final exams.
- ***ExamView*** software that allows teachers to customize their own tests using quizzes and tests from the ***Test Bank.***
- ***AzarGrammar.com,*** a website that provides a variety of supplementary classroom materials, *PowerPoint* presentations for all chapters, and a place where teachers can support each other by sharing their knowledge and experience.

The Student Book is available with or without an answer key in the back. Homework can be corrected as a class or, if appropriate, students can correct it at home with the answer key and bring questions to class. In some cases, the teacher may want to collect the assignments written on a separate piece of paper, correct them, and then highlight common problems in class.

The Azar-Hagen Grammar Series consists of

- *Understanding and Using English Grammar* (blue cover), for upper-level students.
- *Fundamentals of English Grammar* (black cover), for mid-level students.
- *Basic English Grammar* (red cover), for lower or beginning levels.

Tips for Using the New Features in this Text

Warm-Ups

The ***Warm-Up*** exercises are a brief pre-teaching tool for the charts. They highlight the key point(s) that will be introduced in the chart directly following the ***Warm-Up*** exercise. Before beginning the task, teachers will want to familiarize themselves with the material in the chart. Then, with the teacher's guidance, students can discover many or all of the new patterns while completing the ***Warm-Up*** activity. After students finish the exercise, teachers may find that no further explanation is necessary, and the charts can then serve as a useful reference.

Listening

The ***Listening*** exercises have been designed to help students understand American English as it is actually spoken. As such, they include reductions and other phenomena that are part of the natural, relaxed speech of everyday English. Because the pace of speech in the audio may be faster than what students are used to, they may need to hear sentences two or three times as they complete a task.

The ***Listening*** exercises do not encourage immediate pronunciation (unless they are linked to a specific pronunciation task). Receptive skills precede productive ones, and it is essential that students gain receptive familiarity with the speech patterns before they begin using them in their own speech.

Students are encouraged to listen to conversations the first time without looking at their text. Teachers can explain any vocabulary that has not already been clarified. During the second listening, students complete the assigned task. Teachers will want to pause the audio appropriately. Depending on the level of the class, pauses may be needed after every sentence, or even within a sentence.

It is inevitable that sound representations in the text will at times differ from the instructor's speech, whether due to register or regional variation. A general guideline is that if the instructor expects students will *hear* a variation, or if students themselves raise questions, alternate representations can be presented.

A ***Listening Script*** is included in the back of the book.

Reading

The ***Readings*** give students an opportunity to work with the grammar structures in extended contexts. Vocabulary that may be new to students is presented on yellow notes for teachers to introduce. One approach to the reading is to have students read the passage independently the first time through. Then they work in small groups or as a class to clarify vocabulary questions that didn't come up in the notes. A second reading may be necessary. Varied reading tasks allow students to check their comprehension, use the target structures, and expand upon the topic in speaking or writing.

Writing

As students gain confidence in using the target structures, they are encouraged to express their ideas in longer writing tasks. Model paragraphs accompany assignments, and question-prompts help students develop their ideas.

Editing checklists provide guidance for self- or peer-editing. One suggested technique is to pair students, have them exchange papers, and then have the *partner* read the paragraph aloud. The writer can *hear* if the content is what he or she intended. This also keeps the writer from automatically self-correcting while reading aloud. The partner can then offer comments and complete the checklist.

For classes that have not had much experience with writing, the teacher may want students to complete the task in small groups. The group composes a paragraph together, which the teacher then collects and marks by calling attention to beginning-level errors, but not correcting them. The teacher makes a copy for each group member, and each student makes the corrections *individually*.

LET'S TALK

Each ***Let's Talk*** activity is set up as one of the following: **Pairwork**, **Small Group**, **Class Activity**, **Interview**, or **Game**. Language learning is a social activity, and these tasks encourage students to speak with others about their ideas, their everyday lives, and the world around them. Students speak more easily and freely when they can connect language to their own knowledge and experiences.

CHECK YOUR KNOWLEDGE

Toward the end of the chapter, students can practice sentence-level editing skills by correcting errors common to this level. They can work on the sentences for homework or in small groups in class.

This task can easily be set up as a game. The teacher calls out an item number at random. Students work in teams to correct the sentence, and the first team to correctly edit it wins a point.

Please see the ***Teacher's Guide*** for detailed information about teaching from this book, including expansion activities and step-by-step instructions.

Acknowledgments

Our revision began with extensive reviews from many talented professionals. We are grateful for the expertise of the following teachers: Susan Boland, Tidewater Community College; Lee Chen, Palomar College; Gene Hahn, University of Wisconsin, Stevens Point; Kathleen Keeble, Illinois Institute of Art, Chicago; Steven Lasswell, Santa Barbara City College; Michael Pitts, Los Angeles Southwest College; Carla Reible, Riverside City College; Alison Rice, Hunter College; Maria S. Roche, Housatonic Community College; Nelky Rodriguez, Riverside Community College; John Stasinopoulos, College of DuPage; Hallie Wallack, International Language Institute; Robert L. Woods, Central Washington University.

We were assisted throughout the process by a skilled and dedicated editorial staff. We would like to thank Shelley Hartle, managing editor, for her passion for the series and gifted editing and layout skills; Amy McCormick, editorial director, for guiding the project with exceptional judgment, attentiveness, and foresight; Marian Wassner, senior development editor (and grammar master), for her superb editing and thoughtful responses; Robert Ruvo, production manager, for his deft project management, keen eye for design, and unfailing good humor; Janice Baillie, copy-editor, for her stellar editing and remarkable ability to track all manner of detail; Sue Van Etten, business and website manager, for her expert and dedicated counsel.

We'd also like to express our appreciation to the writers of the supplementary texts: Kelly Roberts Weibel, *Test Bank* and Martha Hall, *Teacher's Guide.* Their creative and fresh ideas greatly enrich the series.

Finally, our thanks to our committed leadership team at Pearson Education who oversaw the entire revision: Pietro Alongi, Rhea Banker, and Paula Van Ells.

We are grateful for the artistic talents of Don Martinetti and Chris Pavely — their colorful work brightens every chapter.

Our families, as always, support and encourage our work. They truly inspire us every day.

Betty S. Azar
Stacy A. Hagen

Chapter 1
Using Be

❑ **Exercise 1. Let's talk: class activity.** (Chart 1-1)
Introduce yourself to six classmates. Use this model.

Hi, I am ________________.
(name)

I am from ____________________.
(country or city)

I speak ________________.
(language)

Write down information about six classmates you talk to.

FIRST NAME	COUNTRY OR CITY	LANGUAGE

❑ **Exercise 2. Warm-up.** (Chart 1-1)
Read the sentences and circle *yes* or *no*.

1. He is happy. yes no
2. She is sad. yes no
3. I am happy. yes no

1-1 Singular Pronouns + *Be*

PRONOUN + *BE* (a) *I* *am* late. (b) *You* *are* late. (c) *She* *is* late. (d) *He* *is* late. (e) *It* *is* late.	*Singular* means "one." ***I, you, she, he,*** and ***it*** in (a)—(e) refer to one person. *am, are, is* = forms of ***be***
(f) *Maria* is late. ↓ *She* is late.	Pronouns refer to nouns. In (f): ***She*** (feminine) = Maria
(g) *Tom* is late. ↓ *He* is late.	In (g): ***He*** (masculine) = Tom
(h) *Bus 10* is late. ↓ *It* is late.	In (h): ***It*** = Bus 10

❑ **Exercise 3. Looking at grammar.** (Chart 1-1)
Write the correct pronoun: ***he, she,*** or ***it***. Some items have two answers.

1. Mary ___*she*___
2. David __________
3. Mr. Smith __________
4. Canada __________
5. Dr. Jones __________
6. Ms. Wilson __________
7. Professor Lee __________
8. English __________
9. Robert __________
10. Miss Allen __________

❑ **Exercise 4. Looking at grammar.** (Chart 1-1)
Complete the sentences with ***am, is,*** or ***are***.

1. He ___*is*___ here.
2. You __________ late.
3. It __________ ready.
4. She __________ early.
5. I __________ hot.
6. He __________ cold.

❑ Exercise 5. Let's talk. (Chart 1-1)

Part I. Check (✓) all the words that are true for you right now.

I am . . .

1. ____ happy.	6. ____ sad.
2. ____ hot.	7. ____ cold.
3. ____ nice.	8. ____ nervous.
4. ____ hungry.	9. ____ sick.
5. ____ tired.	10. ____ funny.

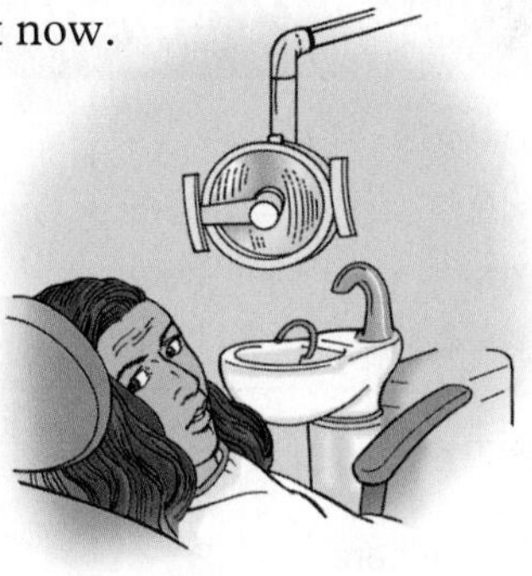

She is nervous.

He is hungry.

She is tired.

Part II. Share some sentences with a partner: "I am ____."

Part III. Tell the class a few things about your partner: "He is ____." OR "She is ____."

❑ Exercise 6. Warm-up. (Chart 1-2)

Circle the correct answer. One sentence has two answers.

How many people?

1. We are ready.	one	two, three, or more
2. You are ready.	one	two, three, or more
3. They are ready.	one	two, three, or more

1-2 Plural Pronouns + *Be*

PRONOUN + *BE*	
(a) *We* *are* here. (b) *You* *are* here. (c) *They* *are* here.	*Plural* means "two, three, or more." ***We***, ***you***, and ***they*** in (a)—(c) refer to two, three, or more persons.
(d) Sam and I are here. ↓ *We* are here.	In (d): ***We*** = Sam and I
(e) Sam and you are here. ↓ *You* are here.	In (e): ***You*** = Sam and you NOTE: ***You*** can be singular or plural.
(f) Sam and Lisa are here. ↓ *They* are here.	In (f): ***They*** = Sam and Lisa

❑ **Exercise 7. Looking at grammar.** (Chart 1-2)
Choose the correct pronoun.

1. Lee and Bill (they) we
2. Alice and I they we
3. Mr. and Mrs. Martin and I they we
4. you and Dr. Taher they you
5. Tony and she they we
6. Tony and you they you

❑ **Exercise 8. Looking at grammar.** (Charts 1-1 and 1-2)
Complete the sentences with ***am***, ***is***, or ***are***.

1. We ___*are*___ ready.
2. I ________ late.
3. He ________ happy.
4. They ________ sick.
5. She ________ homesick.
6. Abdul and Taka ________ homesick.
7. You (one person) ________ funny.
8. You (two persons) ________ early.
9. You and I ________ ready.
10. It ________ hot.
11. Sara and I ________ late.
12. You and Emily ________ tired.

❑ **Exercise 9. Looking at grammar.** (Charts 1-1 and 1-2)
Make complete sentences.

1. He \ here *He is here.*
2. They \ absent ______
3. She \ sick ______
4. I \ homesick ______
5. You and I \ homesick ______
6. We \ late ______
7. Jack \ hungry ______
8. You (one person) \ early ______
9. You (two persons) \ early ______
10. Mr. and Mrs. Nelson \ late ______
11. Amy and I \ late ______

❑ **Exercise 10. Warm-up.** (Chart 1-3)
Read the sentences and circle *yes* or *no*.

1. Canada is a country.	yes	no
2. Toronto is a city.	yes	no
3. Vancouver is an island.	yes	no

1-3 Singular Nouns + *Be*

NOUN + *IS* + NOUN (a) ***Canada is a country.*** *INCORRECT: Canada is country.*	In (a): ***Canada*** = a singular noun ***is*** = a singular verb ***country*** = a singular noun ***A*** frequently comes in front of singular nouns. In (a): ***a*** comes in front of the singular noun ***country***. ***A*** is called an "article."
(b) Bali is ***an*** island. *INCORRECT: Bali is island.*  an island	***A*** and ***an*** have the same meaning. They are both articles. ***A*** is used in front of words that begin with consonants: *b, c, d, f, g, etc.* Examples: *a bed, a cat, a dog, a friend, a girl* ***An*** is used in front of words that begin with the vowels *a, e, i,* and *o.** Examples: *an animal, an ear, an island, an office* 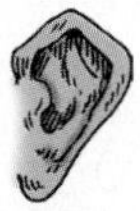 an ear

* ***An*** is sometimes used in front of words that begin with *u*. See Chart 7-2, p. 196.
Vowels = a, e, i, o, u
Consonants = b, c, d, f, g, h, j, k, l, m, n, p, q, r, s, t, v, w, x, y, z

❑ Exercise 11. Looking at grammar. (Chart 1-3)

Write ***a*** or ***an***.

1. ___*a*___ town
2. ________ city
3. ________ island
4. ________ place
5. ________ street
6. ________ avenue
7. ________ ocean
8. ________ continent

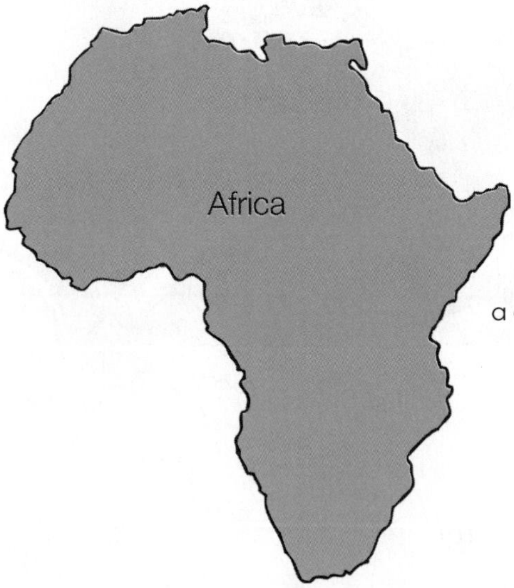

a continent

❑ Exercise 12. Vocabulary and grammar. (Chart 1-3)

Part I. Put the words from the box in the correct column. Some words go in two places.

✓ Arabic	Cuba	Hawaii	Mexico	Russia	Spanish
✓ Beijing	France	Japanese	Moscow	Russian	Taiwan
Chinese	French	Lima	Paris	Saudi Arabia	Tokyo

COUNTRY	LANGUAGE	CITY	ISLAND
	Arabic	*Beijing*	

Part II. Work in small groups. Check your answers. Finish the chart with your own choices. Your teacher will help you. Take turns making sentences. Share some of your sentences with the class.

Example: France, Japanese
STUDENT A: France is a country.
STUDENT B: Japanese is a language.

❑ Exercise 13. Warm-up. (Chart 1-4)

Complete the sentences with ***a book*** or ***books***. What do you notice about the verbs in red?

1. A dictionary is ________________.
2. Textbooks are ________________.
3. Dictionaries and textbooks are ________________.

1-4 Plural Nouns + *Be*

NOUN + *ARE* + NOUN (a) *Cats* *are* *animals*.	***Cats*** = a plural noun ***are*** = a plural verb ***animals*** = a plural noun
(b) SINGULAR: a cat, an animal PLURAL: *cats*, *animals*	Plural nouns end in **-s**. ***A*** and ***an*** are used only with singular nouns.
(c) SINGULAR: a city, a country PLURAL: cit*ies*, countr*ies*	Some singular nouns that end in **-y** have a special plural form: They omit the **-y** and add ***-ies***.*
NOUN and NOUN + *ARE* + NOUN (d) *Canada and China are countries.* (e) *Dogs and cats are animals.*	Two nouns connected by ***and*** are followed by ***are***. In (d): ***Canada*** is a singular noun. ***China*** is a singular noun. They are connected by ***and***. Together they are plural, i.e., "more than one."

*See Chart 3-5, p. 69, for more information about adding ***-s/-es*** to words that end in ***-y***.

❑ Exercise 14. Looking at grammar. (Charts 1-3 and 1-4)

Look at each noun. Is it singular or plural? Choose the correct answer.

1. animals — one — two or more
2. a dog — one — two or more
3. a city — one — two or more
4. cities — one — two or more
5. an island — one — two or more
6. languages — one — two or more
7. a country — one — two or more

❑ Exercise 15. Looking at grammar. (Charts 1-3 and 1-4)

Write the plural form.

1. a book ___*books*___
2. a textbook ____________
3. a pencil ____________
4. an eraser ____________
5. a pen ____________
6. a dictionary ____________

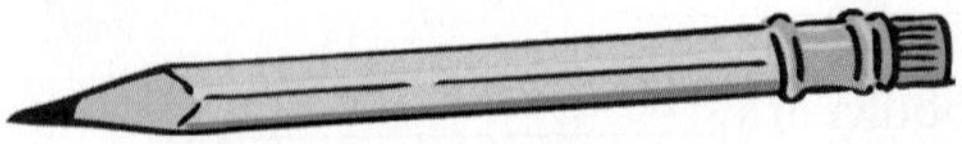

❑ Exercise 16. Looking at grammar. (Charts 1-3 and 1-4)

Complete the sentences. Use ***a*** or ***an*** and the words from the box.

animal	country	language
city	island	sport

1. A bird is ___an animal___. Birds and cats are ___animals___.
2. Tennis is __________. Tennis and soccer are __________.
3. Chicago is __________. Chicago and Berlin are __________.
4. Spanish is __________. Spanish and Italian are __________.
5. Mexico is __________. Mexico and Brazil are __________.
6. A cow is __________. Cows and horses are __________.
7. Hawaii is __________. Hawaii and Taiwan are __________.

❑ Exercise 17. Looking at grammar. (Charts 1-3 and 1-4)

Change the singular sentences to plural sentences.

SINGULAR		PLURAL
1. A chicken is an animal.	→	*Chickens are animals.*

a chicken

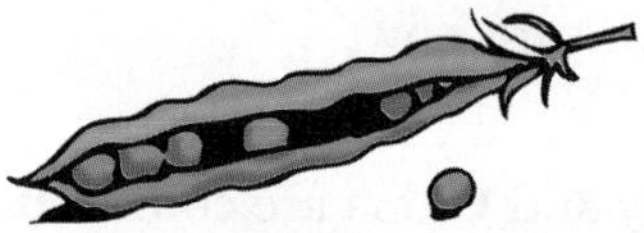

a pea

2. A pea is a vegetable.	→	__________
3. A dictionary is a book.	→	__________
4. An airplane is a machine.	→	__________
5. June is a month. July is a month.	→	__________
6. Winter is a season. Summer is a season.	→	__________
7. Egypt is a country. Indonesia is a country.	→	__________

❑ Exercise 18. Game. (Charts 1-3 and 1-4)

Work in teams. Your teacher will say the beginning of a sentence. As a team, finish the sentence and write it down. The team with the most correct sentences wins the game. Close your book for this activity.

Example:
TEACHER: Spanish . . .
TEAM A: Spanish is a language.

1. A dog . . .
2. Arabic . . .
3. London . . .
4. Summer . . .
5. September and October . . .
6. Mexico and Canada . . .
7. An airplane . . .
8. Winter and summer . . .
9. Peas . . .
10. A car . . .

❑ Exercise 19. Let's talk: pairwork. (Charts 1-3 and 1-4)

Your partner will ask you to name something. Answer in a complete sentence. You can look at your book before you speak. When you speak, look at your partner.

Example:

PARTNER A	PARTNER B
1. a country	1. two countries

PARTNER A: Name a country.
PARTNER B: Brazil is a country.
PARTNER A: Good. Brazil is a country.
Your turn now.

PARTNER B: Name two countries.
PARTNER A: Italy and China are countries.
PARTNER B: Right. Italy and China are countries.
Your turn now.

Remember: You can look at your book before you speak. When you speak, look at your partner.

PARTNER A	PARTNER B
1. a language 2. two languages 3. a machine 4. an animal 5. two seasons	1. two cities 2. an island 3. two countries in Asia 4. a vegetable 5. a street in this city

❑ Exercise 20. Warm-up: listening. (Chart 1-5)

CD 1 Track 2

Listen to the conversation. Notice the words in red. Do you know the long form for them?

A: Hi. My name is Mrs. Smith. I'm the substitute teacher.
B: Hi. I'm Franco.
C: Hi. I'm Lisa. We're in your class.
A: It's nice to meet you.
B: We're glad to meet you too.

1-5 Contractions with *Be*

	PRONOUN + *BE* → CONTRACTION					When people speak, they often push two words together.
AM	*I*	+ *am*	→	***I'm***	(a) ***I'm*** a student.	*A contraction* = two words that are pushed together
IS	*she*	+ *is*	→	***she's***	(b) ***She's*** a student.	Contractions of a *subject pronoun* + **be** are used in both speaking and writing.
	he	+ *is*	→	***he's***	(c) ***He's*** a student.	
	it	+ *is*	→	***it's***	(d) ***It's*** a city.	
ARE	*you*	+ *are*	→	***you're***	(e) ***You're*** a student.	PUNCTUATION: The mark in the middle of a contraction is called an "apostrophe" (').*
	we	+ *are*	→	***we're***	(f) ***We're*** students.	
	they	+ *are*	→	***they're***	(g) ***They're*** students.	

*NOTE: Write an apostrophe above the line. Do not write an apostrophe on the line.

CORRECT: *I'm a student*.

INCORRECT: *I,m a student*.

❑ Exercise 21. Looking at grammar. (Chart 1-5)

Write the contractions.

1. I am *I'm*
2. she is ________
3. you are ________
4. we are ________
5. it is ________
6. they are ________
7. he is ________

❑ Exercise 22. Looking at grammar. (Chart 1-5)

Write the long form for each contraction.

1. They're sick. *They are* sick.
2. He's absent. ________ absent.
3. It's hot. ________ hot.
4. I'm late. ________ late.
5. She's hungry. ________ hungry.
6. We're students. ________ students.
7. You're here. ________ here.

☐ Exercise 23. Looking at grammar. (Chart 1-5)

Complete the sentences with pronouns. Use contractions.

1. *Sara* is a student. ____She's____ in my class.
2. *James* is a student. ______________ in my class.
3. *I* am at school. ______________ in the cafeteria.
4. *Yuri and Anna* are absent. ______________ at home.
5. *Anna* is from Russia. ______________ nice.
6. *Ali and I* are in the same class. ______________ friends.
7. *Yuri, Ali, and Anna* are friends. ______________ funny.

☐ Exercise 24. Listening. (Chart 1-5)

CD 1
Track 3

Part I. Listen to the conversation. Write the contractions.

A: Hello. ___I'm___ (1) Mrs. Brown. ________ (2) the substitute teacher.

B: Hi. ________ (3) Paulo, and this is Marie. ____________ (4) in your class.

A: ________ (5) nice to meet you.

B: ____________ (6) happy to meet you too.

A: ________ (7) time for class. Please take a seat.

Part II. Listen to the conversation again and check your answers.

☐ Exercise 25. Warm-up: pairwork. (Chart 1-6)

Work with a partner. Complete the sentences with <u>all</u> the words from the box that are true. Share a few of your answers with the class.

a baby	a husband	a teacher
a bird	a student	a wife

1. I'm not ______________________________________.
2. You're not ______________________________________.

1-6 Negative with *Be*

	CONTRACTIONS	
(a) I ***am not*** a teacher.	I***'m not***	***Not*** makes a sentence negative.
(b) You ***are not*** a teacher.	you***'re not*** / you ***aren't***	CONTRACTIONS ***Be*** and ***not*** can be contracted.
(c) She ***is not*** a teacher.	she***'s not*** / she ***isn't***	Note that "I am" has only one contraction with ***be***, as in (a), but there are two contractions with ***be*** for (b)—(h).
(d) He ***is not*** a teacher.	he***'s not*** / he ***isn't***	
(e) It ***is not*** a city.	it***'s not*** / it ***isn't***	
(f) We ***are not*** teachers.	we***'re not*** / we ***aren't***	
(g) You ***are not*** teachers.	you***'re not*** / you ***aren't***	
(h) They ***are not*** teachers.	they***'re not*** / they ***aren't***	

❑ **Exercise 26. Looking at grammar.** (Chart 1-6)
Complete the sentences with the negative form of ***be***.

an astronaut

FULL FORM	CONTRACTION
1. I *am not* an astronaut.	I *'m not* an astronaut.
2. He ______ an astronaut.	He ______ an astronaut. OR He ______ an astronaut.
3. They ______ astronauts.	They ______ astronauts. OR They ______ astronauts.
4. You ______ an astronaut.	You ______ an astronaut. OR You ______ an astronaut.
5. She ______ an astronaut.	She ______ an astronaut. OR She ______ an astronaut.
6. We ______ astronauts.	We ______ astronauts. OR We ______ astronauts.

❑ Exercise 27. Looking at grammar. (Charts 1-5 and 1-6)

Make sentences with ***is, isn't, are,*** and ***aren't.***

Examples: Africa \ city . . . It \ continent

Africa isn't a city. It's a continent.

Baghdad and Chicago \ city . . . They \ continent

Baghdad and Chicago are cities. They aren't continents.

1. Canada \ country . . . It \ city

   ____

2. Argentina \ city . . . It \ country

   ____

3. Beijing and London \ city . . . They \ country

   ____

4. Asia \ country . . . It \ continent

   ____

5. Asia and South America \ continent . . . They \ country

   ____

❑ Exercise 28. Vocabulary and listening. (Charts 1-3 and 1-6)

Part I. Write ***a*** or ***an***.

1.	*a*	mother	8.	______	son
2.	______	mom	9.	______	aunt
3.	______	father	10.	______	uncle
4.	______	dad	11.	______	parent
5.	______	sister	12.	______	adult
6.	______	brother	13.	______	child
7.	______	daughter			

Peterson Family Tree

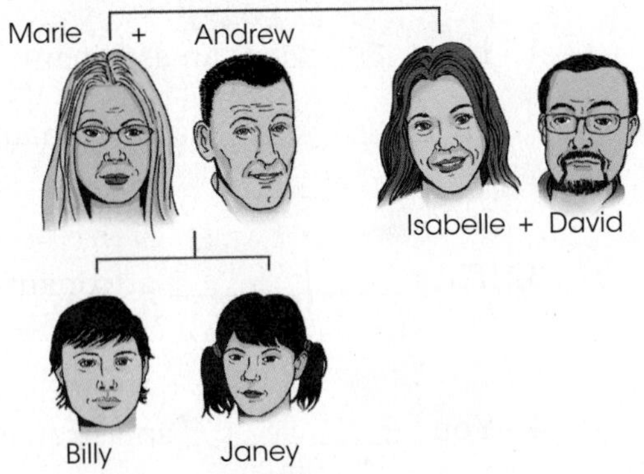

Part II. Listen to the sentences. Choose the correct answer. *Note:* in spoken English, the "t" in negative contractions may be hard to hear.

CD 1 Track 4

1. is	isn't	3. is	isn't	5. are	aren't	7. are	aren't
2. is	isn't	4. is	isn't	6. are	aren't	8. are	aren't

❑ **Exercise 29. Looking at grammar.** (Charts 1-5 and 1-6)

Paul Cox

Gloria Perez

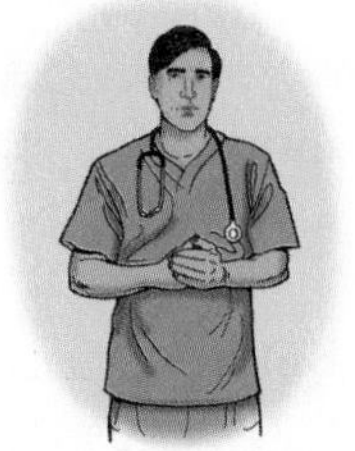
Nurse Lars Jensen

Rick Hayes

Jennifer Evans

Dr. Sana Gupta

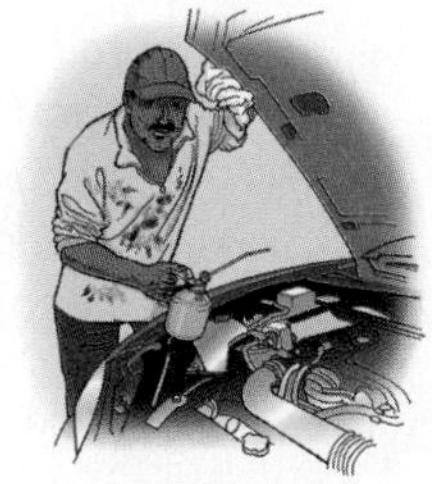
Omar Khan

Joe Davis

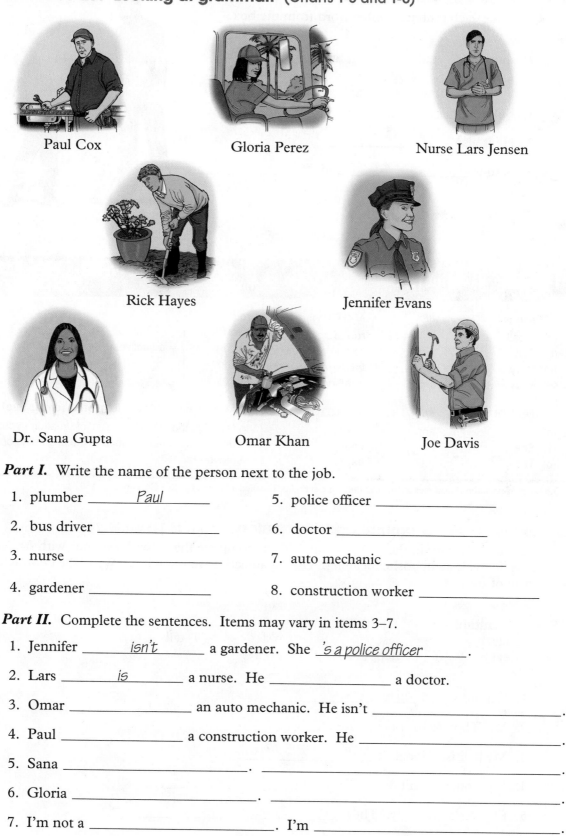

Part I. Write the name of the person next to the job.

1. plumber ____Paul____
2. bus driver ____________
3. nurse ____________
4. gardener ____________
5. police officer ____________
6. doctor ____________
7. auto mechanic ____________
8. construction worker ____________

Part II. Complete the sentences. Items may vary in items 3–7.

1. Jennifer ____isn't____ a gardener. She ____'s a police officer____.
2. Lars ____is____ a nurse. He ____________ a doctor.
3. Omar ____________ an auto mechanic. He isn't ____________.
4. Paul ____________ a construction worker. He ____________.
5. Sana ____________. ____________.
6. Gloria ____________. ____________.
7. I'm not a ____________. I'm ____________.

❑ **Exercise 30. Warm-up.** (Chart 1-7)
Complete each sentence with a word from the box.

short	tall	young	old

1. Bill is ______________.
2. He is also ______________.
3. Sam is ______________ and ______________.

1-7 *Be* + Adjective

NOUN +	*BE* +	ADJECTIVE	
(a) A ball	is	***round***.	*round*
(b) Balls	are	***round***.	*intelligent*
(c) Mary	is	***intelligent***.	*hungry* } = adjectives
(d) Mary and Tom	are	***intelligent***.	*young*
			happy
PRONOUN +	*BE* +	ADJECTIVE	Adjectives often follow a form of **be** *(am, is, are)*. In (a)—(g), the adjectives give information about a noun or pronoun that comes at the beginning of a sentence.*
(e) I	am	***hungry***.	
(f) She	is	***young***.	
(g) They	are	***happy***.	

*The noun or pronoun that comes at the beginning of a sentence is called a "subject." See Chart 6-1, p. 159.

❑ **Exercise 31. Grammar and vocabulary.** (Charts 1-5 and 1-7)
Find the adjective in the first sentence. Then complete the second sentence with ***be*** + *an adjective* with an opposite meaning. Use an adjective from the box. Write the contracted form of ***be***.

beautiful	expensive	noisy	short
clean	fast	old	tall
easy	✓happy	poor	

1. I'm not sad. I *'m happy*.
2. Mr. Thomas isn't rich. He ______________.
3. My hair isn't long. It ______________.
4. My clothes aren't dirty. They ______________.
5. Flowers aren't ugly. They ______________.

6. Cars aren't cheap. They ______________________.
7. Airplanes aren't slow. They ______________________.
8. Grammar isn't difficult. It ______________________.
9. My sister isn't short. She ______________________.
10. My grandparents aren't young. They ______________________.
11. The classroom isn't quiet. It ______________________.

❑ **Exercise 32. Grammar and vocabulary.** (Charts 1-3, 1-4, and 1-7)
Complete each sentence with ***is*** or ***are*** and an adjective from the box.

cold	flat	important	small/little	sweet
dangerous	funny	large/big	sour	wet
dry	✓ hot	round	square	

1. Fire ___*is hot*___.
2. Ice and snow ______________________.
3. A box ______________________.
4. Balls and oranges ______________________.
5. Sugar ______________________.
6. An elephant ______________________, but a mouse ______________________.
7. A rain forest ______________________, but a desert ______________________.
8. A joke ______________________.
9. Good health ______________________.
10. Guns aren't safe. They ______________________.
11. A coin ______________________ small, round, and ______________________.
12. A lemon ______________________.

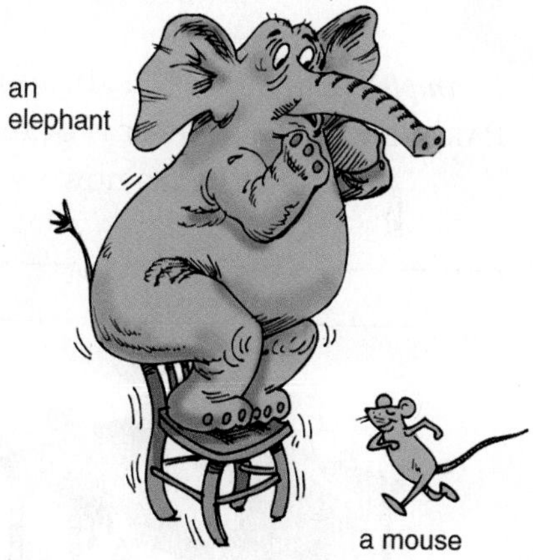

❑ Exercise 33. Let's talk: game. (Chart 1-7)

Work in teams. Your teacher will ask you to name things. Your team will make a list. Share your list with the class. The group with the longest list gets a point. The group with the most points at the end of the game is the winner. Close your book for this activity.

Example: round
TEACHER: Name round things.
TEAM A'S LIST: a ball, an orange, a clock
TEAM B'S LIST: a baseball, a basketball, a soccer ball
TEAM C'S LIST: a ball, a head, an orange, a coin, a ring, a planet
Group C wins a point.

1. hot	4. free	7. beautiful
2. difficult	5. little	8. expensive
3. sweet	6. important	9. cheap

❑ Exercise 34. Let's talk: pairwork. (Charts 1-5 → 1-7)

Work with a partner. Take turns making two sentences for each picture. Use the given adjectives. You can look at your book before you speak. When you speak, look at your partner.

Example: The girl . . . happy/sad
PARTNER A: The girl isn't happy. She's sad.
Your turn now.

Example: The flower . . . beautiful/ugly
PARTNER B: The flower is beautiful. It isn't ugly.
Your turn now.

PARTNER A	PARTNER B
 1. The table . . . clean/dirty.	 1. The man . . . friendly/unfriendly.
 2. The boy . . . sick/well.	 2. The coffee . . . cold/hot.

$x^2 + 5 + 4 = (x + 4)(x + 1)$ 3. The algebra problem . . . easy/difficult.	 3. The woman . . . tall/short.
 4. The cars . . . old/new.	 4. Katie . . . old/young.

❑ Exercise 35. Grammar and vocabulary. (Charts 1-5 → 1-7)

Complete the sentences with ***is*** or ***are*** and the correct pronoun. Use contractions. Some sentences are negative.

1. A pea ___*is*___ green. ___*It isn't*___ red. 

2. Carrots ___*aren't*___ blue. ___*They're*___ orange. 

3. An onion ______________ orange. ______________ brown, white, or green. 

4. A strawberry ______________ black. ______________ red. 

5. Bananas ______________ yellow. ______________ white. 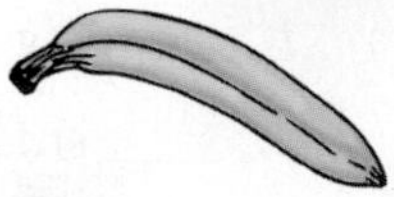

6. A banana ______________ yellow. ______________ white.

7. An orange ______________ orange. ______________ brown. 

8. Apples ______________ red or green. ______________ purple. 

9. A tomato ______________ blue. ______________ red or green. 

❑ Exercise 36. Let's talk: game. (Charts 1-5 → 1-7)

Part I. Check (✓) all the words you know. Your teacher will explain the words you don't know.

1. ____ hungry	11. ____ angry
2. ____ thirsty	12. ____ nervous
3. ____ sleepy	13. ____ friendly
4. ____ tired	14. ____ lazy
5. ____ old	15. ____ hardworking
6. ____ young	16. ____ famous
7. ____ happy	17. ____ sick
8. ____ homesick	18. ____ healthy
9. ____ married	19. ____ friendly
10. ____ single	20. ____ shy

Part II. Sit in a circle. Student A makes a sentence using "I" and the first word. Student B repeats the information about Student A and makes a new sentence using the second word. Continue around the circle until everyone in class has spoken. The teacher is the last person to speak and must repeat the information about everyone in the class.

Example:
STUDENT A: I'm not hungry.
STUDENT B: He's not hungry. I'm thirsty.
STUDENT C: He's not hungry. She's thirsty. I'm sleepy.

❑ Exercise 37. Let's talk: pairwork. (Charts 1-5 → 1-7)

Work with a partner. Check (✓) each adjective that describes this city/town (the city or town where you are studying now). When you finish, compare your work with a partner. Do you and your partner have the same answers? Tell the class about some of your differences.

1. ____ big	11. ____ noisy
2. ____ small	12. ____ quiet
3. ____ clean	13. ____ crowded
4. ____ dirty	14. ____ not crowded
5. ____ friendly	15. ____ hot
6. ____ unfriendly	16. ____ cold
7. ____ safe	17. ____ warm
8. ____ dangerous	18. ____ cool
9. ____ beautiful	19. ____ expensive
10. ____ ugly	20. ____ inexpensive/cheap

❑ **Exercise 38. Warm-up.** (Chart 1-8)

Read the sentences and choose *yes* or *no*.

1. The cat is next to the mousetrap.	yes	no
2. The mouse is under the chair.	yes	no
3. The mouse is behind the cat.	yes	no

1-8 *Be* + a Place

(a) Maria is ***here***. (b) Bob is ***at the library***.	In (a): *here* = a place. In (b): *at the library* = a place. **Be** is often followed by *a place*.
(c) Maria is { ***here***. / ***there***. / ***downstairs***. / ***upstairs***. / ***inside***. / ***outside***. / ***downtown***.	A place may be one word, as in the examples in (c).
PREPOSITION + NOUN (d) Bob is { ***at*** ***the library***. / ***on*** ***the bus***. / ***in*** ***his room***. / ***at*** ***work***. / ***next to*** ***Maria***.	A place may be a prepositional phrase (*preposition* + *noun*), as in (d).

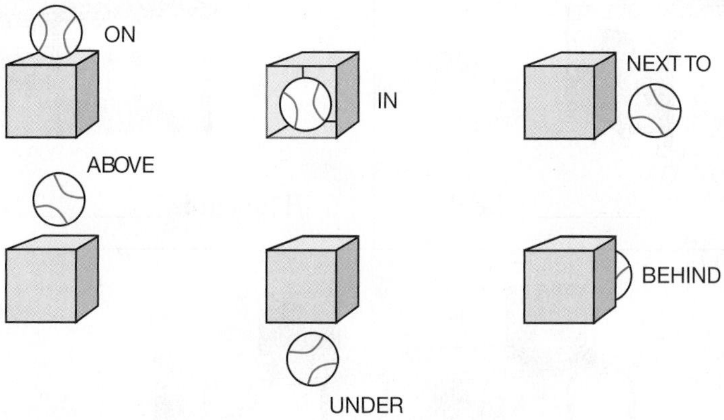

SOME COMMON PREPOSITIONS

above	behind	from	next to	under
at	between	in	on	

❑ Exercise 39. Looking at grammar. (Chart 1-8)

Complete each sentence with a preposition from the box.

above	between	next to	under
behind	✓ in	on	

1. The cat is ______*in*______ the desk.

2. The cat is ________________ the desk.

3. The cat is ________________ the desk.

4. The cat is ________________ the desk.

5. The cat is ________________ the desk.

6. The cat is ________________ the desk.

7. The cat is ________________ the desks.

❑ **Exercise 40. Let's talk: pairwork.** (Chart 1-8)

Work with a partner. Follow your partner's instructions.

Example:
PARTNER A: Put your hand under your chair.
PARTNER B: (*Partner B performs the action.*)

PARTNER A	PARTNER B
Put your pen . . .	*Put a piece of paper . . .*
1. on your book.	1. behind your back.
2. in your hand.	2. between two fingers.
3. next to your thumb.	3. next to your thumb.
4. under your desk.	4. in the air.

❑ **Exercise 41. Listening.** (Charts 1-1 → 1-8)

Listen to the sentences. Write the words you hear. Some answers have contractions.

CD 1
Track 5

The First Day of Class

Paulo ___*is a student*___ (1) from Brazil. Marie __________ (2) student from France. __________ (3) the classroom. Today __________ (4) exciting day. __________ (5) the first day of school, but they __________ (6) nervous. __________ (7) to be here. Mrs. Brown __________ (8) the teacher. She __________ (9) in the classroom right now. __________ (10) late today.

❑ **Exercise 42. Reading and writing.** (Charts 1-1 → 1-8)

Read the paragraph. Then complete the sentences with true answers. Several answers are possible for each item.

A Substitute Teacher

Today is Monday. It is the first day of English class. Mr. Anderson is an English teacher, but he isn't in class today. He is at home in bed. Mrs. Anderson is in the classroom today. Mrs. and Mr. Anderson are husband and wife. Mrs. Anderson is a good teacher. The students are a little nervous, but they're happy. Mrs. Anderson is very funny, and her explanations are clear. It's a good class.

1. Mr. Anderson is ___*an English teacher, sick, etc.*___.
2. Mrs. Anderson is not ______________________________.
3. Mr. and Mrs. Anderson are ______________________________.
4. The students are ______________________________.
5. The English class is ______________________________.

1-9 Summary: Basic Sentence Patterns with *Be*

SUBJECT + *BE* + NOUN (a) I am *a student.*	The noun or pronoun that comes at the beginning of a sentence is called the "subject."
SUBJECT + *BE* + ADJECTIVE (b) He is *intelligent.*	***Be*** is a "verb." Almost all English sentences have a subject and a verb.
SUBJECT + *BE* + A PLACE (c) We are *in class.* (d) She is *upstairs.*	Notice in the examples: There are three basic completions for sentences that begin with a *subject* + *the verb* ***be:*** • *a noun,* as in (a) • *an adjective,* as in (b) • *an expression of place,** as in (c) and (d)

*An expression of place can be a *preposition* + *noun,* or it can be one word: *upstairs.*

❑ **Exercise 43. Looking at grammar.** (Chart 1-9)

Write the form of ***be*** (***am, is,*** or ***are***) that is used in each sentence. Then write the grammar structure that follows ***be***.

	BE	+	COMPLETION
1. We're students.	*are*	+	*noun*
2. Anna is in Rome.	*is*	+	*place*
3. I'm hungry.	*am*	+	*adjective*
4. Dogs are animals.	______	+	______________
5. Jack is at home.	______	+	______________
6. He's sick.	______	+	______________
7. They're in class.	______	+	______________
8. I'm a mechanic.	______	+	______________
9. Gina is upstairs.	______	+	______________
10. The peas are good.	______	+	______________
11. Dan and I are nurses.	______	+	______________
12. Nora is downstairs.	______	+	______________
13. We aren't homesick.	______	+	______________
14. They are astronauts.	______	+	______________

❑ Exercise 44. Listening. (Chapter 1)

CD 1
Track 6

Is and ***are*** are often contracted with nouns in spoken English. Listen to the sentences. Practice saying them yourself. *Note:* ***'s*** and ***'re*** can be hard to hear.

1. Grammar is easy. → Grammar's easy.
2. My name is Josh.
3. My books are on the table.
4. My brother is 21 years old.
5. The weather is cold today.
6. The windows are open.
7. My money is in my wallet.
8. Mr. Smith is a teacher.
9. My parents are at work now.
10. The food is good.
11. Tom is sick today.
12. My roommates are from Chicago.
13. My sister is a student in high school.

❑ Exercise 45. Looking at grammar. (Chapter 1)

Choose the correct completion.

Example: My friend _____ from South Korea.
a. he (b.) 's c. Ø*

1. The test _____ easy.
a. are b. is c. Ø

2. My notebook _____ on the table.
a. is b. are c. Ø

3. My notebooks _____ on the table.
a. is b. are c. Ø

4. Sue _____ a student.
a. is b. she c. Ø

5. The weather _____ warm today.
a. is b. it c. Ø

6. My friends _____ from Cuba.
a. are b. is c. Ø

7. My book _____ on my desk.
a. it b. is c. Ø

8. The teachers _____ in class.
a. is b. are c. Ø

9. The teacher _____ nice.
a. 's b. are c. Ø

10. Dinner _____ ready.
a. it b. is c. Ø

---

*Ø = nothing

❑ Exercise 46. Reading and writing. (Chapter 1)

Part I. Read the paragraph. Look at new vocabulary with your teacher first.

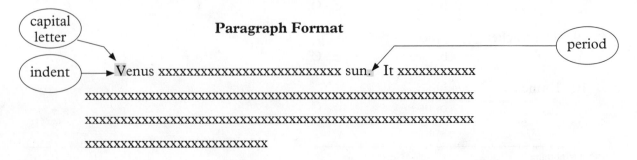

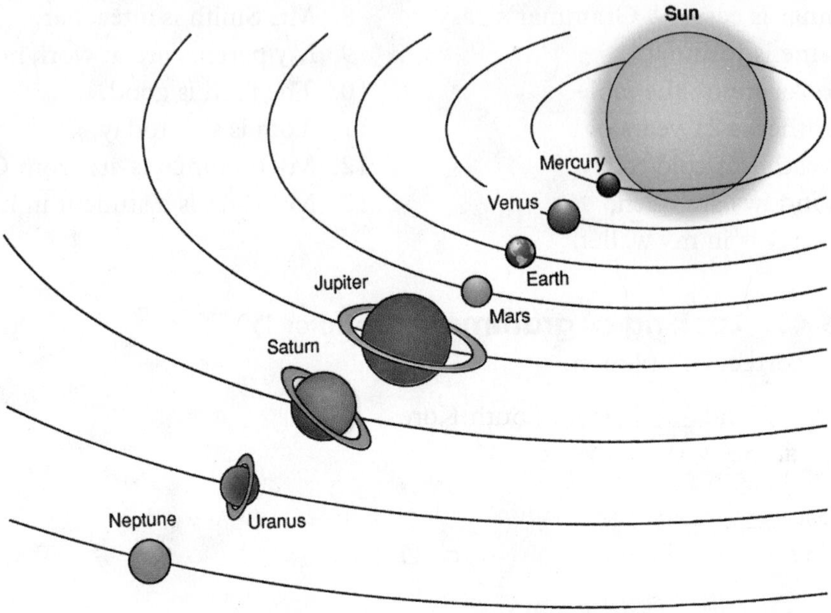

Venus

Venus is the second planet from the sun. It isn't big and it isn't small. It is between Earth and Mercury. It is an interesting planet. It is very bright at night. It is rocky and dusty. It is also hot. The temperature on Venus is 464 degrees Celsius or 867 degrees Fahrenheit.

Do you know these words?
bright
at night
rocky
dusty
temperature

Part II. Write a paragraph about Mars. Use the following information.

Facts:

- 4th (fourth) planet from the sun
- small
- between Earth and Jupiter
- red
- very rocky
- very dusty
- very cold (-55° C / -67° F)
- interesting?

Before you begin, look at the paragraph format.

Paragraph Format

capital letter

indent → Venus xxxxxxxxxxxxxxxxxxxxxxxxxxx sun. It xxxxxxxxxxx

period

xxxxxxxxxxxxxxxxxxxxxxxxxxxxxxxxxxxxxxxxxxxxxxxxxxxxxx
xxxxxxxxxxxxxxxxxxxxxxxxxxxxxxxxxxxxxxxxxxxxxxxxxxxxxx
xxxxxxxxxxxxxxxxxxxxxxxxx

Part III. Editing check: Work individually or change papers with a partner. Check (✓) for the following:

1. ____ capital letter at the beginning of each sentence
2. ____ period at the end of each sentence
3. ____ paragraph indent
4. ____ a verb (for example, ***is*** or ***are***) in every sentence
5. ____ correct spelling (use a dictionary or spell-check)

Chapter 2

Using Be *and* Have

❑ **Exercise 1. Warm-up.** (Chart 2-1)
Answer the questions.

1.	Is the weather nice today?	yes	no
2.	Are you in a classroom right now?	yes	no
3.	Are you hungry?	yes	no

2-1 Yes/No Questions with *Be*

	QUESTION			STATEMENT			
	BE +	SUBJECT		SUBJECT +	*BE*		In a question, ***be*** comes in front of the subject.
(a)	*Am*	*I*	early?	*I*	*am*	early.	PUNCTUATION
(b)	*Is*	*Ana*	a student?	*Ana*	*is*	a student.	A question ends with a question mark (?).
(c)	*Are*	*they*	at home?	*They*	*are*	at home.	A statement ends with a period (.).

❑ **Exercise 2. Looking at grammar.** (Chart 2-1)
Complete the questions with ***am, is,*** or ***are.***

1. ____________ you tired?
2. ____________ he late?
3. ____________ they here?
4. ____________ we early?
5. ____________ she at home?
6. ____________ I a new student?
7. ____________ they new students?
8. ____________ you and Bill ready?
9. ____________ Mr. Rivera sick?
10. ____________ Mr. and Mrs. Rivera sick?

❑ Exercise 3. Looking at grammar. (Chart 2-1)

Make questions.

1. A: *Is Mrs. Han a teacher?*
   B: Yes, Mrs. Han is a teacher.

2. A: ______________________________
   B: Yes, carrots are vegetables.

3. A: ______________________________
   B: Yes, Mr. Wang is absent today.

4. A: ______________________________
   B: Yes, planets are big.

5. A: ______________________________
   B: Yes, Amy and Mika are here today.

6. A: ______________________________
   B: Yes, English grammar is fun.

7. A: ______________________________
   B: Yes, I am ready for the next exercise.

❑ Exercise 4. Listening. (Chart 2-1)

Listen to the sentences. Write the words you hear.

CD 1 Track 7

Example: You will hear: A: Elena's absent today.
B: Is she sick?
You will write: B: *Is* she sick?

A: Elena's absent today.
B: ________ she sick? (1)
A: No.
B: ________ her husband sick? (2)
A: No.
B: ________ her children sick? (3)
A: No.
B: ________ she homesick? (4)
A: No.
B: So? What's the matter?
A: Her turtle ________ sick. (5)
B: Are you serious? That's crazy!

a turtle

❑ Exercise 5. Warm-up. (Chart 2-2)

Answer the questions. In b., both answers are possible. Which negative contraction do you prefer?

1. Is the classroom cold?
   a. Yes, it is. b. No, it isn't. / No, it's not.

2. Are the chairs in the classroom comfortable?
   a. Yes, they are. b. No, they aren't. / No, they're not.

2-2 Short Answers to Yes/No Questions

QUESTION		SHORT ANSWER	
			Spoken contractions are not used in short answers that begin with *yes*.
(a) *Is Kari* a student?	→	Yes, *she is*.	In (a): INCORRECT: *Yes, she's.*
	→	No, *she's not*.	
	→	No, *she isn't*.	
(b) *Are they* at home?	→	Yes, *they are*.	In (b): INCORRECT: *Yes, they're.*
	→	No, *they aren't*.	
		No, *they're not*.	
(c) *Are you* ready?	→	Yes, *I am*.	In (c): INCORRECT: *Yes, I'm.*
	→	No, *I'm not*.*	

**Am* and *not* are not contracted.

❑ Exercise 6. Looking at grammar. (Chart 2-2)

Make questions and give short answers.

1. A: *Are you tired?*
   B: *No, I'm not.* (I'm not tired.)

2. A: *Is Alma in your class?*
   B: *Yes, she is.* (Alma is in my class.)

3. A: ______________________
   B: ______________ (I'm not homesick.)

4. A: ______________________
   B: ______________ (Kareem is homesick.)

5. A: ______________________
   B: ______________ (Kara isn't here today.)

6. A: ______________________
   B: ______________ (The students in this class are smart.)

7. A: ____

B: ____________________ (The chairs in this room aren't comfortable.)

8. A: ____

B: ____________________ (I'm not single.)

9. A: ____

B: ____________________ (We're married.)

❑ **Exercise 7. Let's talk: pairwork.** (Chart 2-2)

Work with a partner. Ask and answer questions. You can look at your book before you speak. When you speak, look at your partner.

Example: dolphins: intelligent/dumb

PARTNER A: Are dolphins intelligent?

PARTNER B: Yes, they are.

OR

PARTNER A: Are dolphins dumb?

PARTNER B: No, they aren't.

a dolphin

PARTNER A	PARTNER B
1. a mouse: big/little	1. diamonds: expensive/cheap
2. lemons: sweet/sour	2. your grammar book: light/heavy
3. the world: flat/round	3. butterflies: beautiful/ugly
4. the weather: cool today/warm today	4. English grammar: easy/difficult
5. your dictionary: with you/at home	5. turtles: fast/slow
6. your shoes: comfortable/uncomfortable	6. the floor in this room: clean/dirty

❑ **Exercise 8. Looking at grammar.** (Charts 2-1 and 2-2)

Complete the conversations with your own words.

1. A: ___*Are*___ you a student at this school?

B: Yes, ___*I am*___.

A: __________ you from ______________?

B: No, ______________ from ______________.

2. A: Are you a/an ______________?

B: No, ______________ not. I'm a/an ______________.

3. A: Are ______________________ expensive?

B: Yes, ______________________.

A: Is ______________________ expensive?

B: No, ______________________.

4. A: ________________ Vietnam and Cambodia countries in Asia?

B: Yes, ________________ are.

A: ______________________________ a country in South America?

B: Yes, ________________ is.

A: ______________________________ a country in Africa?

B: No, ________________ not. It's a country in ______________________.

❑ Exercise 9. Warm-up. (Chart 2-3)

Choose the correct answer for each question.

On your head	No, they aren't

A: Are my glasses in the kitchen?

B: ______________________________.
(1)

A: Where are they?

B: ______________________________!
(2)

2-3 Questions with *Be*: Using *Where*

Where asks about place. ***Where*** comes at the beginning of the question, in front of ***be***.

		QUESTION			SHORT ANSWER	(LONG ANSWER)
		BE +	SUBJECT			
(a)		*Is*	***the book*** on the table?	→	Yes, ***it is***.	(*The book is on the table.*)
(b)		*Are*	***the books*** on the table?	→	Yes, ***they are***.	(*The books are on the table.*)
	WHERE +	*BE* +	SUBJECT			
(c)	***Where***	***is***	***the book?***	→	***On the table.***	(*The book is on the table.*)
(d)	***Where***	***are***	***the books?***	→	***On the table.***	(*The books are on the table.*)

❑ **Exercise 10. Looking at grammar.** (Chart 2-3)
Choose the correct question for each response.

Question	Response
1. a. Is Sami absent? b. Where is Sami?	At home.
2. a. Where are the boxes? b. Are the boxes in the closet?	Yes, they are.
3. a. Are you outside? b. Where are you?	No, I'm not.
4. a. Is the mail on the kitchen counter? b. Where is the mail?	On the kitchen counter.

❑ **Exercise 11. Looking at grammar.** (Chart 2-3)
Make questions.

1. A: *Is Sara at home?*
   B: Yes, she is. (Sara is at home.)
2. A: *Where is Sara?*
   B: At home. (Sara is at home.)
3. A: ______________________
   B: Yes, it is. (Cairo is in Egypt.)
4. A: ______________________
   B: In Egypt. (Cairo is in Egypt.)

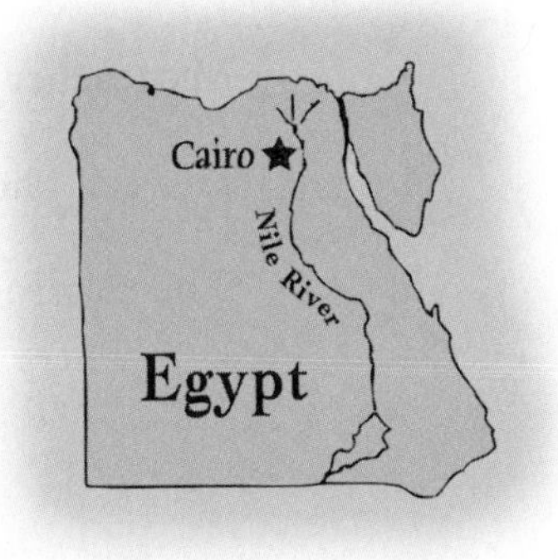

5. A: ______________________
   B: Yes, they are. (The students are in class today.)
6. A: ______________________
   B: In class. (The students are in class today.)
7. A: ______________________
   B: On Main Street. (The post office is on Main Street.)
8. A: ______________________
   B: Yes, it is. (The train station is on Grand Avenue.)
9. A: ______________________
   B: Over there. (The bus stop is over there.)
10. A: ______________________
    B: At work. (Ali and Jake are at work now.)

❑ **Exercise 12. Let's talk: pairwork.** (Chart 2-3)

Work with a partner. Ask and answer questions. Use ***where***. You can look at your book before you speak. When you speak, look at your partner.

Example:

PARTNER A: Where is your pen?

PARTNER B: It's in my hand. (*or any other true answer*)

PARTNER A	PARTNER B
1. your money	1. your wallet
2. your books	2. your glasses or sunglasses
3. your coat	3. your family
4. your pencil	4. your apartment
5. (*name of a classmate*)	5. (*names of two classmates*)
6. your hometown	6. your hometown
7. (*name of a city in the world*)	7. (*name of a country in the world*)

❑ **Exercise 13. Warm-up.** (Chart 2-4)

Check (✓) the true sentences.

1. ____ I have a dictionary on my desk.
2. ____ Many students have backpacks.
3. ____ My teacher has a cell phone.
4. ____ Her cell phone has a case.
5. ____ The classroom has a globe.

a globe

2-4 Using *Have* and *Has*

SINGULAR			PLURAL					
(a) *I*	***have***	a pen.	(f) *We*	***have***	pens.	I, you, we, they	+	***have***
(b) *You*	***have***	a pen.	(g) *You*	***have***	pens.			
(c) *She*	***has***	a pen.	(h) *They*	***have***	pens.	she, he, it	+	***has***
(d) *He*	***has***	a pen.						
(e) *It*	***has***	blue ink.						

❑ **Exercise 14. Looking at grammar.** (Chart 2-4)

Complete the sentences with ***have*** or ***has***.

1. You ____________ a bike.
2. I ____________ a bike.
3. She ____________ a small car.
4. They ____________ trucks.
5. We ____________ trucks.
6. You and I ____________ bikes.
7. The business ____________ a van.
8. He ____________ a motorcycle.
9. Radek ____________ a motorcycle.
10. The Molinas ____________ two motorcycles.

❑ **Exercise 15. Looking at grammar.** (Chart 2-4)

Choose the correct answer.

1. We has / (have) a daughter.
2. Venita has / have two daughters.
3. She has / have twin daughters.
4. The Leons are grandparents. They has / have one grandchild.
5. Hiro has / have an interesting job. He's a journalist.
6. You has / have a good job too.
7. You and I has / have good jobs.
8. I has / have a laptop computer.
   It has / have a small screen.
9. Samir is a website designer. He
   has / have a laptop and a desktop.
10. A laptop has / have a battery.
11. Laptops has / have batteries.

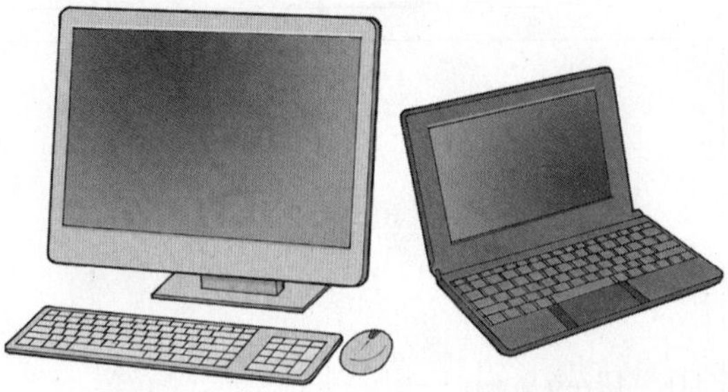

❑ Exercise 16. Vocabulary and grammar. (Chart 2-4)

Complete each sentence with ***have*** or ***has*** and words from the box.

backaches	a fever	a sore throat
the chills	✓ a headache	a stomachache
a cold	high blood pressure	toothaches
coughs		

1. Mr. Kasim has a headache.

2. The patients ______________________.

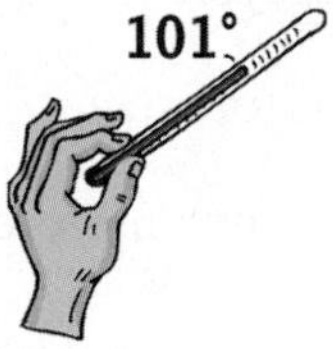

3. I ____________.

4. Mrs. Ramirez ____________.

5. You ______________.

6. The workers ______________________.

7. Olga ______________________.

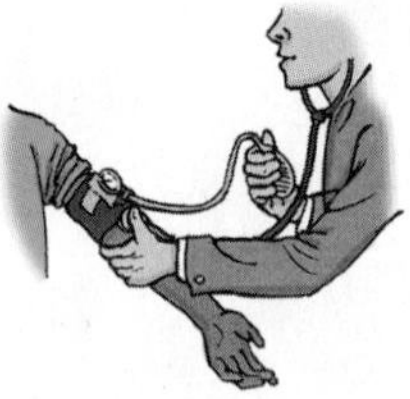

8. You ______________________________.

9. Alan ______________________.

10. They ______________________________.

❑ **Exercise 17. Let's talk: pairwork.** (Chart 2-4)

Complete the conversations with a partner. You can look at your book before you speak. When you speak, look at your partner. Use this model.

Partner A: How ________?

Partner B: Not so good. ________.

Partner A: That's too bad.

Example: Jamal? . . . a toothache.
PARTNER A: How's Jamal?
PARTNER B: Not so good. He has a toothache.
PARTNER A: That's too bad. Your turn now.

1. you? . . . a headache.
2. you? . . . a sore tooth.
3. your mother? . . . a sore back.
4. Mr. Park? . . . a backache.
5. your parents? . . . colds.
6. the patients? . . . stomachaches.
7. your little brother? . . . a sore throat.
8. Mrs. Luna? . . . a fever.

❑ **Exercise 18. Looking at grammar.** (Charts 1-1 and 2-4)

Rewrite the paragraph. Change "I" to "he." You will also need to change the verbs in **bold**.

Dr. Lee

I **am** a doctor. I **am** 70 years old, so I **have** many years of experience. I **have** many patients. Some are very sick. I **have** a clinic downtown. I also **have** patients at the hospital. It is hard work, and I **am** often very tired. But I **am** also happy. I help many people.

He is a doctor. ____
____
____
____
____ *He helps many people.*

❑ **Exercise 19. Looking at grammar.** (Charts 1-1, 1-2, and 2-4)

Part I. Complete the sentences with ***is*** or ***has***.

I have a college roommate, Tia. She . . .

1. ____*is*____ from a small town.
2. ____________ nice.
3. ____________ a motorcycle.
4. ____________ a smart phone.
5. ____________ smart.
6. ____________ homework every night.
7. ____________ homesick.
8. ____________ a large family.
9. ____________ quiet.
10. ____________ a boyfriend.
11. ____________ a pet bird at home.
12. ____________ serious.

Part II. Complete the sentences with ***are*** or ***have***.

The two students in the room next to us . . .

1. ____________ a TV.
2. ____________ two computers.
3. ____________ noisy.
4. ____________ messy.
5. ____________ from a big city.
6. ____________ busy.
7. ____________ a lot of friends.
8. ____________ friendly.
9. ____________ parties on weekends.
10. ____________ low grades.

❑ Exercise 20. Warm-up. (Chart 2-5)

Complete each sentence with a word from the box.

Her	His	My	Their

1. __________ name is Evita.
2. __________ name is Paulo.

Her	His	My	Their

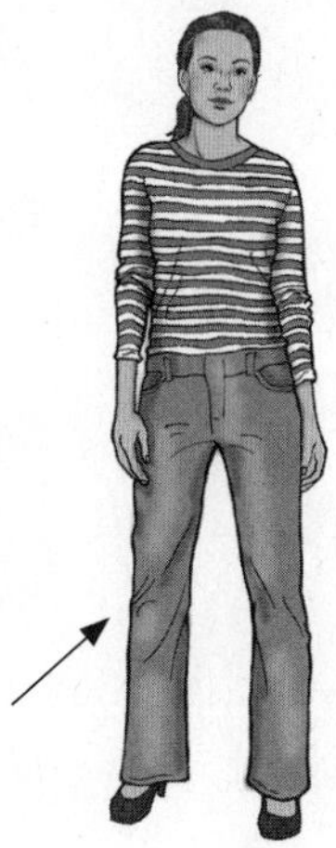

3. __________ name is Natalie.

4. __________ names are Natalie and Paulo.

2-5 Using *My, Your, Her, His, Our, Their*

SINGULAR	PLURAL	SUBJECT FORM → POSSESSIVE FORM
(a) **I** have a book. ***My*** book is red.	(e) **We** have books. ***Our*** books are red.	I → my you → your she → her he → his we → our they → their
(b) **You** have a book. ***Your*** book is red.	(f) **You** have books. ***Your*** books are red.	I *possess* a book. = I *have* a book. = It is *my* book.
(c) **She** has a book. ***Her*** book is red.	(g) **They** have books. ***Their*** books are red.	*My, your, her, his, our,* and *their* are called "possessive adjectives." They come in front of nouns.
(d) **He** has a book. ***His*** book is red.		

❑ **Exercise 21. Looking at grammar.** (Chart 2-5)
Complete each sentence with a word from the box.

her	his	my	our	their	your

1. You're next. It's ___*your*___ turn.
2. Susana's next. It's __________ turn.

her	his	my	our	their	your

3. Bruno and Maria are next. It's ______________ turn.
4. My aunt is next. It's ______________ turn.
5. I'm next. It's ______________ turn.
6. The children are next. It's ______________ turn.
7. You and Mohamed are next. It's ______________ turn.
8. Marcos and I are next. It's ______________ turn.
9. Bill's next. It's ______________ turn.
10. Mrs. Sung is next. It's ______________ turn.

❑ **Exercise 22. Vocabulary and grammar.** (Chart 2-5)
Complete the sentences with the information on the ID cards.

What information do you know about this person from his ID card?

1. __________ last name is ______________.
2. __________ first name is ______________.
3. __________ middle initial is ______________.

What information do the ID cards give you about Don and Kathy Johnson?

4. __________ zip code is ______________.
5. __________ area code is ______________.

What do you know about Dr. Nelson?

6. ____________ birthdate is ________________.
7. ____________ birthday is ________________.
8. ____________ middle name is ________________.

Write about yourself.

9. ____________ first name is ________________________.
10. ____________ last name is ________________________.
11. ____________ middle name is ________________________.
12. ____________ middle initial is ________________.
13. ____________ area code is ________________.
14. ____________ phone number is ____________________.
15. ____________ zip code is ________________.
16. ____________ birthday is ____________________.

April
Sun. Mon. Tues. Wed. Thurs. Fri. Sat.
1 2 3
4 5 6 7 8 9 10
11 12 13 14 15 16 17
18 19 20 21 22 23 24
25 26 27 28 29 30
HAPPY BIRTHDAY

❑ Exercise 23. Vocabulary: pairwork. (Chart 2-5)

Work with a partner. Look at the vocabulary. Put a check (✓) beside the words you know. Ask your partner about the ones you don't know. Your teacher can help you. The picture on the next page shows clothes and jewelry.

Vocabulary Checklist

COLORS	CLOTHES	JEWELRY
__ black	__ belt	__ bracelet
__ blue, dark blue, light blue	__ blouse	__ earrings
__ blue green	__ boots	__ necklace
__ brown, dark brown, light brown	__ coat	__ ring
__ gold	__ dress	__ watch
__ gray, dark gray, light gray	__ gloves	
__ green, dark green, light green	__ hat	
__ orange	__ jacket	
__ pink	__ jeans	
__ purple	__ pants	
__ red	__ sandals	
__ silver	__ shirt	
__ tan, beige	__ shoes	
__ white	__ skirt	
__ yellow	__ socks	
	__ suit	
	__ sweater	
	__ tie, necktie	
	__ T-shirt	

❑ Exercise 24. Looking at grammar. (Chart 2-5)

Complete the sentences with ***my, your, her, his, our,*** or ***their***.

1. Malena has on* a blouse. ___Her___ blouse is light blue.
2. Tomas has on a shirt. __________ shirt is yellow and brown.
3. I have on jeans. __________ jeans are blue.
4. Kiril and Oleg have on boots. __________ boots are brown.
5. Diana and you have on dresses. __________ dresses are red.

---

* ***has on*** and ***have on*** = wear (clothes)

6. Salma and I have on sweaters. ____________ sweaters are green.

7. You have on shoes. ____________ shoes are dark brown.

8. Nora has on a skirt. ____________ skirt is black.

9. Leo has on a belt. ____________ belt is white.

10. Sashi and Akira have on socks. ____________ socks are gray.

11. Arturo has on pants. ____________ pants are dark blue.

12. I have on earrings. ____________ earrings are gold.

❏ Exercise 25. Listening. (Charts 2-4 and 2-5)

CD 1 Track 8

Listen to the sentences. Write the words you hear.

Example: You will hear: She has on boots.
You will write: *She has* on boots.

Anna's clothes

1. ____________ boots ____________ zippers.
2. ____________ a raincoat.
3. ____________ raincoat ____________ buttons.
4. ____________________ small.
5. ____________ sweater ____________ long sleeves.
6. ____________________ earrings on ____________ ears.
7. ________________________ silver.
8. ____________________ on jeans.
9. ____________ jeans ____________ pockets.

❏ Exercise 26. Looking at grammar. (Charts 2-4 and 2-5)

Complete the sentences. Use ***have*** or ***has*** and ***my, your, her, his, our,*** or ***their***.

1. You *have* a big family. *Your* family is nice.
2. You and Tina ____________ many cousins. ____________ cousins are friendly.
3. I ____________ a brother. ____________ brother is in college.
4. William ____________ a sister. ____________ sister is a doctor.

5. Lisa ____________ a twin sister. ____________ sister is disabled.

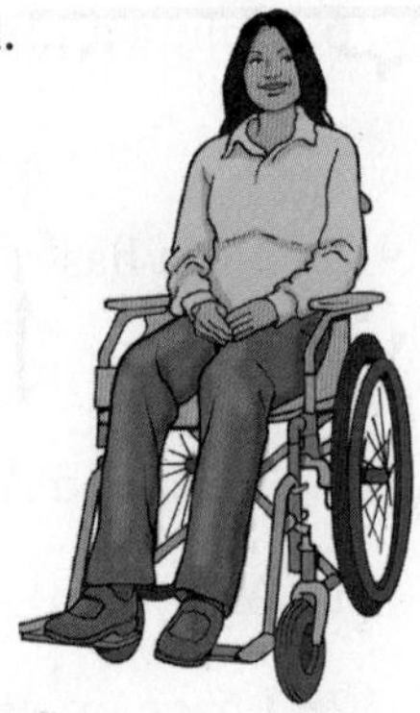

6. Iman and Amir are married. They ____________ a baby. ____________ baby is six months old.

7. Anton and I ____________ a son. ____________ son is seven years old.

8. Pietro and Julieta ____________ a daughter. ____________ daughter is ten years old.

9. I ____________ an adopted brother. ____________ brother is thirty.

10. Lidia is single. She ____________ a brother. ____________ brother is single too.

❑ **Exercise 27. Reading and grammar.** (Chapter 1 and Charts 2-4 and 2-5)

Part I. Read the story and answer the questions. Look at new vocabulary with your teacher first.

One Big Happy Family

Do you know these words?
- sibling
- adopted
- pilot
- overnight
- stay-at-home father

Kanai is 13 years old. She has a big family. She has four sisters and five brothers. Kanai and her siblings are adopted. They are from several different countries. She likes her brothers and sisters. They have a good time. They are always busy. Kanai's parents are busy too. Her mother is an airline pilot. She goes away overnight fifteen days a month. Kanai's dad is a stay-at-home father. He has a lot of work, but the older kids are helpful. Kanai's parents love children. They are one big happy family.

1. Kanai is a girl.	yes	no
2. Only the girls are adopted.	yes	no
3. Kanai's father is home a lot.	yes	no
4. Her mother is home every night.	yes	no

Part II. Complete the sentences with ***her***, ***his***, or ***their***. One sentence has two possible answers.

1. Kanai is adopted. ____________ brothers and sisters are adopted too.
2. Her parents are busy. ____________ mother is an airline pilot. ____________ father is a stay-at-home dad.
3. She has nine siblings. ____________ family is very large.
4. Kanai's dad is very busy. ____________ children are helpful.

Part III. Complete the story with ***is, are, has,*** or ***have***.

One Big Happy Family

Kanai ____________ (1) 13 years old. She ____________ (2) a big family. She ____________ (3) four sisters and five brothers. Kanai and her siblings are adopted. They ____________ (4) from several different countries. She likes her brothers and sisters. They ____________ (5) a good time. They ____________ (6) always busy. Kanai's parents ____________ (7) busy too. Her mother ____________ (8) an airline pilot. She ____________ (9) away overnight fifteen days a month. Kanai's dad ____________ (10) a stay-at-home father. He ____________ (11) a lot of work, but the older kids are helpful. Kanai's parents love children. They are one big happy family.

❑ **Exercise 28. Warm-up.** (Chart 2-6)
Match the sentences to the pictures.

Picture A

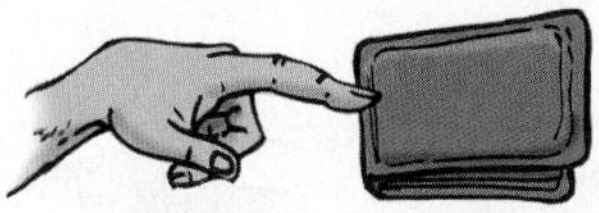

Picture B

1. This is my wallet. ____

2. That is your wallet. ____

2-6 Using *This* and *That*

(a) I have a book in my hand. ***This book*** is red. (b) I see a book on your desk. ***That book*** is blue. (c) ***This*** is my book. (d) ***That*** is your book.	*this* book = the book is near me. *that* book = the book is not near me.
(e) ***That's*** her book.	CONTRACTION: *that is* = *that's*
(f) ***This is*** (***"This's"***) her book.	In spoken English, *this is* is usually pronounced as *"this's."* It is not used in writing.

❑ **Exercise 29. Looking at grammar.** (Chart 2-6)

Complete the sentences with ***this*** or ***that***.

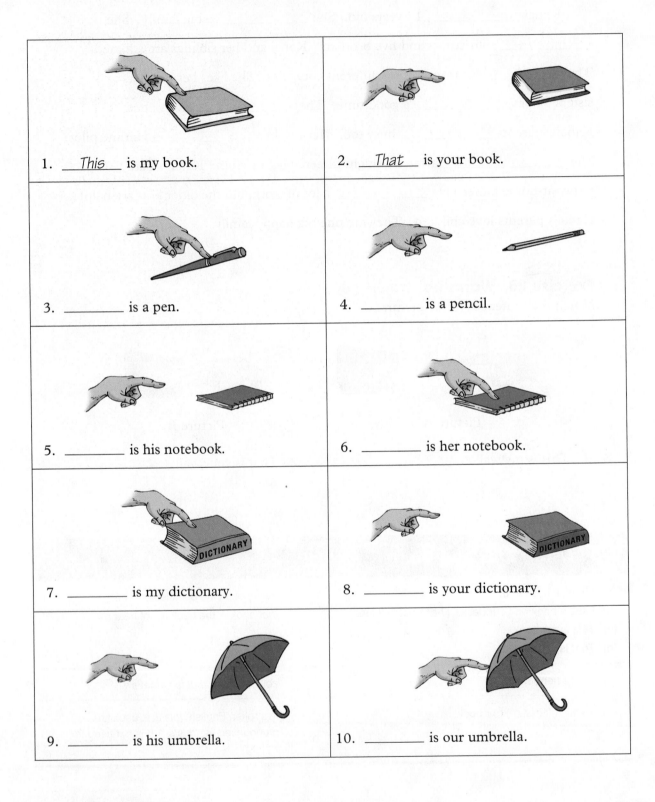

 1. ___This___ is my book.	 2. ___That___ is your book.
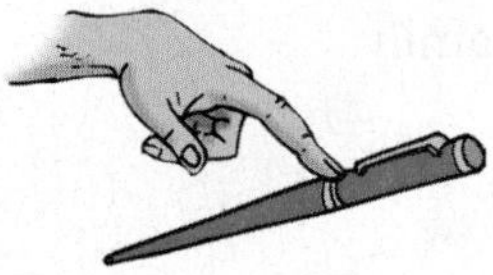 3. ________ is a pen.	 4. ________ is a pencil.
 5. ________ is his notebook.	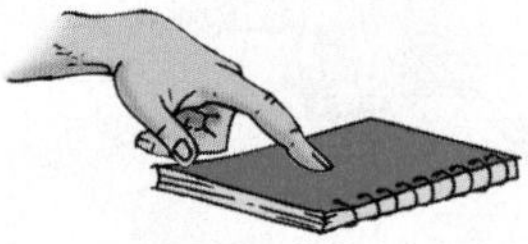 6. ________ is her notebook.
 7. ________ is my dictionary.	 8. ________ is your dictionary.
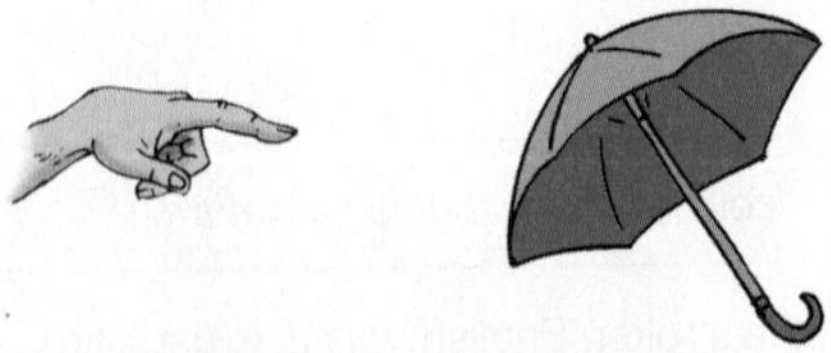 9. ________ is his umbrella.	 10. ________ is our umbrella.

❑ Exercise 30. Let's talk: pairwork. (Chart 2-6)

Part I. Work with a partner. Take turns. Make a sentence with ***this*** or ***that*** for each picture.

Example:
Partner A: That is a backpack.
Your turn.

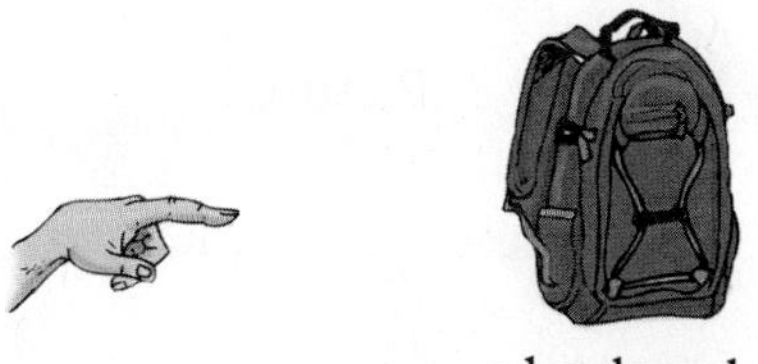

a backpack

PARTNER A	PARTNER B
 1. a credit card	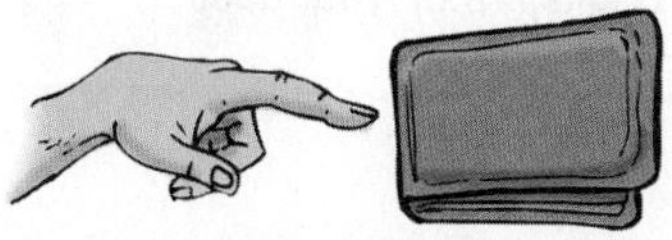 2. a wallet
 3. a credit card	 4. a checkbook
 5. a business card	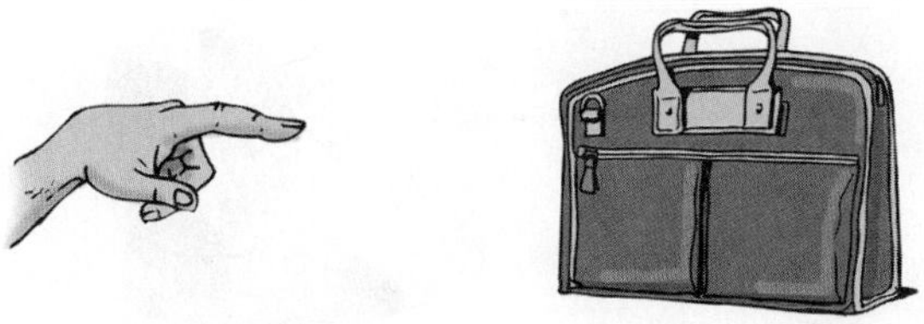 6. a computer bag

Part II. Put items from a school bag, a bookbag, or a purse on a desk or table. Put some near you and some at a distance. Point to them, and your partner will make sentences with ***this*** or ***that***.

❑ Exercise 31. Warm-up. (Chart 2-7)
Match the sentences to the pictures.

 Picture A	 Picture B

1. Those are my keys. ____
2. These are your keys. ____

2-7 Using *These* and *Those*

(a) My books are on my desk. *These* are my books. (b) Your books are on your desk. *Those* are your books.	SINGULAR → PLURAL *this* → *these* *that* → *those*

❑ Exercise 32. Looking at grammar. (Chart 2-7)
Complete the sentences with ***these*** or ***those***.

 1. ____________ are my books.	 2. ____________ are your pencils.
 3. ____________ are his boots.	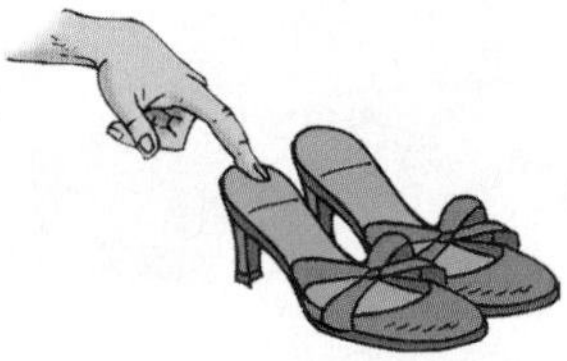 4. ____________ are her shoes.
 5. ____________ are your hats.	 6. ____________ are their jackets.

❑ Exercise 33. Vocabulary and grammar. (Charts 2-6 and 2-7)

Look at the vocabulary in the picture. Choose the correct verb.

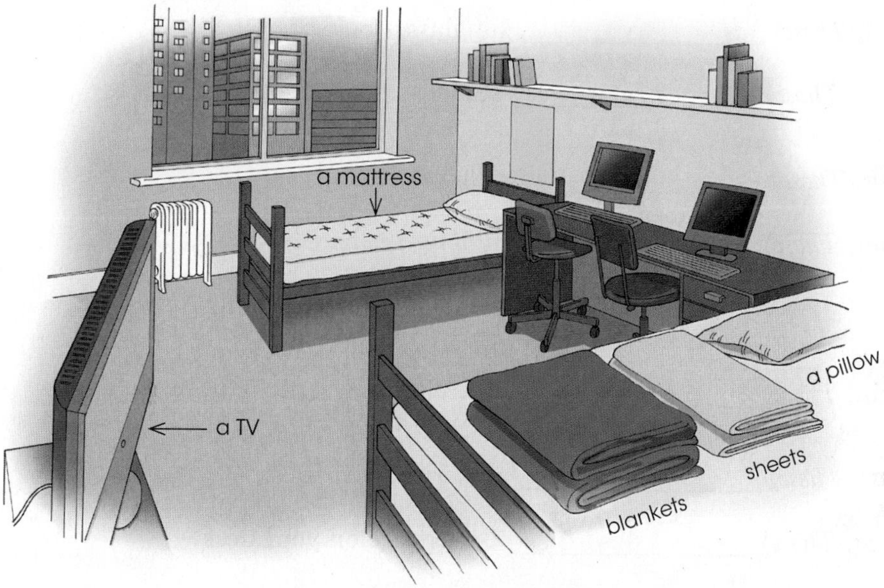

In our dorm room

1. This (is) / are my pillow.
2. That is / are your pillow.
3. Those sheets is / are for you.
4. These blankets is / are for me.
5. That TV is / are broken.
6. This chair is / are new.
7. Those mattresses is / are soft.
8. This mattress is / are uncomfortable.

❑ Exercise 34. Looking at grammar. (Charts 2-6 and 2-7)

Complete the sentences. Use the words in parentheses.

1. (*This, These*) ___This___ pencil belongs to Alex.

   (*That, Those*) ___That___ pencil belongs to Olga.

2. (*This, These*) __________ notepads belong to me.

   (*That, Those*) __________ notepad belongs to Kate.

3. (*This, These*) _______________ coat is waterproof.

(*That, Those*) _______________ coats are not.

4. (*This, These*) _______________ sunglasses belong to me.

(*That, Those*) _______________ sunglasses belong to you.

5. (*This, These*) _______________ pillows are soft.

(*That, Those*) _______________ pillows are hard.

6. (*This, These*) _______________ exercise is easy.

(*That, Those*) _______________ exercises are hard.

7. (*This, These*) _______________ eraser is on my desk.

(*That, Those*) _______________ erasers are on your desk.

❑ **Exercise 35. Let's talk: pairwork.** (Charts 2-6 and 2-7)

Work with a partner. Make a sentence for each picture using ***this, that, these,*** or ***those.*** Take turns.

Examples:

PARTNER A: That is a cap.
Your turn now.

a cap

PARTNER B: These are caps.
Your turn now.

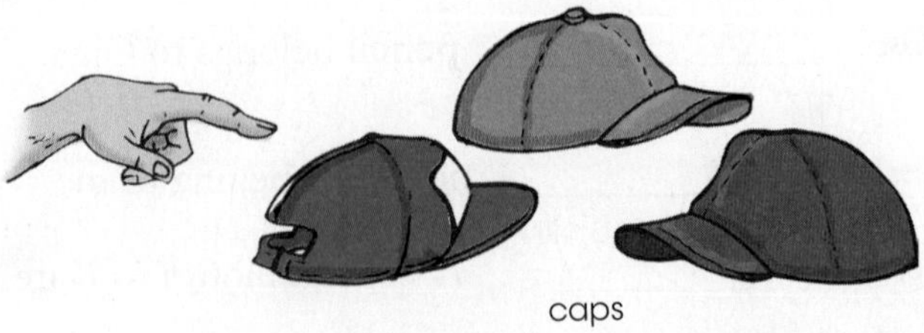

caps

PARTNER A	PARTNER B
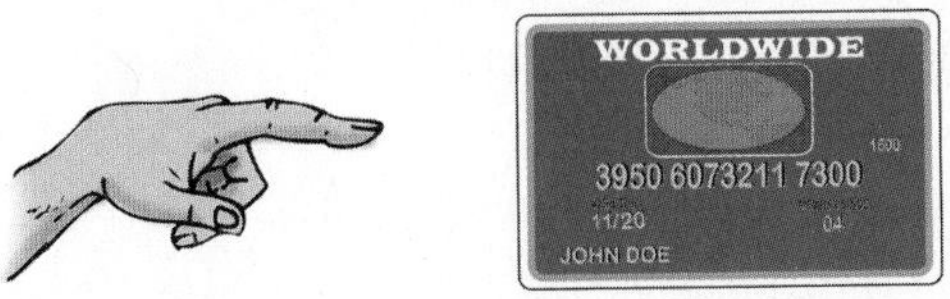 1. a debit card	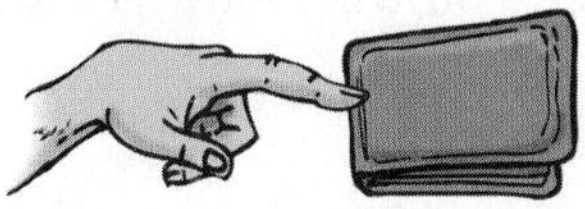 2. a wallet
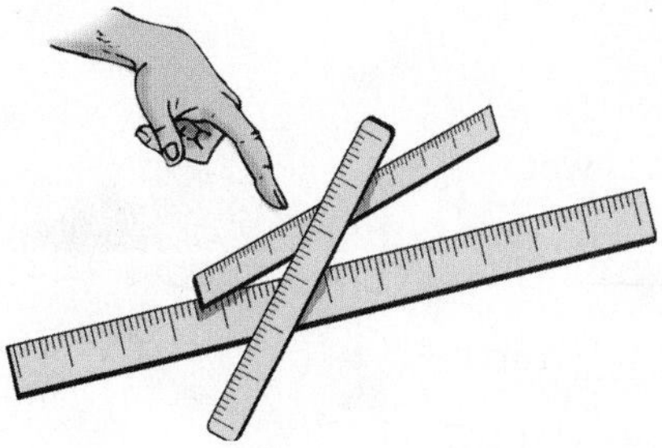 3. rulers	 4. paper clips
 5. a notepad	 6. checks
 7. checkbooks	 8. a folder
 9. a stapler	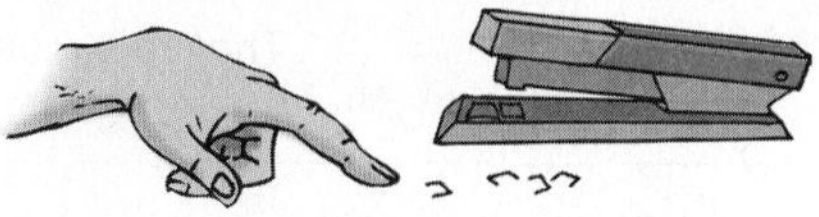 10. staples

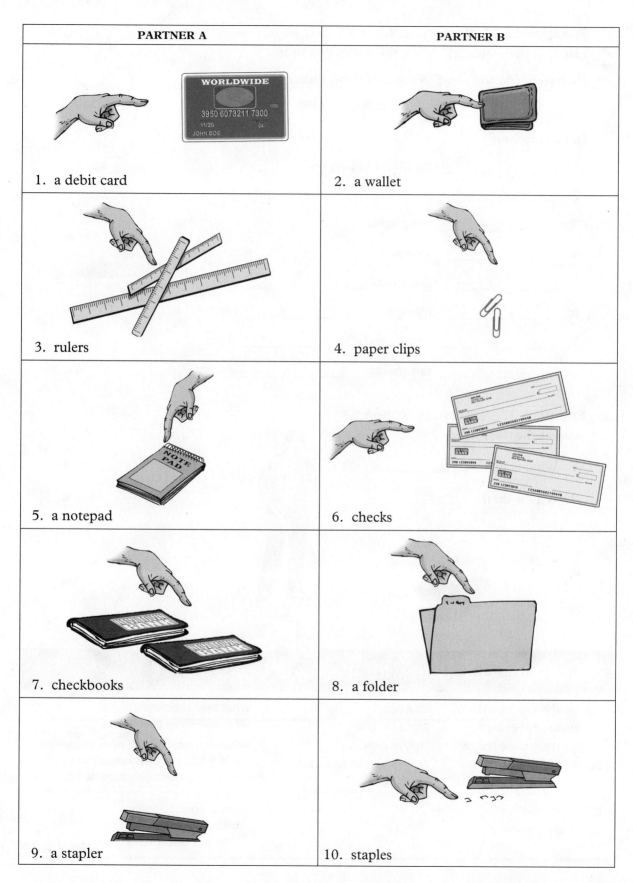

❑ Exercise 36. Listening. (Charts 2-6 and 2-7)

CD 1 Track 9

Listen to the sentences. Write the words you hear.

Example: You will hear: Those are clean dishes.

You will write: *Those are* clean dishes.

In the kitchen

1. ______________ my coffee cup.
2. ______________ your dessert.
3. ______________ our plates.
4. ______________ sponges ______________ wet.
5. ______________ dishcloths ______________ dry.
6. ______________ frying pan ______________ dirty.
7. ______________ frying pan ______________ clean.
8. ______________ salt shaker ______________ empty.

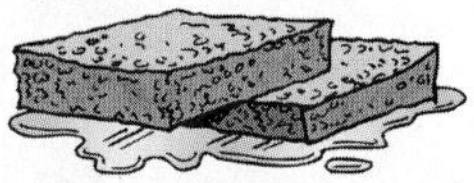

sponges

❑ Exercise 37. Warm-up. (Chart 2-8)

Answer the questions.

1. What is that? ______________
2. Who is that? ______________

a beetle

Tim

2-8 Asking Questions with *What* and *Who* + *Be*

(a) ***What is*** this (thing)?	It's a pen.	***What*** asks about things.
(b) ***Who is*** that (man)?	That's Mr. Lee.	***Who*** asks about people.
(c) ***What are*** those (things)?	They're pens.	Note: In questions with ***what*** and ***who***,
(d) ***Who are*** they?	They're Mr. and Mrs. Lee.	• ***is*** is followed by a singular word. • ***are*** is followed by a plural word.
(e) ***What's*** this?		CONTRACTIONS:
(f) ***Who's*** that man?		*what is* = *what's* *who is* = *who's*

❑ Exercise 38. Looking at grammar. (Chart 2-8)

Complete the questions with ***what*** or ***who*** and ***is*** or ***are***.

1. A: ___Who is___ that woman?
   B: She's my sister. Her name is Sonya.

2. A: ____________ those things?
   B: They're erasers.

3. A: ____________ that?
   B: That's Ms. Walenski.

4. A: ____________ this?
   B: That's my new camera. It's really small.

5. A: ____________ those people?
   B: I'm not sure, but I think they're new students from Thailand.

6. A: ____________ your name?
   B: Anita.

7. A: ____________ your grammar teacher?
   B: Mr. Walker.

8. A: ____________ your favorite teachers?
   B: Mr. Walker and Ms. Rosenberg.

9. A: ____________ an only child?
   B: It's a child with no brothers or sisters.

10. A: ____________ bats?
    B: They're animals with wings. They fly at night. They're not birds.

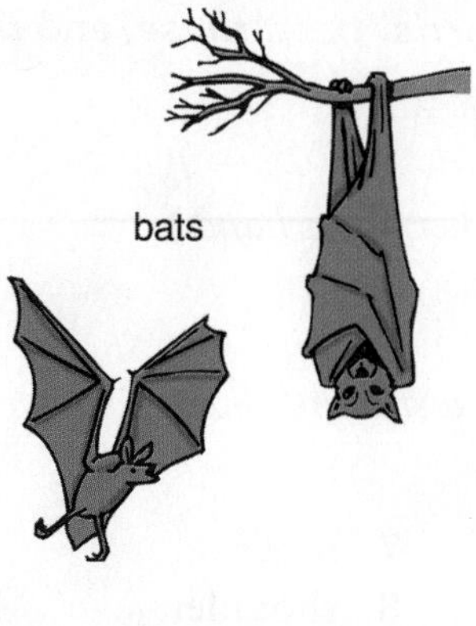

❑ Exercise 39. Vocabulary and speaking: pairwork. (Chart 2-8)

Part I. Work with a partner. Write the names of the parts of the body on the pictures below. Use the words from the box.

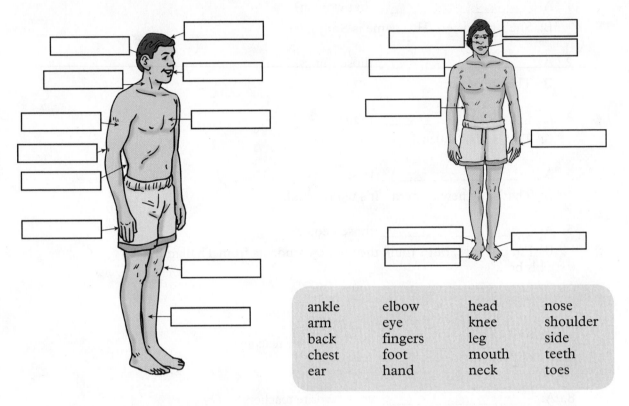

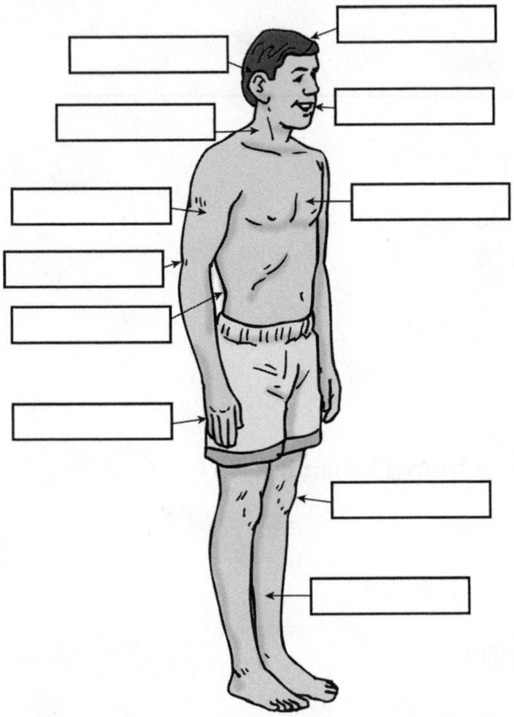

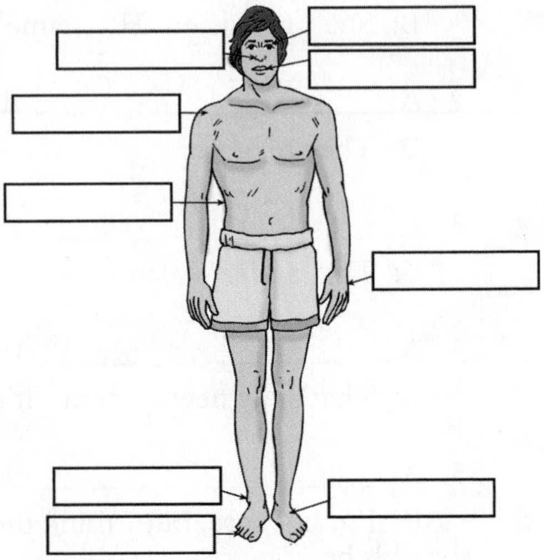

ankle	elbow	head	nose
arm	eye	knee	shoulder
back	fingers	leg	side
chest	foot	mouth	teeth
ear	hand	neck	toes

Part II. With your partner, take turns asking questions with ***this, that, these,*** and ***those.***
Note: Both partners can ask about both pictures.

Example:
PARTNER A: What is this?
PARTNER B: This is his leg. (*to Partner A*) What are those?
PARTNER A: Those are his fingers.

❑ Exercise 40. Let's talk: class activity. (Chart 2-8)

Your teacher will ask questions. Answer with ***this, that, these,*** and ***those.*** Close your book for this activity.

Example: hand
TEACHER: What is this? (*The teacher indicates her or his hand.*)
STUDENT: That is your hand.
OR
TEACHER: What is that? (*The teacher indicates a student's hand.*)
STUDENT: This is my hand.

1. nose	3. arm	5. legs	7. foot	9. fingers
2. eyes	4. elbow	6. knee	8. shoulder	10. ears

❑ **Exercise 41. Check your knowledge.** (Chapter 2)

Correct the mistakes.

has
1. She ~~have~~ a headache.
2. What are that?
3. Roberto he is a student in your class?
4. I am have a backache.
5. This is you dictionary. I my dictionary is at home.
6. Where my keys?
7. I am a sore throat.
8. He's father is from Cuba.
9. This books are expensive.
10. Where is the teachers?
11. A: Are you tired?

    B: Yes, I'm.

❑ **Exercise 42. Looking at grammar.** (Chapter 2)

Choose the correct completion.

1. Carla _____ a grammar book.
   a. have   b. is   (c.) has
2. This floor _____.
   a. dirty is   b. dirty   c. is dirty
3. _____ yellow.
   a. A banana are   b. A banana is   c. Bananas is
4. Lucas is _____ engineer.
   a. a   b. an   c. Ø
5. _____ books are really expensive.
   a. Those   b. They   c. This
6. Give this to Kathleen. It is _____ math book.
   a. she   b. an   c. her

7. That is _____.
   a. a mistakes   b. mistakes   c. a mistake

8. PABLO: _____ is your apartment?
   BLANCA: It's on Forest Street.
   a. What   b. Where   c. Who

9. YOKO: _____ these?
   GINA: My art books. I'm taking an art history class.
   a. What are   b. Who are   c. What is

10. MALIK: Are you hungry?
    LAYLA: Yes, _____.
    a. I'm   b. I'm not   c. I am

11. TINA: _____ that?
    LUIS: That's Paul Carter.
    a. Who's   b. What's   c. Where's

12. PAUL: _____ in your class?
    ERIC: No.
    a. Mr. Kim   b. Is Mr. Kim   c. Mr. Kim is he

❑ **Exercise 43. Looking at grammar.** (Chapter 2)

Complete the sentences with ***am, is,*** or ***are.*** Use ***not*** if necessary.

1. Apples _______________ vegetables.
2. An apple _______________ a kind of fruit.
3. I _______________ from the United States.
4. We _______________ human beings.
5. Balls _______________ square.
6. Chickens _______________ birds, but bats _______________ birds.
7. Lemons _______________ sweet. They _______________ sour.
8. Soccer _______________ a sport.
9. Soccer and basketball _______________ sports.
10. Africa _______________ a country. It _______________ a continent.

❑ Exercise 44. Looking at grammar. (Chapter 2)

Complete the conversations with any words that make sense.

1. A: Where ____________ your book?
   B: Hiroko ____________ it.
   A: Where ____________ your notebooks?
   B: Nasir and Angela ____________ them.

2. A: ____________ this?
   B: It ____________ a picture of my family.
   A: ____________ this?
   B: That's ____________ father.
   A: ____________ they?
   B: My brother and sister.

3. A: What's ____________?
   B: I don't know. Ask the teacher.
   A: What's ____________?
   C: It's ____________.

4. A: Where ____________?
   B: He's ____________.
   A: Where ____________?
   B: They're ____________.

❑ Exercise 45. Grammar and writing. (Chapter 2)

Part I. Complete the sentences in the composition by Carlos.

My name ___*is*___ (1) Carlos. ___*I am* OR *I'm*___ (2) from Mexico. ____________ (3) a student. ____________ (4) twenty years old.

My family lives in Mexico City. ____________ (5) father ____________ (6) a businessman. ____________ (7) fifty-one years old. ____________ (8) mother ____________ (9) an accountant. ____________ (10) forty-nine years old.

I ____________ (11) two sisters and one brother. The names of my sisters ____________ (12) Rosa and Patricia. Rosa ____________ (13) a teacher. ____________ (14) twenty-eight years old. Patricia ____________ (15) a student.

_______________ eighteen years old. My brother _______________ an engineer. His
16 / 17

name _______________ Pedro. He is married. He _______________ two children.
18 / 19

I live in a dormitory. _______________ a tall building on Pine Street. My address
20

_______________ 3225 Pine St. I live with my roommate. _______________ name is
21 / 22

Bob. _______________ from Chicago. _______________ nineteen years old.
23 / 24

I like my classes. They _______________ interesting. I like _______________
25 / 26

classmates. _______________ friendly.
27

Part II. Write about yourself. Follow the style below. Use your own paper.

PARAGRAPH I: **Information about you**:
your name, hometown, age (*optional*)

PARAGRAPH II: **Information about your parents (if they are alive)**:
their ages, jobs

PARAGRAPH III: **Information about other family or people in your life**:
your siblings: names, ages, jobs OR
your husband/wife: name, job OR
your roommate/partner/friend: name, job

PARAGRAPH IV: **Additional information**:
your home (apartment/dormitory/house): I live in a/an ____.
your classes
your classmates

Part III. Editing check: Work individually or change papers with a partner. Check (✓) for the following:

1. ____ capital letter at the beginning of each sentence
2. ____ capital letter at the beginning of a person's name
3. ____ period at the end of each sentence
4. ____ paragraph indents
5. ____ a verb in every sentence
6. ____ correct use of ***be*** and ***have***
7. ____ correct spelling (use a dictionary or computer spell-check)

Chapter 3
Using the Simple Present

❑ **Exercise 1. Warm-up.** (Chart 3-1)
Read the paragraph. Write the verb forms for *take, post,* and *share.*

I often take videos of my family and friends. I post them online. I share them with my family and friends. My brother Mario is a science teacher. He takes videos of his students and their experiments. He posts them online. He shares them with his classes.

take	***post***	***share***
1. I ___________	3. I ___________	5. I ___________
2. Mario ___________	4. He ___________	6. He ___________

3-1 Form and Basic Meaning of the Simple Present Tense

I *talk.* You *talk.* He *talks.* She *talks.* It *rains.* We *talk.* They *talk.*	The verb after 3rd person singular (***she***, ***he***, ***it***) has a final **-*s*:** *talks*. SINGULAR / PLURAL 1st person: I *talk* / we *talk* 2nd person: you *talk* / you *talk* 3rd person: she *talks* / they *talk* he *talks* it *rains*
(a) I ***eat*** breakfast **every morning**. (b) Olga ***speaks*** English **every day**. (c) We ***sleep*** **every night**. (d) They ***go*** to the beach **every weekend**.	The simple present tense expresses habits. In (a): Eating breakfast is a habit, a usual activity. *Every morning* = Monday morning, Tuesday morning, Wednesday morning, Thursday morning, Friday morning, Saturday morning, and Sunday morning.
 She wakes up every morning at 7:00.	 He shaves every morning.

❑ Exercise 2. Looking at grammar. (Chart 3-1)

Complete the sentences with ***speak*** or ***speaks***.

1. Martin ____________________ English.
2. I ____________________ German.
3. Erika ____________________ several languages.
4. Her husband ____________________ Thai and Vietnamese.
5. My friends and I ____________________ a little Persian.
6. My friends ____________________ Arabic.
7. They ____________________ Arabic fluently.
8. You ____________________ Spanish well.
9. You and I ____________________ Spanish well.
10. We ____________________ it well.
11. You and Peter ____________________ it well.

❑ Exercise 3. Let's talk: pairwork. (Chart 3-1)

Part I. Look at the list of habits. Check (✓) your habits every morning. Put them in order. What do you do first, second, third, etc.? Write them on the lines.

HABITS		MY HABITS EVERY MORNING
____ eat breakfast	1.	*I turn off the alarm clock.*
____ go to class	2.	____________________
____ put on my clothes	3.	____________________
____ drink a cup of coffee/tea	4.	____________________
____ shave	5.	____________________
____ put on my make-up	6.	____________________
____ take a shower/bath	7.	____________________
____ get up	8.	____________________
____ pick up my books	9.	____________________
____ walk to the bathroom	10.	____________________
____ watch TV	11.	____________________
____ look in the mirror	12.	____________________
_✓_ turn off the alarm clock	13.	____________________
____ go to the kitchen/the cafeteria	14.	____________________
____ brush/comb my hair	15.	____________________

____ say good-bye to someone — 16. ______________________

____ brush my teeth — 17. ______________________

____ do exercises — 18. ______________________

____ wash my face — 19. ______________________

Part II. Work with a partner. Talk about your habits every morning. Close your book for this activity.

❑ Exercise 4. Listening. (Chart 3-1)

Listen to the sentences. Choose the verbs you hear.

CD 1
Track 10

1.	(wake)	wakes	6.	watch	watches
2.	wake	wakes	7.	take	takes
3.	get	gets	8.	take	takes
4.	go	goes	9.	take	takes
5.	do	does	10.	talk	talks

❑ Exercise 5. Looking at grammar. (Chart 3-1)

Choose the correct completion.

1. My mother and father ____*eat*____ breakfast at 7:00 every day.
   eat / eats
2. My mother ______________ tea with her breakfast.
   drink / drinks

3. I ______________ a bath every morning.
   take / takes
4. My sister ______________ a shower.
   take / takes
5. I ______________ English with my friends.
   study / studies
6. We ______________ to school together every morning.
   walk / walks
7. Class ______________ at 9:00 every day.
   begin / begins
8. It ______________ at 12:00 for lunch.
   stop / stops
9. We ______________ in the cafeteria.
   eat / eats
10. You ______________ your lunch from home every day.
    bring / brings
11. My friends and I ______________ home at 3:00 every afternoon.
    go / goes
12. You and Jamal ______________ to the library after school every day.
    go / goes

❑ Exercise 6. Warm-up. (Chart 3-2)

Which sentence is true for you?

1. I always do my homework.
2. I usually do my homework.
3. I sometimes do my homework.
4. I never do my homework.

3-2 Frequency Adverbs

100%	*always*	(a) Ivan *always* eats breakfast.	SUBJECT + { *always* / *usually* / *often* / *sometimes* / *seldom* / *rarely* / *never* } + VERB
↑	*usually*	(b) Maria *usually* eats breakfast.	
	often	(c) They *often* watch TV.	
50%	*sometimes*	(d) We *sometimes* watch TV.	
	seldom	(e) Sam *seldom* drinks milk.	
↓	*rarely*	(f) Rita *rarely* drinks milk.	
0%	*never*	(g) I *never* drink milk.	The words in this list are called "frequency adverbs." They come between the subject and the simple present verb.*

OTHER FREQUENCY EXPRESSIONS

(h) I drink tea { once *a day*. / two times / twice *a day*. / three times *a day*. / four times *a day*. / etc. } (i) I see my grandparents three times *a week*. (j) I see my aunt once *a month*. (k) I see my cousin Sam twice *a year*.	We can express frequency by saying how many times something happens ***a day***. ***a week***. ***a month***. ***a year***.
(l) I see my doctor every *year*.	*Every* is singular. The noun that follows (e.g., *morning*) must be singular. INCORRECT: *every mornings*

* Some frequency adverbs can also come at the beginning or at the end of a sentence. For example:
Sometimes *I get up at seven.* *I* ***sometimes*** *get up at seven.* *I get up at seven* ***sometimes***.
Also: See Chart 3-3, for the use of frequency adverbs with ***be***.

☐ **Exercise 7. Looking at grammar.** (Chart 3-2)

Complete each sentence with a word from the box.

always	often	never	rarely	sometimes	usually

	SUN.	MON.	TUES.	WED.	THURS.	FRI.	SAT.
1. Ana _____ drinks tea with lunch.							
2. Kenji _____ drinks tea with lunch.							
3. Clara _____ drinks tea with lunch.							
4. Igor _____ drinks tea with lunch.							
5. Sonya _____ drinks tea with lunch.							
6. Sami _____ drinks tea with lunch.							

☐ **Exercise 8. Looking at grammar.** (Chart 3-2)

Write "S" over the subject and "V" over the verb in each sentence. Rewrite the sentences, adding the given frequency adverbs.

1. always — *S V* I eat breakfast in the morning.
   I always eat breakfast in the morning.
2. never — I eat carrots for breakfast.
   _______________ for breakfast.
3. seldom — I watch TV in the morning.
   _______________ in the morning.
4. sometimes — I have dessert after dinner.
   _______________ after dinner.
5. usually — Kiri eats lunch at the cafeteria.
   _______________ at the cafeteria.
6. often — We listen to music after dinner.
   _______________ after dinner.
7. always — The students speak English in class.
   _______________ in class.

❑ Exercise 9. Let's talk: class activity. (Chart 3-2)

Your teacher will ask you to talk about your morning, afternoon, and evening activities. Close your book for this activity.

Tell me something you . . .

1. always do in the morning.
2. never do in the morning.
3. sometimes do in the morning.
4. usually do in the afternoon.
5. seldom do in the afternoon.
6. never do in the afternoon.
7. often do in the evening.
8. sometimes do in the evening.
9. rarely do in the evening.
10. sometimes do on weekends.

❑ Exercise 10. Looking at grammar. (Chart 3-2)

Use the information in the chart to complete the sentences.

	SUN.	MON.	TUES.	WED.	THURS.	FRI.	SAT.
Hamid							
Yoko							
Victoria							
Pavel							
Mr. Wu							
Mrs. Cook							

How often do the people in the chart take the bus during the week?

1. Hamid takes the bus ___*seven times*___ a week. That means he ___*always*___ takes the bus.
2. Yoko takes the bus ____________________ a week. That means she ____________________ takes the bus.
3. Victoria takes the bus ____________________ a week. That means she ____________________ takes the bus.
4. Pavel takes the bus ____________________ a week. That means he ____________________ takes the bus.
5. Mr. Wu ____________________ takes the bus.
6. Mrs. Cook takes the bus ____________________ a week. That means she ____________________ takes the bus.

❑ Exercise 11. Warm-up. (Chart 3-3)

Choose the correct answer. What do you notice about the placement of the verb and the frequency adverb?

1. It often rains here.	yes	no
2. It sometimes snows.	yes	no
3. It is often cold here.	yes	no
4. It is sometimes hot.	yes	no

3-3 Position of Frequency Adverbs

SUBJECT + ***BE*** + FREQUENCY ADVERB	Frequency adverbs come after the simple present tense forms of ***be***: ***am***, ***is***, and ***are***.
I am / You are / He is / She is / It is / We are / They are + {*always* / *usually* / *often* / *sometimes* / *seldom* / *rarely* / *never*} + late.	
SUBJECT + FREQUENCY ADVERB + OTHER SIMPLE PRESENT VERBS	Frequency adverbs come before all simple present verbs except ***be***.
Tom + {*always* / *usually* / *often* / *sometimes* / *seldom* / *rarely* / *never*} + *comes* late.	

❑ Exercise 12. Looking at grammar. (Chart 3-3)

Add the frequency adverbs to the sentences.

1. always	Anita is on time for class. → *Anita is always on time for class.*
2. always	Anita comes to class on time. → *Anita always comes to class on time.*
3. often	Liliana is late for class.
4. often	Liliana comes to class late.
5. never	It snows in my hometown.
6. never	It is very cold in my hometown.
7. usually	Hiroshi is at home in the evening.
8. usually	Hiroshi stays at home in the evening.
9. seldom	Thomas studies at the library in the evening.
10. seldom	His classmates are at the library in the evening.
11. sometimes	I skip breakfast.
12. rarely	I have time for a big breakfast.

❑ **Exercise 13. Let's talk: class activity.** (Chart 3-3)

Part I. Check (✓) the boxes to describe your activities after 5:00 P.M.

	ALWAYS	*USUALLY*	*OFTEN*	*SOMETIMES*	*RARELY*	*NEVER*
1. eat dinner						
2. go to a movie						
3. go shopping						
4. go swimming						
5. spend time with friends						
6. go to class						
7. be at home						
8. watch videos or DVDs						
9. study English						
10. send emails						
11. surf the Internet						
12. drink coffee after 9:00						
13. be in bed at ten o'clock						
14. go to bed late						

Part II. Exchange books with a partner. Your partner will tell the class two things about your evening.

Example: (Carlos) is usually at home. He sometimes sends emails.
(Olga) sometimes drinks coffee after 9:00 P.M. She usually goes to bed late.

❑ **Exercise 14. Writing.** (Chart 3-3)

Write about a typical day in your life, from the time you get up in the morning until you go to bed. Use the following words to show the order of your activities: ***then, next, at . . . o'clock, after that, later.***

Writing sample: I usually get up at 7:30. I shave, brush my teeth, and take a shower. Then I put on my clothes and go to the student cafeteria for breakfast. After that, I go back to my room. I sometimes watch the news on TV. At 8:15, I leave the dormitory. I go to class. My class begins at 8:30. I'm in class from 8:30 to 11:30. After that, I eat lunch. I usually have a sandwich and a cup of tea for lunch. (Continue until you complete your day.)

❑ **Exercise 15. Warm-up: listening.** (Chart 3-4)

Listen to the words. Decide if they have one syllable or two.

CD 1 Track 11

1. eat	one	two	4. pushes	one	two
2. eats	one	two	5. sleeps	one	two
3. push	one	two	6. fixes	one	two

3-4 Spelling and Pronunciation of Final *-es*

			SPELLING	PRONUNCIATION	
-sh	(a) push	→	*pushes*	*push*/əz/	Ending of verb: ***-sh***, ***-ch***, ***-ss***, ***-x***.
-ch	(b) teach	→	*teaches*	*teach*/əz/	Spelling: add ***-es***.
-ss	(c) kiss	→	*kisses*	*kiss*/əz/	Pronunciation: /əz/.
-x	(d) fix	→	*fixes*	*fix*/əz/	

❑ **Exercise 16. Looking at grammar.** (Chart 3-4)

Use the correct form of the given verbs to complete the sentences.

1. brush — Arianna ___*brushes*___ her hair every morning.
2. teach — Alex ______________ English.
3. fix — Pedro ______________ his breakfast every morning. He makes eggs and toast.
4. drink — Sonya ______________ tea every afternoon.
5. watch — Joon Kee often ______________ television at night.
6. kiss — Viktor always ______________ his children goodnight.
7. wear — Tina usually ______________ jeans to class.
8. wash — Eric seldom ______________ dishes.
9. walk — Jenny ______________ her dog twice each day.
10. stretch, yawn — When Jack gets up in the morning, he ______________ and ______________.

❑ **Exercise 17. Listening.** (Chart 3-4)

Listen to the sentences and choose the verbs you hear.

CD 1 Track 12

1. teach	(teaches)	6. watch	watches
2. teach	teaches	7. brush	brushes
3. fix	fixes	8. brush	brushes
4. fix	fixes	9. wash	washes
5. watch	watches	10. wash	washes

❑ **Exercise 18. Looking at grammar.** (Charts 3-1 and 3-4)

Complete the sentences. Use the words from the box and add ***-s*** or ***-es***. Practice reading the story aloud. Work with a partner or in small groups.

brush	get	take	wash
cook	✓ leave	turn	watch
fall	read	sit	

Laura ___*leaves*___ (1) her office every night at 5:00 and ________ (2) on a bus to go home. She has the same schedule every evening. She ________ (3) dinner and then ________ (4) down to eat at 6:00. After she ________ (5) the dishes, she ________ (6) on the TV. She usually ________ (7) the news and then a movie. At 9:00, she ________ (8) a shower. She always ________ (9) her teeth after her shower. Then she picks up a book and ________ (10) in bed for a while. She usually ________ (11) asleep before 10:00.

❑ **Exercise 19. Warm-up.** (Chart 3-5)

What kind of ending does each verb have? Put the verbs from the box in the correct column.

b***uy***	f***ly***	pl***ay***	stu***dy***

CONSONANT + ***-y***	VOWEL + ***-y***
________	________
________	________

3-5 Adding Final *-s/-es* to Words That End in *-y*

(a) *cry* → *cries* *try* → *tries*	ENDING OF VERB: consonant + **-y** SPELLING: change ***y*** to ***i***, add **-es**
(b) *pay* → *pays* *enjoy* → *enjoys*	ENDING OF VERB: vowel + **-y** SPELLING: add **-s**

❑ **Exercise 20. Looking at grammar.** (Chart 3-5)
Complete the chart with the correct form of each verb.

1. I try.	He _____ *tries* _____ .
2. We study.	She __________ .
3. They say.	It __________ .
4. I enjoy games.	Ann __________ games.
5. You worry a lot.	My mother __________ a lot.
6. We pay bills.	Gina __________ bills.
7. You stay awake.	Paul __________ awake.
8. We fly.	A bird __________ .
9. Students buy books.	My brother __________ books.
10. I play music. ♪♪	My friend __________ music.

❑ **Exercise 21. Looking at grammar.** (Chart 3-5)
Complete each sentence with the simple present form of a verb from the box.

buy	cry	pay	stay
carry	employ	✓ play	study

1. Monique likes sports. She _____ *plays* _____ tennis and soccer several times a week.
2. The school cafeteria is cheap. Rob __________ his lunch there every day.
3. My company is big. It __________ 2,000 people.
4. Elizabeth is always tired. Her new baby __________ during the night.

5. Mr. Garcia travels every week. He ____________________ in small hotels.

6. Some airplanes are very big. A large airplane ____________________ 400 to 500 passengers.

7. I usually pay with a debit card, but my husband ____________________ in cash.

8. Zara is a medical student. She ____________________ every night and on weekends.

❑ **Exercise 22. Warm-up.** (Chart 3-6)

Read the information about Milos and complete the chart.

Milos is a college student. He **has** a part-time job. He **does** the breakfast dishes at his dorm. Then he **goes** to class.

HAVE	*DO*	*GO*
I **have**	I **do**	I **go**
you **have**	you **do**	you **go**
he __________	he __________	he __________
she __________	she __________	she __________
it __________	it __________	it __________
we **have**	we **do**	we **go**
they **have**	they **do**	they **go**

3-6 Irregular Singular Verbs: *Has, Does, Goes*

(a) I ***have*** a book. (b) He ***has*** a book.	*she*, *he*, *it* } + ***has*** /hæz/	***Have***, ***do***, and ***go*** have irregular forms for 3rd person singular: *have* → *has* *do* → *does* *go* → *goes* Note that final **-s** is pronounced /z/ in these verbs.
(c) I ***do*** my work. (d) She ***does*** her work.	*she*, *he*, *it* } + ***does*** /dəz/	
(e) They ***go*** to school. (f) She ***goes*** to school.	*she*, *he*, *it* } + ***goes*** /gowz/	

❑ **Exercise 23. Looking at grammar.** (Chart 3-6)

Use the correct form of the given verbs to complete the sentences.

1. do Pierre always ___*does*___ his homework.

2. do We always ___do___ our homework.

3. have Yoko and Hamid __________ their books.

4. have Mrs. Chang __________ a car.

5. go Andy __________ to school every day.

6. do Sara seldom __________ her homework.

7. do We __________ exercises in class every day.

8. go, go Roberto __________ downtown every weekend. He and his wife __________ shopping.

9. play My friends often __________ volleyball at the beach.

❑ Exercise 24. Listening. (Chart 3-6)

Listen to the story. Complete the sentences with ***is, has, does,*** or ***goes.***

CD 1
Track 13

Marco ___is___ (1) a student. He ___has___ (2) an unusual schedule. All of his classes are at night. His first class __________ (3) at 6:00 P.M. every day. He takes a break from 7:30 to 8:00. Then he __________ (4) classes from 8:00 to 10:00.

He leaves school and __________ (5) home at 10:00. After he __________ (6) dinner, he watches TV. Then he __________ (7) his homework from midnight to 3:00 or 4:00 in the morning.

Marco __________ (8) his own computer at home. When he finishes his homework, he usually goes on the Internet. He often stays at his computer until the sun comes up. Then he __________ (9) a few exercises, __________ (10) breakfast, and __________ (11) to bed. He sleeps all day. Marco thinks his schedule __________ (12) great, but his friends think it __________ (13) strange.

❑ Exercise 25. Looking at grammar. (Charts 3-1 → 3-6)

Complete the sentences with the words in parentheses. Use the simple present tense. Pay special attention to singular and plural and to the spelling of final ***-s/-es***.

1. The students (*ask, often*) ____*often ask*____ questions in class.
2. Pablo (*study, usually*) ________________ at the library every evening.
3. Olga (*bite*) ____________ her fingernails when she is nervous.
4. Donna (*cash*) ____________ a check at the bank once a week.
5. Sometimes I (*worry*) ____________ about my grades at school. Sonya (*worry, never*) ________________ about her grades. She (*study*) ____________ hard.
6. Ms. Fernandez and Mr. Anderson (*teach*) ____________ at the local high school. Ms. Fernandez (*teach*) ____________ math.
7. Birds (*fly*) __________. They (*have*) __________ wings.
8. A bird (*fly*) __________. It (*have*) __________ wings.
9. Emilio (*do, always*) ________________ his homework. He (*go, never*) ______________ to bed until his homework is finished.
10. Mr. Cook (*say, always*)* ________________ hello to his neighbor.
11. Ms. Chu (*pay, always*)* ________________ attention in class. She (*answer*) ______________ questions. She (*listen*) ______________ to the teacher. She (*ask*) ____________ questions.

❑ Exercise 26. Let's talk: game. (Charts 3-1 → 3-6)

Part I. Your teacher will assign you a verb from the list. Make a sentence with that verb. Walk around the room. Say your sentence to other students. Listen to other students say their sentences.

1. eat	4. brush	7. get up	10. do	13. put on
2. go	5. have	8. watch	11. listen to	14. carry
3. drink	6. study	9. speak	12. wash	15. kiss

Part II. Work in teams of five to eight students. Write as many sentences as you can remember. Each team will have one paper. The team with the most correct sentences wins.

*Pronunciation of ***says*** = /sɛz/. Pronunciation of ***pays*** = /peyz/.

❑ Exercise 27. Let's talk: pairwork. (Charts 3-1 → 3-6)

Work with a partner. Use frequency adverbs like ***sometimes, rarely,*** etc.

Part I. Yuri, Levi, and Peter do many things in the evening. How often do they do the things in the list? Pay attention to final ***-s***.

Example: Yuri rarely/seldom does homework.

	YURI	LEVI	PETER
DO HOMEWORK	once a week	6 days a week	every day
SURF THE INTERNET	every day	once a week	once a month
WATCH TV	3–4 days a week	3–4 days a week	3–4 days a week
READ FOR PLEASURE	5 days a week	5 days a week	5 days a week
GO TO BED EARLY	once a week	5–6 nights a week	6–7 nights a week

Part II. For homework, write ten sentences about the activities of Yuri, Levi, and Peter.

❑ Exercise 28. Looking at grammar. (Charts 3-1 → 3-6)

Add ***-s*** or ***-es*** where necessary.

Abdul and Pablo

(1) My friend Abdul live^s in an apartment near school. (2) He walk to school almost every day. (3) Sometimes he catch a bus, especially if it's cold and rainy outside. (4) Abdul share the apartment with Pablo. (5) Pablo come from Venezuela. (6) Abdul and Pablo go to the same school. (7) They take English classes. (8) Abdul speak Arabic as his first language, and Pablo speak Spanish. (9) They communicate in English. (10) Sometimes Abdul try to teach Pablo to speak a little Arabic, and Pablo give Abdul Spanish lessons. (11) They laugh a lot during the Arabic and Spanish lessons. (12) Abdul enjoy his roommate, but he miss his family back in Saudi Arabia.

❑ Exercise 29. Speaking and writing: pairwork. (Charts 3-1 → 3-6)

Work with a partner. Tell your partner five to ten things you do every morning. Use the list you made in Exercise 3. Your partner will also give you information about his/her morning. Take notes. Then write a paragraph about your partner's morning activities. Pay special attention to the use of final ***-s/-es***. Ask your partner to read your paragraph and to check your use of final ***-s/-es***.

❑ Exercise 30. Warm-up. (Chart 3-7)

Which sentences are true for you?

1. I like to speak English. yes no
2. I need to learn English. yes no
3. I want to speak English fluently. yes no

3-7 *Like To, Want To, Need To*

VERB + INFINITIVE	
(a) I ***like*** ***to travel***. It's fun. (b) I ***want*** ***to travel***. I have vacation time next month. (c) I ***need*** ***to travel*** for my job. I have no choice.	***Like***, ***want***, and ***need*** can be followed by an infinitive. infinitive = ***to*** + *the base form of the verb.** ***Need to*** is stronger than ***want to***. ***Need to*** = necessary, important.

* The base form of a verb = a verb without *-s*, *-ed*, or *-ing*. Examples of the base form of a verb: *come, help, answer, write*. Examples of infinitives: *to come, to help, to answer, to write*. The base form is also called the simple form of a verb.

❑ **Exercise 31. Looking at grammar.** (Chart 3-7)
Make complete sentences. Pay attention to the final ***-s*** ending on singular verbs.

1. Maya \ need \ study ___*Maya needs to study.*___
2. We \ want \ go home ______________________
3. Bill and I \ like \ eat sweets ______________________
4. You \ need \ speak more quietly ______________________
5. She \ like \ talk on the phone ______________________
6. Her friends \ like \ text ______________________
7. They \ need \ save money ______________________
8. He \ want \ travel ______________________

❑ **Exercise 32. Reading and grammar.** (Charts 3-1 → 3-7)
Part I. Read the story.

A Wonderful Cook

Roberto is a wonderful cook. He often tries new recipes. He likes to cook for friends. He frequently invites my girlfriend and me to dinner. When we arrive, we go to the kitchen. He usually has three or four pots on the stove. He makes a big mess when he cooks. We like to watch him, and he wants to tell us about each recipe. His dinners are delicious. After dinner, he needs to clean the kitchen. We want to help him because we want him to invite us back soon.

Part II. Complete each sentence with a word from the box.

help	invite	is	like	likes to	wash

1. Roberto ____________________ a great cook.
2. He ____________________ try new recipes.
3. He likes to ____________________ friends to dinner.
4. After dinner, he needs to ____________________ the pots, and his friends ____________________ him.
5. His friends ____________________ his food.

❑ **Exercise 33. Let's talk: game.** (Chart 3-7)

Work in teams. What do you know about mosquitoes? Choose the correct answer. The team with the most correct answers wins.*

1. They like to look for food during the day.	yes	no
2. They like to look for food at night.	yes	no
3. They need to lay their eggs in water.	yes	no
4. They like to travel.	yes	no
5. They need to sleep in water.	yes	no
6. Male mosquitoes need to bite.	yes	no
7. Female mosquitoes need to bite.	yes	no

❑ **Exercise 34. Warm-up.** (Chart 3-8)

Which sentences are true for you?

1. a. I like vegetables. b. I don't like vegetables.
2. a. I drink tea. b. I don't drink tea.
3. a. I eat meat. b. I don't eat meat.

---

*See *Let's Talk: Answers,* p. 277.

3-8 Simple Present Tense: Negative

(a) I *do not* drink coffee. You *do not* drink coffee. We *do not* drink coffee. They *do not* drink coffee. (b) He *does not* drink coffee. She *does not* drink coffee. It *does not* drink coffee.	NEGATIVE: *I / You / We / They* + ***do not*** + *main verb* *He / She / It* + ***does not*** + *main verb* ***Do*** and ***does*** are called "helping verbs." Notice in (b): In 3rd person singular, there is no ***-s*** on the main verb, ***drink;*** the final ***-s*** is part of the helping verb, ***does***. INCORRECT: *She does not drinks coffee.*
(c) I ***don't*** drink coffee. He ***doesn't*** drink coffee.	CONTRACTIONS: ***do not*** = ***don't*** ***does not*** = ***doesn't*** People usually use contractions when they speak. People often use contractions when they write.

❑ **Exercise 35. Looking at grammar.** (Chart 3-8)
Choose the correct verb.

1.	We	does not / (do not)	have a TV.
2.	She	does not / do not	like milk.
3.	They	does not / do not	play soccer.
4.	I	does not / do not	understand.
5.	It	does not / do not	rain much here.
6.	You	does not / do not	understand.
7.	He	doesn't / don't	work hard.
8.	You	doesn't / don't	need help.
9.	They	doesn't / don't	live here.
10.	She	doesn't / don't	speak English.
11.	We	doesn't / don't	have time.
12.	I	doesn't / don't	study every day.

❑ Exercise 36. Looking at grammar. (Chart 3-8)

Use the given words to make negative sentences. Use contractions.

1. like, not — Ingrid ___*doesn't like*___ tea.
2. like, not — I ___*don't like*___ tea.
3. know, not — Mary and Jim are strangers. Mary ______________ Jim.
4. speak, not — I ______________ French.
5. need, not — It's a nice day today. You ______________ your umbrella.

an umbrella

6. live, not — Dogs ______________ long.
7. have, not — A dog ______________ a long life.
8. have, not — We ______________ class every day.
9. have, not — This city ______________ nice weather in the summer.
10. snow, not — It ______________ in Bangkok in the winter.
11. rain, not — It ______________ every day.

❑ Exercise 37. Let's talk: pairwork. (Chart 3-8)

Work with a partner. Make two sentences about each picture.

Example:

PARTNER A: Isabel takes showers. She doesn't take baths.
Your turn now.

PARTNER B: Omar has a dog. He doesn't have a cat.
Your turn now.

YES | NO

1. (Isabel \ take)
showers
baths

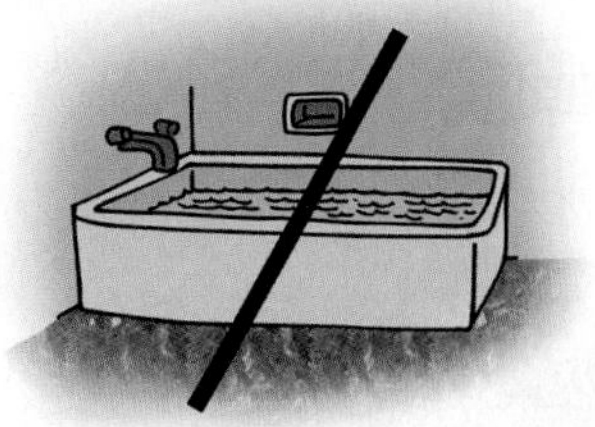

2. (Omar \ have)
a cat
a dog

YES | NO

3. (I \ drink)
tea
coffee

4. (Rob and Ed \ live)
an apartment
a house

5. (Julia \ drive)
a new car
an old car

6. (I \ play)
soccer
tennis

7. (Mr. Ortiz \ teach)
English
French

8. (we \ use)
typewriters
computers

9. (Inga \ watch)
news reports
old movies

10. (Marco \ study)
history
physics

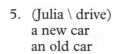

❑ **Exercise 38. Let's talk: game.** (Chart 3-8)

Sit in a circle. Use any of the verbs from the box. Make sentences with ***not***.

Example: like
STUDENT A: I don't like bananas.
STUDENT B: (*Student A*) doesn't like bananas. I don't have a dog.
STUDENT C: (*Student A*) doesn't like bananas. (*Student B*) doesn't have a dog.
I don't play baseball.

have	like	need	play	read	speak

Continue around the circle. Each time, repeat the information of your classmates before you say your sentence. If you have trouble, your classmates can help you. Your teacher will be the last one to speak.

❑ **Exercise 39. Looking at grammar.** (Chart 3-8)

Use verbs from the box to complete the sentences. Make all of the sentences negative by using ***does not*** or ***do not***. You can use contractions (***doesn't/don't***). Some verbs may be used more than one time.

do	eat	make	shave	speak
drink	go	put on	smoke	

1. Ricardo *doesn't go* to school every day.
2. My roommates are from Japan. They ______________ Spanish.
3. Roberto has a beard. He ______________ in the morning.

4. We ______________ to class on Sunday.
5. Camilla is healthy. She ______________ cigarettes.
6. Nadia and Anton always have lunch at home. They ______________ in the cafeteria.
7. Sometimes I ______________ my homework in the evening. I watch TV instead.
8. My sister likes tea, but she ______________ coffee.
9. Hamid is a careful writer. He ______________ spelling mistakes when he writes.
10. Sometimes Julianna ______________ her shoes when she goes outside. She likes to go barefoot.

❑ **Exercise 40. Looking at grammar.** (Charts 1-6, 1-7, and 3-8)
Complete the chart with the correct form of the given verbs.

SIMPLE PRESENT: *BE*	SIMPLE PRESENT: *EAT*
1. I ___*am not*___ hungry.	1. I ___*do not eat*___ meat.
2. You ___________ hungry.	2. You ___________ meat.
3. She ___________ hungry.	3. She ___________ meat.
4. We ___________ hungry.	4. We ___________ meat.
5. It ___________ hungry.	5. It ___________ meat.
6. They ___________ hungry.	6. They ___________ meat.
7. He ___________ hungry.	7. He ___________ meat.
8. Raj ___________ hungry.	8. Raj ___________ meat.
9. You and I ___________ hungry.	9. You and I ___________ meat.

❑ **Exercise 41. Looking at grammar.** (Charts 1-6, 1-7, and 3-8)
Choose the correct verb.

1.	I	(am not) / do not	late.
2.	They	are not / do not	drink coffee.
3.	He	is not / does not	do his homework.
4.	You	are not / do not	poor.
5.	She	is not / does not	do her homework.
6.	The key	is not / does not	work.
7.	It	is not / does not	in the car.
8.	I	am not / do not	like vegetables.
9.	We	are not / do not	live here.
10.	We	are not / do not	citizens.

❑ **Exercise 42. Let's talk: class activity.** (Charts 1-6, 1-7, and 3-8)
Part I. Use the given words to make true sentences for each pair.

Example: a. Grass \ be blue.
b. Grass \ be green

STUDENT A: Grass isn't blue.
STUDENT B: Grass is green.

Example: a. Dogs \ have tails
b. People \ have tails.
STUDENT C: Dogs have tails.
STUDENT D: People* don't have tails.

1. a. A restaurant \ sell shoes.
   b. A restaurant \ serve food.

2. a. People \ wear clothes.
   b. Animals \ wear clothes.

3. a. A child \ need love, food, and care.
   b. A child \ need a driver's license.

4. a. Refrigerators \ be hot inside.
   b. Refrigerators \ be cold inside.

5. a. A cat \ have whiskers.
   b. A bird \ have whiskers.

Part II. Make true sentences.

6. Doctors in my country \ be expensive.
7. A bus \ carry people from one place to another.
8. It \ be cold today.
9. English \ be an easy language to learn.
10. People in this city \ be friendly.
11. It \ rain a lot in this city.

❑ Exercise 43. Warm-up. (Chart 3-9)

What do you notice about the questions with ***have*** and ***need***?

Are you okay?
Are you sick?
Do you have a fever?
Do you need a doctor?

***People* is a plural noun. It takes a plural verb.

3-9 Simple Present Tense: Yes/No Questions

DO/DOES + SUBJECT + MAIN VERB	QUESTION FORMS, SIMPLE PRESENT
(a) *Do* *I* *work?* (b) *Do* *you* *work?* (c) *Does* *he* *work?* (d) *Does* *she* *work?* (e) *Does* *it* *work?* (f) *Do* *we* *work?* (g) *Do* *they* *work?*	***Do I*** ***Do you*** ***Does he*** ***Does she*** } + *main verb* (base form) ***Does it*** ***Do we*** ***Do they*** Notice in (c), (d), and (e): The main verb in the question does not have a final **-s**. The final **-s** is part of ***does***. INCORRECT: *Does she works?*
(h) *Am I* late? (i) *Are you* ready? (j) *Is he* a teacher? (k) *Are we* early? (l) *Are they* at home? (m) *Are you* a student? INCORRECT: *Do you be a student?*	When the main verb is a form of ***be***, ***do*** is NOT used. See Chart 2-1, p. 28, for question forms with ***be***.
QUESTION → SHORT ANSWER (n) *Do* you *like* fish? → Yes, I *do*. / No, I *don't*. (o) *Does* Liam *like* fish? → Yes, he *does*. / No, he *doesn't*.	***Do, don't, does***, and ***doesn't*** are used in the short answers to yes/no questions in the simple present.
(p) Brad *does* his homework. (q) *Does* Brad *do* his homework?	Note that ***do*** can also be a main verb, as in (p) and (q).

❑ **Exercise 44. Looking at grammar.** (Chart 3-9)

Make questions. Choose the correct answer.

1. A: *like \ you \ tea* Do you like tea?
   B: (a.) Yes, I do.
   b. Yes, I like.

2. A: *speak \ Anita \ Italian* ____________
   B: a. Yes, she does.
   b. Yes, she speaks.

3. A: *speak \ Thomas and Sierra \ Arabic* ____________
   B: a. No, they don't.
   b. No, they don't speak.

4. A: *rain \ it \ in April* ______________________________
   B: a. Yes, it does.
      b. Yes, it rains.

5. A: *do \ he \ his homework* ______________________________
   B: a. No, he doesn't.
      b. No, he doesn't do.

6. A: *do \ you \ your homework* ______________________________
   B: a. No, I don't.
      b. No, I don't do.

7. A: *have \ they \ enough money* ______________________________
   B: a. Yes, they do.
      b. Yes, they have.

❑ Exercise 45. Speaking and grammar: pairwork. (Charts 2-1, 2-2, and 3-9)

Part I. Work with a partner. Take turns making questions and giving short answers. Use the names of your classmates in the questions. *Note: Part I* is speaking practice. Do not write the answers until *Part II*.

Example:
PARTNER A: ______________________________
PARTNER B: ______________________ (He is in class today.)
PARTNER A: Is Ali in class today?
PARTNER B: Yes, he is.

Example:
PARTNER B: ______________________________
PARTNER A: ______________________ (She doesn't speak Spanish.)
PARTNER B: Does Akiko speak Spanish?
PARTNER A: No, she doesn't.

1. PARTNER A: ______________________________
   PARTNER B: ______________________ (He speaks English in class every day.)
2. PARTNER B: ______________________________
   PARTNER A: ______________________ (She comes to class every day.)
3. PARTNER A: ______________________________
   PARTNER B: ______________________ (They're in class today.)
4. PARTNER B: ______________________________
   PARTNER A: ______________________ (He wears jeans every day.)
5. PARTNER A: ______________________________
   PARTNER B: ______________________ (They aren't from Australia.)

6. PARTNER B: ______________________________

PARTNER A: ______________ (They don't have dictionaries on their desks.)

7. PARTNER A: ______________________________

PARTNER B: ______________________ (They speak English.)

Part II. Now write the questions and answers in your book.

❑ **Exercise 46. Vocabulary and speaking.** (Chart 3-9)

Part I. Check (✓) the activities you do at least once a week.

1. ____ take a nap
2. ____ take a break
3. ____ take a shower
4. ____ take a bath
5. ____ take a bus/train/taxi
6. ____ make breakfast
7. ____ make lunch
8. ____ make dinner
9. ____ make a snack
10. ____ make my bed
11. ____ do my homework
12. ____ do the dishes
13. ____ do the laundry

Part II. Walk around the room. Ask questions using these phrases. For each question, find someone who can answer ***yes***. *Note:* Remember to change ***my*** to ***your***.

Example:

To STUDENT A: Do you take a nap in the afternoon?
STUDENT A: No.
To STUDENT B: Do you take a nap in the afternoon?
STUDENT B: Yes.
To STUDENT C: Do you make your bed every day?
STUDENT C: Yes.

❑ **Exercise 47. Looking at grammar.** (Chapters 1 and 2; Charts 3-1 and 3-7 → 3-9)

Complete each sentence with the correct form of the given verb. Use the full form or contractions for the negative.

Part I. Statement Forms

	LIVE	***BE***
1.	I ___*live*___ here.	I ___*am*___ here.
2.	They __________ here.	They __________ here.
3.	He __________ here.	He __________ here.
4.	You __________ here.	You __________ here.
5.	She __________ here.	She __________ here.
6.	We __________ here.	We __________ here.

Part II. Negative Forms

7. They <u>do not / don't live</u> here. They <u>are not / aren't</u> here.
8. I ______________ here. I ______________ here.
9. She ______________ here. She ______________ here.
10. You ______________ here. You ______________ here.
11. He ______________ here. He ______________ here.
12. We ______________ here. We ______________ here.

Part III. Question Forms

13. <u>Do</u> you <u>live</u> here? <u>Are</u> you here?
14. ______ they ______________ here? ______ they here?
15. ______ he ______________ here? ______ he here?
16. ______ we ______________ here? ______ we here?
17. ______ she ______________ here? ______ she here?

❑ Exercise 48. Let's talk: game. (Charts 2-1 and 3-9)

Work in teams. Complete the sentences with ***is***, ***are***, ***do***, or ***does***. Answer the questions with *yes* or *no*. The team with the most correct answers wins.

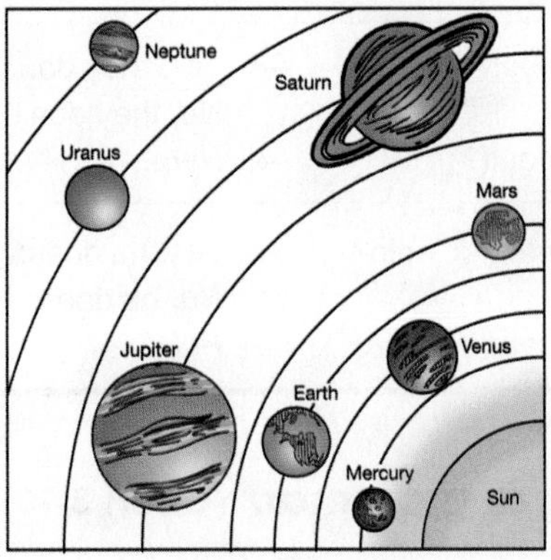

1. <u>Does</u> the moon go around the Earth? (yes) no
2. ______ the sun go around the Earth? yes no
3. ______ the planets go around the sun? yes no
4. ______ the sun a planet? yes no
5. ______ stars planets? yes no
6. ______ Venus hot? yes no
7. ______ Neptune easy to see? yes no

8.	____________	Jupiter windy?	yes	no
9.	____________	Venus and Mercury go around the sun?	yes	no
10.	____________	Saturn and Uranus have moons?	yes	no

❑ **Exercise 49. Warm-up.** (Chart 3-10)
Match the questions with the correct answers.

1. Where is the lost-and-found? ___ — a. The lost-and-found.
2. Is the lost-and-found office in this building? ___ — b. Yes, it is.
3. What is in this building? ___ — c. Down the hall.

3-10 Simple Present Tense: Asking Information Questions with *Where* and *What*

	(WHERE/ WHAT) +	DO/ DOES +	SUBJECT +	MAIN VERB			SHORT ANSWER	
(a)		Do	they	*live*	in Miami?	→	**Yes,** they do. **No,** they don't.	(a) = a yes/no question (b) = an information question **Where** asks for information about a place. The form of yes/no questions and information questions is the same: ***Do/Does*** + *subject* + *main verb*
(b)	***Where***	*do*	they	*live?*		→	***In Miami.***	
(c)		Does	Gina	*live*	in Rome?	→	**Yes,** she does. **No,** she doesn't.	
(d)	***Where***	*does*	Gina	*live?*		→	***In Rome.***	
(e)		Do	they	*need*	help?	→	**Yes,** they do. **No,** they don't.	***What*** asks for information about a thing.
(f)	***What***	*do*	they	*need?*		→	***Help.***	
(g)		Does	Lee	*need*	help?	→	**Yes,** he does. **No,** he doesn't.	
(h)	***What***	*does*	Lee	*need?*		→	***Help.***	

❑ **Exercise 50. Looking at grammar.** (Chart 3-10)
Make questions.

1. A: *Does Hana eat lunch in the cafeteria every day?*
   B: Yes, she does. (Hana eats lunch in the cafeteria every day.)
2. A: *Where does Hana eat lunch every day?*
   B: In the cafeteria. (Hana eats lunch in the cafeteria every day.)
3. A: ______________________________
   B: Rice. (She eats rice for lunch every day.)
4. A: ______________________________
   B: At the post office. (Alfonso works at the post office.)

5. A: ____
   B: Yes, he does. (Alfonso works at the post office.)

6. A: ____
   B: Yes, I do. (I live in an apartment.)

7. A: ____
   B: In an apartment. (I live in an apartment.)

8. A: ____
   B: Popcorn. (Hector likes popcorn for a snack.)

9. A: ____
   B: At the University of Toronto. (Ming goes to school at the University of Toronto.)

10. A: ____
    B: Biology. (Her major is biology.)

11. A: ____
    B: To class. (I go to class every morning.)

12. A: ____
    B: In class. (The students are in class right now.)

❑ **Exercise 51. Let's talk: pairwork.** (Chart 3-10)
Work with a partner. Ask and answer questions with ***where***.

Example: live
→ Where do you live?

PARTNER A	PARTNER B
1. live	1. buy your clothes
2. eat lunch every day	2. go on weekends
3. go after class	3. sit during class
4. study at night	4. eat dinner
5. go to school	5. do your homework
6. buy school supplies	6. go on vacation

❑ **Exercise 52. Reading.** (Chart 3-10)
Read the story and answer the questions.

Opposite Roommates

I have two roommates. One of them, Fernando, is always neat and clean. He washes his clothes once or twice a week. My other roommate, Matt, is the opposite of Fernando. For example, Matt doesn't change the sheets on his bed. He keeps the same sheets week after week. He never washes his clothes. He wears the same dirty jeans every day. He doesn't care if his clothes smell! Fernando's side of the room is always neat. He makes his bed, hangs up his clothes, and puts everything away. Matt's side of the room is always a mess. He doesn't make his bed, hang up his clothes, or put things away. What habits do you think I prefer?

1. What are some of Fernando's habits?
2. What are some of Matt's habits?
3. Who is a good roommate for you? Why?

❏ Exercise 53. Let's talk: class activity. (Chart 3-10)

Ask your teacher questions to get more information about each person's life.* Decide who has the best life and why.

Example:
STUDENT A: Where does Antonio live?
TEACHER: On a boat.
STUDENT B: What does Lena do?
TEACHER: She teaches skiing.
STUDENT C: What pets does Lisa have?
TEACHER: She has a snake.

Continue asking questions until your chart is complete.

	Where does she/he live?	**What does he/she do?**	**Where does she/he work?**	**What pets does he/she have?**
ANTONIO	*on a boat*			
LENA		*teaches skiing*		
KANE			*at a jewelry store*	
LISA				*a snake*
JACK				

❏ Exercise 54. Warm-up. (Chart 3-11)

Answer the questions.

1. What time does Alberto's alarm clock go off? ____________
2. When does Alberto get out of bed? ____________

8:00 A.M.

8:30 A.M.

*Teacher: See *Let's Talk: Answers,* p. 277.

3-11 Simple Present Tense: Asking Information Questions with *When* and *What Time*

	QUESTION* WORD	+ *DO/ DOES*	+ SUBJECT	+ MAIN VERB			SHORT ANSWER	
(a)	*When*	do	you	go	to class?	→	*At nine o'clock.*	***When*** and ***what time*** ask for information about time.
(b)	*What time*	do	you	go	to class?	→	*At nine o'clock.*	
(c)	*When*	does	Anna	eat	dinner?	→	*At six* P.M.	
(d)	*What time*	does	Anna	eat	dinner?	→	*At six* P.M.	

(e) *What time* do you *usually* go to class?	The frequency adverb usually comes immediately after the subject in a question: *Question word* + **does/do** + *subject* + **usually** + *main verb*

* *Where, when, what, what time, who,* and *why* are examples of question words.

❑ Exercise 55. Looking at grammar. (Chart 3-11)

Make questions.

1. A: *When/What time do you eat breakfast?*
   B: At 7:30. (I eat breakfast at 7:30 in the morning.)

2. A: *When/What time do you usually eat breakfast?*
   B: At 7:00. (I usually eat breakfast at 7:00.)

3. A: ______________________________
   B: At 6:45. (I usually get up at 6:45.)

4. A: ______________________________
   B: At 6:30. (Maria usually gets up at 6:30.)

5. A: ______________________________
   B: At 8:15. (The movie starts at 8:15.)

6. A: ______________________________
   B: Around 11:00. (I usually go to bed around 11:00.)

7. A: ______________________________
   B: At 12:30. (I usually eat lunch at 12:30.)

8. A: ______________________________
   B: At 5:30. (The restaurant opens at 5:30.)

9. A: ______________________________
   B: At 9:05. (The train leaves at 9:05.)

10. A: ______________________________
    B: Between 6:30 and 8:00. (I usually eat dinner between 6:30 and 8:00.)

11. A: ______________________________
    B: At a quarter after eight. (Classes begin at a quarter after eight.)

12. A: ______________________________
    B: At 10:00 P.M. (The library closes at 10:00 P.M. on Saturday.)

❑ Exercise 56. Let's talk: interview. (Chart 3-11)

Walk around the room. Ask a question beginning with ***when*** or ***what time***. Write the answer and your classmate's name. Then ask another classmate a different question with ***when*** or ***what time***. Share a few of your answers with the class.

Example: eat breakfast
STUDENT A: When/What time do you eat breakfast?
STUDENT B: I usually eat breakfast around seven o'clock.

ACTIVITY	NAME	ANSWER
1. wake up		
2. usually get up		
3. eat breakfast		
4. leave home in the morning		
5. usually get to class		
6. eat lunch		
7. get home from school		
8. have dinner		
9. usually study in the evening		
10. go to bed		

❑ **Exercise 57. Looking at grammar.** (Chapter 3)
Use the information about Professor Vega to make questions and answers.

Professor Vega
Office hours: Tuesday and Thursday 3:00 - 4:00
Classes: Psychology 101, Room 213 9:00 - 10:00 daily
Child Psychology 205, Room 201 11:00 - 12:50 Tuesday and Thursday

1. *be \ he \ a physics teacher*

   Is he a physics teacher?

   No, he isn't.

2. *what \ teach \ he*

   What does he teach?

   He teaches Psychology 101 and Child Psychology 205.

3. *teach \ he \ Psychology 102*

   ________________? ________________

4. *where \ teach \ he \ Child Psychology 205*

   ________________? ________________

5. *be \ he \ in his office \ every day*

   ________________? ________________

6. *be \ he \ in his office \ at 9:00*

   ________________? ________________

7. *teach \ he \ at 7:00 A.M.*

   ________________? ________________

8. *what time \ leave \ he \ the office on Tuesdays and Thursdays*

   ________________? ________________

9. *be \ he \ a professor*

   ________________? ________________

❑ **Exercise 58. Looking at grammar.** (Chapter 3)
Complete the questions in the conversations. Use ***is, are, does,*** or ***do***.

CONVERSATION 1:

A: What time ___does___ (1) the movie start?

B: Seven-fifteen. ________ (2) you want to go with us?

A: Yes. What time __________ it now?
3

B: Almost seven o'clock. __________ you ready to leave?
4

A: Yes, let's go.

CONVERSATION 2:

A: Where __________ my keys to the car?
5

B: I don't know. Where __________ you usually keep them?
6

A: In my purse. But they're not there.

B: Are you sure?

A: Yes. __________ you see them?
7

B: No. __________ they in one of your pockets?
8

A: I don't think so.

B: __________ your husband have them?
9

A: No. He has his own set of car keys.

B: Well, good luck!

A: Thanks.

CONVERSATION 3:

A: __________ you go to school?
10

B: Yes.

A: __________ your brother go to school too?
11

B: No, he works full-time.

A: Where __________ he work?
12

B: At a hotel.

A: __________ he happy?
13

B: Yes, he loves his job.

❑ Exercise 59. Check your knowledge. (Chapter 3)

Correct the mistakes.

1. Niko ~~live~~ *lives* in Greece.
2. Lisa comes usually to class on time.
3. Diego use his cell phone often.
4. Amira carry a notebook computer to work every day.
5. She enjoy her job.
6. Miguel don't like milk. He never drink it.
7. Tina doesn't speaks Chinese. She speakes Spanish.
8. You a student?
9. Does your roommate sleeps with the window open?
10. Where your parents live?
11. What time is your English class begins?
12. Olga isn't need a car. She have a bicycle.
13. I no speak English.
14. Omar speak English every day.
15. A: Do you like strong coffee?

    B: Yes, I like.

❑ Exercise 60. Looking at grammar. (Chapter 3)

Make questions. Use your own words.

1. A: ____?

   B: No, I don't.

2. A: ____?

   B: Yes, I am.

3. A: ____?

   B: In an apartment.

4. A: ____?

   B: Six-thirty.

5. A: ____ ?
   B: Monday.

6. A: ____ ?
   B: No, he doesn't.

7. A: ____ ?
   B: No, she isn't.

8. A: ____ ?
   B: South of the United States.

9. A: ____ ?
   B: Yes, it is.

10. A: ____ ?
    B: Yes, they do.

11. A: ____ ?
    B: In Southeast Asia.

12. A: ____ ?
    B: Yes, I do.

❑ **Exercise 61. Speaking and writing: pairwork.** (Chapter 3)

Part I. Work with a partner. Take turns asking about things you have and don't have (for example, a car, a computer, a pet, children, a TV set, a briefcase, etc.). Take notes.

Example:
PARTNER A: Do you have a car?
PARTNER B: No.
PARTNER A: Do you have a computer?
PARTNER B: Yes, but it's not here. It's in my country.
Etc.

Part II. Take turns asking about things you like and don't like.

Example:
PARTNER B: Do you like pizza?
PARTNER A: Yes.
PARTNER B: Do you like the music of (name of a group or singer)?
PARTNER A: No, I don't.
Etc.

Part III. Write about your partner.

- Give a physical description.
- Write about things this person has and doesn't have.
- Write about things this person likes and doesn't like.

Here is some vocabulary to help you describe your partner.

HAIR TYPE	HAIR COLOR		EYE COLOR
straight	brown	blond	brown
curly	black	dark	blue
wavy	red	light	green
bald			gray

straight

curly

wavy

bald

Writing sample:

My partner is Jin. He is very tall. He has brown eyes and black hair, and he has a nice smile. He is very friendly.

Jin has an apartment near school. He doesn't have a car, but he has a bike. He rides his bike to school. He has a laptop computer. His family doesn't live here. He talks to them by video a few times a week.

He is often homesick. He likes to watch movies from his country in the evening. He enjoys comedy and drama. He likes many kinds of music. He listens to music on his cell phone. He doesn't really like the food here. He likes spicy food. The food here is not spicy. Unfortunately, he is not a good cook, so he doesn't cook much. He likes to eat with his friends. They are good cooks.

Part IV. Editing check: Work individually or change papers with a partner. Check (✓) for the following:

1. ____ capital letter at the beginning of each sentence
2. ____ capital letter at the beginning of a person's name
3. ____ period at the end of each sentence
4. ____ paragraph indents
5. ____ a verb in every sentence
6. ____ correct use of ***doesn't*** or ***isn't*** in negative sentences
7. ____ correct spelling (use a dictionary or spell-check)

Chapter 4
Using the Present Progressive

❑ **Exercise 1. Warm-up.** (Chart 4-1)
Complete the sentences with the given words.

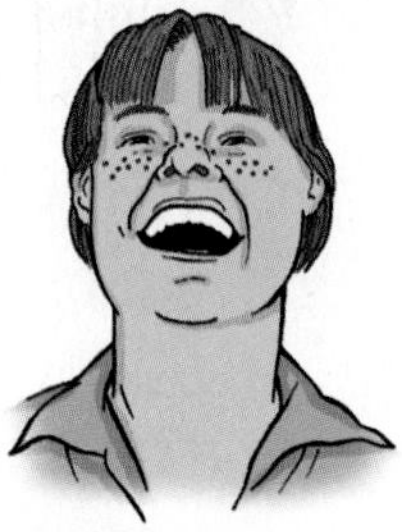

David

Nancy

	happy/sad	***laughing/crying***
1.	David is ______________________.	He is ______________________.
2.	Nancy is ______________________.	She is ______________________.

4-1 *Be* + *-ing*: the Present Progressive

am + ***-ing***	(a) I ***am sitting*** in class right now.	In (a): When I say this sentence, I am in class. I am sitting. I am not standing. The action (sitting) is happening right now, and I am saying the sentence at the same time.
is + ***-ing***	(b) Rita ***is sitting*** in class right now.	***am, is, are*** = helping verbs ***sitting*** = the main verb
are + ***-ing***	(c) You ***are sitting*** in class right now.	***am, is, are*** + ***-ing*** = the present progressive*

* The present progressive is also called the "present continuous."

❑ Exercise 2. Looking at grammar. (Chart 4-1)

Complete the sentences with the correct form of ***be*** (***am, is,*** or ***are***).

Right now . . .

1. it ___is___ raining outside.
2. we ________ sitting in the college library.
3. you ________ writing.
4. some students ________ studying.
5. I ________ looking out the window.
6. two women ________ waiting for a bus.
7. they ________ talking.
8. a bus ________ coming.

❑ Exercise 3. Looking at grammar. (Chart 4-1)

Complete each sentence with the present progressive of the verb in *italics*.

1. *stand* She ___is standing___________.
2. *sleep* You ____________________.
3. *read* He ____________________.
4. *eat* I ____________________.
5. *help* We ____________________.
6. *play* They ____________________.
7. *snow* It ____________________.

❑ Exercise 4. Let's talk: class activity. (Chart 4-1)

Your teacher will act out some verbs. Answer questions about these actions. Close your book for this activity.

Example: read
TEACHER: (*acts out reading*) I am reading. What am I doing?
STUDENT: You are reading.

1. write
2. sit
3. stand
4. count
5. wave
6. look at the ceiling

❑ **Exercise 5. Let's talk: pairwork.** (Chart 4-1)

Work with a partner. Take turns describing the pictures. Use the present progressive form of the verbs from the box.

Example:

PARTNER A: The woman is driving a car.
PARTNER B: (*points to the picture*)
PARTNER A: Your turn.

fish	get on (a bus)	laugh	sing	swim
fix (a computer)	kick (a soccer ball)	read	sleep	walk

1

2

3

4

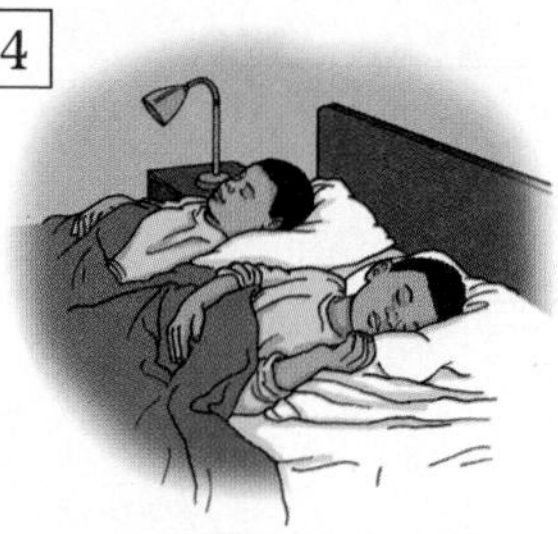

5

6

7

8

9

10

❑ **Exercise 6. Let's talk: class activity.** (Chart 4-1)

Act out the directions your teacher gives you. Describe the actions using the present progressive. Continue the action during the description. Close your book for this activity.

Example:

TEACHER TO STUDENT A:	Please smile. What are you doing?
STUDENT A:	I'm smiling.
TEACHER TO STUDENTS A + B:	Please smile. (*Student A*), what are you and (*Student B*) doing?
STUDENT A:	We're smiling.
TEACHER TO STUDENT B:	What are you and (*Student A*) doing?
STUDENT B:	We're smiling.
TEACHER TO STUDENT C:	What are (*Student A* and *Student B*) doing?
STUDENT C:	They're smiling.
TEACHER TO STUDENT B:	What is (*Student A*) doing?
STUDENT B:	He/She is smiling.

1. Stand up.
2. Sit down.
3. Sit in the middle of the room.
4. Stand in the back of the room.
5. Stand between (____) and (____).
6. Touch your desk.
7. Look at the ceiling.
8. Hold up your right hand.
9. Hold up your left hand.
10. Clap your hands.

❑ **Exercise 7. Listening.** (Chart 4-1)

CD 1
Track 14

Read the story. Then listen to each sentence and look at the picture of Tony. Circle the correct answer. Compare your answers with your classmates' answers.

Tony is not a serious student. He is lazy. He doesn't go to class much. He likes to sit in the cafeteria. Sometimes he sits alone, and sometimes he visits with friends from his country. He is in the cafeteria right now. What is he doing?

Example: Tony is talking on his cell phone. (yes) no

1. yes no
2. yes no
3. yes no
4. yes no
5. yes no
6. yes no
7. yes no
8. yes no
9. yes no
10. yes no

❑ **Exercise 8. Warm-up.** (Chart 4-2)
Answer the questions.

count   ride   sleep   stop

1. Which verb ends in a consonant + ***-e***? __________
2. Which verb ends in two consonants? __________
3. Which verb ends in two vowels + one consonant? __________
4. Which verb ends in one vowel + one consonant? __________

4-2 Spelling of *-ing*

	END OF VERB	→	*-ING* FORM
RULE 1	A CONSONANT* + ***-e***	→	DROP THE ***-e*** AND ADD ***-ing***
	smil*e*	→	smil*ing*
	wri*te*	→	wri*ting*
RULE 2	ONE VOWEL* + ONE CONSONANT	→	DOUBLE THE CONSONANT AND ADD ***-ing*****
	s*it*	→	s*itting*
	r*un*	→	r*unning*
RULE 3	TWO VOWELS + ONE CONSONANT	→	ADD ***-ing;*** DO NOT DOUBLE THE CONSONANT
	r*ead*	→	r*eading*
	r*ain*	→	r*aining*
RULE 4	TWO CONSONANTS	→	ADD ***-ing;*** DO NOT DOUBLE THE CONSONANT
	sta*nd*	→	sta*nding*
	pu*sh*	→	pu*shing*

*Vowels = *a, e, i, o, u.* Consonants = *b, c, d, f, g, h, j, k, l, m, n, p, q, r, s, t, v, w, x, y, z.*
**Exception to Rule 2: Do not double *w, x,* and *y*. *snow → snowing; fix → fixing; say → saying*

❑ **Exercise 9. Looking at spelling.** (Chart 4-2)
Write the ***-ing*** form of the given verbs.

1. take ___*taking*___
2. come __________
3. dream __________
4. bite __________
5. hit __________
6. rain __________
7. hurt __________
8. plan __________
9. bake __________
10. snow __________
11. study __________
12. stop __________

❑ Exercise 10. Looking at spelling. (Chart 4-2)

Your teacher will act out a sentence. On a separate piece of paper, write the word that ends in ***-ing***. Close your book for this activity.

Example: wave

TEACHER: (*waves*) I'm waving.

STUDENT: (*writes*) ___*waving*___

1. smile	4. sit	7. write	10. sneeze
2. read	5. eat	8. fly	11. cut a piece of paper
3. drink	6. clap	9. sleep	12. cry

❑ Exercise 11. Looking at grammar. (Chart 4-2)

Complete the sentences. Use the present progressive form of the verbs from the box.

call	charge	eat	search	send	wait

At work

1. People are standing in the lobby. They ___*are waiting*___ for the elevator.
2. A secretary _______________ an email to the staff.
3. A customer is using an office phone. He _______________ his office.
4. Several people are in the lunchroom. They _______________ lunch.
5. A manager has his cell phone on his desk. He _______________ his battery.
6. An employee needs information. She _______________ the Internet.

❑ Exercise 12. Warm-up. (Chart 4-3)

Choose the correct completion.

1. The birds are / aren't flying.
2. They are / aren't sitting on a telephone wire.
3. A car is / isn't driving by.

4-3 Present Progressive: Negatives

(a) I ***am not** sleeping*. I am awake. (b) Ben ***isn't** listening*. He's daydreaming. (c) Mr. and Mrs. Silva ***aren't** watching* TV. They're reading.	Present progressive negative: ***am*** / ***is*** / ***are*** } + ***not*** + ***-ing***

Ben

Mr. and Mrs. Silva

❑ **Exercise 13. Looking at grammar.** (Chart 4-3)

Make two sentences about each situation, one negative and one affirmative. Use the present progressive.

Example: Sandra: standing up / sitting down

Sandra *isn't standing up.*

She *'s sitting down.*

SITUATION 1:

Otto: watching TV / talking on the phone

Otto ______________________________

He ______________________________

SITUATION 2:
Anita: listening to music / playing soccer

Anita ____

She ____

SITUATION 3:
Sofia and Bruno: reading / eating lunch

Sofia and Bruno ____

They ____

SITUATION 4:
Ted: making photocopies / fixing the photocopy machine

Ted ____

He ____

❑ **Exercise 14. Looking at grammar.** (Chart 4-3)

Part I. Read the paragraph.

Jamal is a car mechanic. He owns a car repair business. He is very serious and works very hard.

Right now Jamal is at work. What is he doing? Check (✓) the phrases that make sense.

1. __✓__ talk to customers
2. ____ play soccer in a park
3. ____ change the oil in a car
4. ____ watch a movie in a theater
5. ____ put on a new tire
6. ____ answer the office phone
7. ____ give a customer a bill
8. ____ repair an engine
9. ____ eat at a restaurant
10. ____ replace a windshield wiper

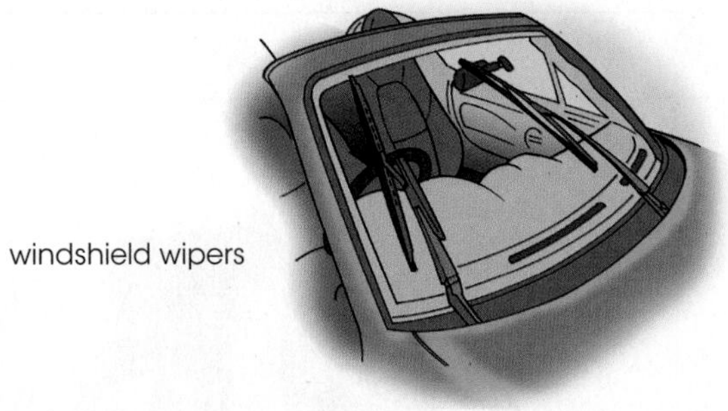

Part II. Make true sentences about Jamal.

1. *He is talking to customers.*
2. *He isn't playing soccer in a park.*
3. ______________________________
4. ______________________________
5. ______________________________
6. ______________________________
7. ______________________________
8. ______________________________
9. ______________________________
10. ______________________________

❑ **Exercise 15. Let's talk.** (Chart 4-3)
Work in small groups. Take turns making sentences about the people in the list. Say what they are doing right now and what they are not doing right now.

Example: a neighbor
→ Mrs. Martinez is working in her office right now.
→ She is not working in her garden.

1. someone in your family
2. your favorite actor, writer, or sports star
3. a friend from childhood
4. a classmate
5. the leader of your country

❑ **Exercise 16. Warm-up.** (Chart 4-4)
Choose the correct answer.

1. Are you lying on a bed?
   a. Yes, I am. b. No, I'm not.
2. Is your teacher dancing?
   a. Yes, he/she is. b. No, he/she isn't.
3. Are the students in your class singing?
   a. Yes, they are. b. No they aren't.

4-4 Present Progressive: Questions

	QUESTION					SHORT ANSWER (LONG ANSWER)	
		BE +	SUBJECT +	*-ING*			
(a)		*Is*	Marta	*sleeping?*	→	Yes, *she is.*	(She's sleeping.)
					→	No, *she's not.*	(She's not sleeping.)
					→	No, *she isn't.*	(She isn't sleeping.)
(b)		*Are*	you	*watching* TV?	→	Yes, *I am.*	(I'm watching TV.)
					→	No, *I'm not.*	(I'm not watching TV.)
	QUESTION WORD +	BE +	SUBJECT +	*-ING*			
(c)	*Where*	*is*	Marta	*sleeping?*	→	*In bed.*	(She's sleeping in bed.)
(d)	*What*	*is*	Ted	*watching?*	→	*A movie.*	(Ted is watching a movie).
(e)	*Why*	*are*	you	*watching* TV?	→	*Because I like this program.*	(I'm watching TV because I like this program.)

❑ Exercise 17. Looking at grammar. (Chart 4-4)

Make questions.

1. A: *Is the teacher helping* students?
   B: Yes, she is. (The teacher is helping students.)
2. A: ______________________________?
   B: Yes, he is. (Ivan is talking on his phone.)
3. A: ______________________________?
   B: No, I'm not. (I'm not sleeping.)
4. A: ______________________________ TV?
   B: No, they aren't. (The students aren't watching TV.)
5. A: ______________________________ outside?
   B: No, it isn't. (It isn't raining outside.)
6. A: ______________________________?
   B: Yes, he is. (John is riding a bike.)

❑ Exercise 18. Vocabulary and speaking: pairwork. (Chart 4-4)

Part I. Work with a partner. Check (✓) the expressions you know. Your teacher will explain the ones you don't know.

do	***make***	***take***
____ do the dishes	____ make breakfast	____ take a nap
____ do the laundry	____ make a bed	____ take a shower
____ do homework	____ make a phone call	____ take a bath
____ do the ironing	____ make a mess	____ take a test
		____ take a break
		____ take medicine

Part II. With your partner, take turns asking and answering questions about the pictures. Find the differences. You can look at your book before you speak. When you speak, look at your partner. Partner A: Use the pictures on p. 107. Partner B: Use the pictures in Let's Talk: Answers, p. 277.

Example:

PARTNER A	PARTNER B

PARTNER A: Is the girl in your picture taking a test?
PARTNER B: No, she isn't.
PARTNER A: What is she doing?
PARTNER B: She's taking a break.

PARTNER A		
1 	2 	3 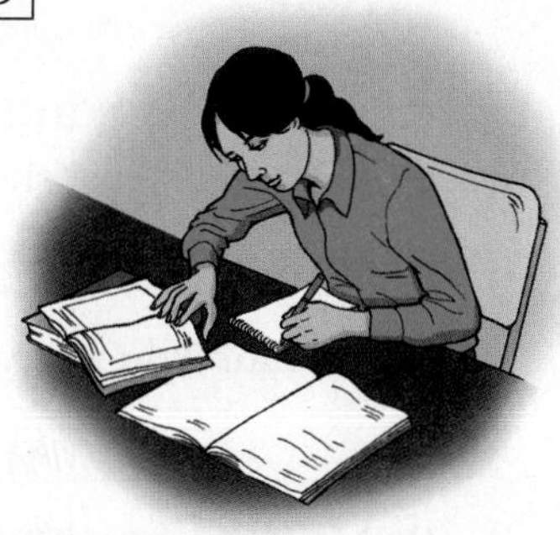
4 	5 	6 

❑ Exercise 19. Looking at grammar. (Chart 4-4)

Make questions with ***where***, ***why***, and ***what***.

1. A: ___*What are you reading?*___

   B: My grammar book. (I'm reading my grammar book.)

2. A: ________________________________

   B: Because we're doing an exercise. (I'm reading my grammar book because we're doing an exercise.)

3. A: ________________________________

   B: A sentence. (I'm writing a sentence.)

4. A: ________________________________

   B: In the back of the room. (Yoshi is sitting in the back of the room.)

5. A: ________________________________

   B: In a hotel. (I'm staying in a hotel.)

6. A: ________________________________

   B: Jeans and a sweatshirt. (Jonas is wearing jeans and a sweatshirt today.)

7. A: ________________________________

   B: Because I'm happy. (I'm smiling because I'm happy.)

❑ Exercise 20. Looking at grammar. (Chart 4-4)

Make questions. Give short answers to yes/no questions.

1. A: What ___*are you writing?*___

   B: A thank-you note. (I'm writing a thank-you note.)

2. A: ___*Is Ali reading a book?*___

   B: No, ___*he isn't / he's not.*___ (Ali isn't reading a book.)

3. A: ________________________________

   B: Yes, ________________________ (Magda is eating lunch.)

4. A: Where ____
   B: At the Sunrise Café. (She's eating lunch at the Sunrise Café.)

5. A: ____
   B: No, ______________________ (Sam isn't drinking a cup of coffee.)

6. A: What ____
   B: A glass of lemonade. (He's drinking a glass of lemonade.)

7. A: ____
   B: No, ______________________ (The girls aren't playing in the street.)

8. A: Where ____
   B: In the park. (They're playing in the park.)

9. A: Why ____
   B: Because they don't have school today. (They're playing in the park because they don't have school today.)

10. A: ____
    B: Yes. (The girls are playing together.)

11. A: ____?
    B: No. (A parent isn't watching them.)

❑ **Exercise 21. Warm-up.** (Chart 4-5)

Answer the questions with *yes* or *no*.

1. Do you eat breakfast every day?
2. Do you talk on the phone every day?
3. Do you study English every day?
4. Are you eating breakfast right now?
5. Are you talking on the phone right now?
6. Are you studying English right now?

4-5 Simple Present Tense vs. the Present Progressive

	SIMPLE PRESENT	PRESENT PROGRESSIVE
	The simple present expresses habits or usual activities. Common time words are ***every day***, ***every year***, ***every month***, ***often***, ***sometimes***, and ***never***. The simple present uses ***do*** and ***does*** in negatives and questions.	The present progressive expresses actions that are happening right now, while the speaker is speaking. Common time words are ***now***, ***right now***, and ***today***. The present progressive uses ***am***, ***is***, and ***are*** in negatives and questions.
STATEMENT	I *talk* You *talk* He, She, It *talks* We *talk* They *talk* } *every day.*	I *am talking* You *are talking* He, She, It *is talking* We *are talking* They *are talking* } *now.*
NEGATIVE	I *don't talk.* You *don't talk.* He, She, It *doesn't talk.* We *don't talk.* They *don't talk.*	I *am not talking.* You *are not talking.* He, She, It *is not talking.* We *are not talking.* They *are not talking.*
QUESTION	*Do* I *talk?* *Do* you *talk?* *Does* he, she, it *talk?* *Do* we *talk?* *Do* they *talk?*	*Am* I *talking?* *Are* you *talking?* *Is* he, she it *talking?* *Are* we *talking?* *Are* they *talking?*

❑ **Exercise 22. Looking at grammar.** (Chart 4-5)

Choose the correct completion.

1. Mari is working — (now.) — every day.
2. Mari works at a pharmacy — now. — every day.
3. I am working — today. — every day.
4. It's snowing — now. — every day.
5. You are making breakfast — today. — every day.
6. You make breakfast — right now. — every day.
7. We eat vegetables — right now. — every day.
8. We are eating outside — right now. — every day.

❑ Exercise 23. Looking at grammar. (Chart 4-5)

Complete the sentences with the correct form of the words in parentheses.

1. Ahmed (*talk*) ____talks____ to his classmates every day in class.

   Right now he (*talk*) ____is talking____ to Yoko. He (*talk, not*) ______________ to his friend Omar right now.

2. It (*rain*) ______________ a lot in this city, but it (*rain, not*) ______________ right now. The sun (*shine*) ______________. (*it, rain*) ______________ a lot in your hometown?

3. Hans and Anna (*sit*) ______________ next to each other in class every day, so they often (*help*) ______________ each other with their grammar exercises. Right now Anna (*help*) ______________ Hans with an exercise on verbs.

4. Roberto (*cook*) ______________ his own dinner every evening. Right now he is in his kitchen. He (*cook*) ______________ rice and beans. (*he, cook*) ______________ meat for his dinner tonight too? No, he is a vegetarian. He (*eat, never*) ______________ meat. (*you, eat*) ______________ meat? (*you, be*) ______________ a vegetarian?

❑ Exercise 24. Listening. (Chart 4-5)

Listen to each sentence. Choose the correct completion.

CD 1 Track 15

Examples: You will hear: Pedro is sleeping late . . .
You will choose: (now) every day

1. now every day
2. now every day
3. now every day
4. now every day
5. now every day
6. now every day
7. now every day
8. now every day

❑ **Exercise 25. Let's talk: pairwork.** (Chart 4-5)

Work with a partner. Take turns asking and answering questions about Isabel's activities. Use the present progressive and the simple present.

Example: check her phone for messages
PARTNER A: Is Isabel checking her phone for messages?
PARTNER B: Yes, she is.
PARTNER A: Does she check her phone for messages every day?
PARTNER B: Yes, she does.
PARTNER A: Your turn now.

drink tea	ride her bike	take a walk
listen to music	say "hi" to her neighbor	talk on her phone
play her guitar	write a report	text
play tennis	swim	watch TV

1

2

3

4

5

6

7

8

9

10

11

12

❑ Exercise 26. Looking at grammar. (Chart 4-5)

Complete each question with all the correct answers.

a teacher	at school	early	sick	study	studying	work

1. a. Are you *a teacher / early / studying / at school / sick*?
   b. Do you *work / study*?

angry	a dancer	cook	dance	driving	ready	understand

2. a. Do you ______________________?
   b. Are you ______________________?

a problem	help	here	new	raining	ready	true	work

3. a. Is it ______________________?
   b. Does it ______________________?

❑ Exercise 27. Looking at grammar. (Chart 4-5)

Complete the sentences with ***Do, Does, Is,*** or ***Are***.

On the subway

1. *Do* you have your ticket?
2. *Is* your ticket in your wallet?
3. ____________ the train usually leave on time?
4. ____________ the train on time?
5. ____________ the tickets cheap?
6. ____________ you looking at a map?
7. ____________ you have enough money?
8. ____________ the train here?
9. ____________ we have extra time?
10. ____________ the train leaving?
11. ____________ the conductor check for tickets?

❑ Exercise 28. Listening. (Chart 4-5)

Listen to the conversation. Complete the sentences with the words you hear.

CD 1 Track 16

Example: You will hear: Are you doing an exercise?

You will write: ___Are you doing___ an exercise?

A: What are you doing? _______________(1) on your English paper?

B: No. _______________(2). _______________(3) an email to my sister.

A: _______________(4) to her often?

B: Yes, but I _______________(5) a lot of emails to anyone else.

A: _______________(6) to you often?

B: No, but she _______________(7) me a lot.

❑ Exercise 29. Looking at grammar. (Chart 4-5)

Complete the sentences with the correct form of the words in parentheses.

1. A: Tom is on the phone.

   B: (*he, talk*) ___Is he talking___ to his wife?

   A: Yes.

   B: (*he, talk*) ___Does he talk___ to her often?

   A: Yes, he (*talk*) ___talks___ to her every day during his lunch break.

2. A: I (*walk*) _______________ to school every day. I (*take, not*) _______________ the bus. (*you, take*) _______________ the bus?

   B: No, I don't.

3. A: Selena is in the hallway.

   B: (*she, talk*) _______________ to her friends?

   A: No, she isn't. She (*run*) _______________ to her next class.

4. A: I (*read*) _______________ the newspaper every day.

   B: (*you, read*) _______________ it online?

   A: No, I don't. I (*read, not*) _______________ it online.

5. A: What (*you, read*) _______________ right now?

   B: I (*read*) _______________ my grammar book.

6. A: (*you, want*) _______________ your coat?

   B: Yes.

   A: (*be, this*) _______________ your coat?

   B: No, my coat (*hang*) _______________ in the closet right now.

❑ Exercise 30. Reading and grammar. (Chart 4-5)

Part I. Read the paragraph. Look at new vocabulary with your teacher first.

Reni's Job

Reni is a server at a restaurant. She works long hours, and the restaurant pay is minimum wage. She earns extra money from tips. Reni is an excellent server. She is friendly and fast. Customers leave her good tips. Fifteen percent is average, but often she gets twenty percent. Today Reni is working an extra shift. A co-worker is sick, so Reni is taking her hours. Reni is feeling tired at the moment, but she is also happy because the tips are good. She is earning a lot of extra money today.

Do you know these words?

- server
- minimum wage
- tips
- average
- shift
- co-worker

Part II. Complete the sentences with ***Is, Do,*** or ***Does.***

1. ____Is____ Reni a good server?
2. __________ the restaurant pay Reni a lot of money?
3. __________ customers leave her good tips?
4. __________ Reni work extra hours every day?
5. __________ Reni working extra hours today?
6. __________ she happy today?
7. __________ she earning extra money?
8. __________ she usually get good tips?
9. __________ servers earn a lot of money from tips?

Part III. Discuss possible answers to these questions.

1. In your opinion, what are some important qualities for a restaurant server? Check (✓) the items.

____ fast	____ formal
____ friendly	____ speaks other languages
____ talkative	____ smiles a lot
____ polite	____ has a good memory

2. Do customers leave tips at restaurants in your country? If yes, what percentage is an average tip? Do you like to leave tips?
3. What is more important for you at a restaurant: the food or the service?
4. In some countries, a usual workday is eight hours, and a usual workweek is 40 hours. What is the usual workday and workweek in your country?

❑ **Exercise 31. Warm-up.** (Chart 4-6)
Read the sentences. What do you notice about the verbs in red?

Right now, I am waiting at a bus stop. I see an ambulance. I hear a siren. A car and a motorcycle are stopping. The ambulance is going fast.

4-6 Non-Action Verbs Not Used in the Present Progressive

	Some verbs are NOT used in the present progressive. They are called "non-action verbs."
(a) I'm hungry ***right now***. I ***want*** an apple. INCORRECT: *I am wanting an apple.*	In (a): ***Want*** is a non-action verb. *Want* expresses a physical or emotional need, not an action.
(b) I ***hear*** a siren. ***Do*** you ***hear*** it too? INCORRECT: *I'm hearing a siren. Are you hearing it too?*	In (b): ***Hear*** is a non-action verb. *Hear* expresses a sensory experience, not an action.

NON-ACTION VERBS

dislike	hear	believe
hate	see	know
like	smell	think (*meaning* believe)*
love	taste	understand
need		
want		

*Sometimes *think* is used in progressive verbs. See Chart 4-8 for a discussion of *think about* and *think that.*

❑ **Exercise 32. Looking at grammar.** (Chart 4-6)
Complete the sentences. Use the simple present or the present progressive form of the verbs in parentheses.

1. Alicia is in her room right now. She (*listen*) ___is listening___ to a podcast. She (*like*) ___likes___ the podcast.
2. It (*snow*) ______________ right now. It's beautiful! I (*like*) ______________ this weather.
3. I (*know*) ______________ Jessica Santos. She's in my class.
4. The teacher (*talk*) ______________ to us right now. I (*understand*) ______________ everything she's saying.
5. Emilio is at a restaurant right now. He (*eat*) ______________ dinner. He (*like*) ______________ the food. It (*taste*) ______________ good.
6. Sniff-sniff. I (*smell*) ______________ gas. (*you, smell*) ______________ it?

7. Taro (*tell*) _________________________ us a story right now. I (*believe*) ________________ his story.

8. Ugh! Someone (*smoke*) _________________________ a cigar. It (*smell*) ________________ terrible! I (*hate*) ________________ cigars.

9. Look at Mr. Gomez. He (*hold*) _________________________ a kitten in his hand. He (*love*) ________________ the kitten. Mr. Gomez (*smile*) _________________________.

❑ Exercise 33. Let's talk: interview. (Chart 4-6)

Ask two students each question. Write their answers in the chart. Share some of their answers with the class.

QUESTION	STUDENT A	STUDENT B
1. What \ you \ like?		
2. What \ babies \ around the world \ like?		
3. What \ you \ want?		
4. What \ children around the world \ want?		
5. What \ you \ love?		
6. What \ teenagers around the world \ love?		
7. What \ you \ dislike or hate?		
8. What \ people around the world \ dislike or hate?		
9. What \ you \ need?		
10. What \ elderly people around the world \ need?		

❑ **Exercise 34. Warm-up.** (Chart 4-7)

Complete the sentences with the given phrases.

1. *am looking at / am watching*

   a. I ______________________________ my cell phone. It is 10:00 P.M.

   b. I ______________________________ a movie. It is very funny.

2. *hear / am listening to*

   a. I ______________________________ the teacher carefully. She is explaining grammar to me.

   b. Shh! I ______________________________ a noise. Maybe someone is downstairs!

4-7 *See, Look At, Watch, Hear,* and *Listen To*

SEE, LOOK AT, and *WATCH* (a) I **see** many things in this room.	In (a): ***see*** = a non-action verb. Seeing happens because my eyes are open. Seeing is a physical reaction, not a planned action.
(b) I'***m looking at*** the clock. I want to know the time.	In (b): ***look at*** = an action verb. Looking is a planned or purposeful action. Looking happens for a reason.
(c) Bob ***is watching*** TV.	In (c): ***watch*** = an action verb. I *watch* something for a long time, but I *look at* something for a short time.
HEAR and *LISTEN TO* (d) I'm in my apartment. I'm trying to study. I ***hear*** music from the next apartment. The music is loud.	In (d): ***hear*** = a non-action verb. Hearing is an unplanned act. It expresses a physical reaction.
(e) I'm in my apartment. I'm studying. I have an iPod. I'***m listening to*** music. I like to listen to music when I study.	In (e): ***listen*** (***to***) = an action verb. Listening happens for a purpose.

❑ **Exercise 35. Let's talk: class activity.** (Chart 4-7)

Your teacher will ask you questions. Close your book for this activity.

Example:
TEACHER: Look at the floor. What do you see?
STUDENT: I see shoes/dirt/etc.

1. What do you see in this room? Now look at something. What are you looking at?
2. Turn to p. 107 of this book. What do you see? Now look at one thing on that page. What are you looking at?
3. Look at the board. What do you see?
4. What programs do you like to watch on TV?
5. What sports do you like to watch?

6. What animals do you like to watch when you go to the zoo?
7. What do you hear at night in the place where you live?
8. What do you listen to when you go to a concert?
9. What do you listen to when you are at home?

❑ **Exercise 36. Looking at grammar.** (Chart 4-7)

Complete the sentences. Use the simple present or the present progressive form of the verbs in parentheses.

SITUATION 1:

I (*sit*) ___am sitting___ (1) in class right now. I (*sit, always*) ___always sit___ (2) in the same seat every day. Rashid is my partner today. We (*do*) __________ (3) a pairwork exercise. Right now we (*speak*) __________ (4) English. We both (*know*) __________ (5) French, so sometimes we (*speak*) __________ (6) French to each other. Of course, our teacher (*want*) __________ (7) us to speak English.

Sandro is in the corner of the room. He (*work, not*) __________ (8). He (*look*) __________ (9) around the room. Kim (*check*) __________ (10) the answer key in his grammar book. Francisco (*stare*) __________ (11) at the clock. Abdullah (*smile*) __________ (12). Lidia (*tap*) __________ (13) her foot. Hans (*chew*) __________ (14) gum.

SITUATION 2:

The person on the bench in the picture on page 120 is Caroline. She's an accountant. She (*work*) __________ (1) for the government. She (*have*) __________ (2) an hour for lunch every day. She (*eat, often*) __________ (3) lunch in the park. She (*bring, usually*) __________ (4) a sandwich and some fruit with her to the park. She (*sit, usually*) __________ (5) on a bench, but sometimes she (*sit*) __________ (6) on the grass and (*watch*) __________ (7) people and animals. She (*sees, often*) __________ (8) joggers and squirrels. She (*relax*) __________ (9) when she eats at the park.

Right now I (*look*) ________________ (10) at the picture of Caroline. She (*be, not*) ________________ (11) at home in the picture. She (*be*) ________________ (12) at the park. She (*sit*) ________________ (13) on a bench. She (*eat*) ________________ (14) her lunch. A jogger (*run*) ________________ (15) on a path through the park. A squirrel (*sit*) ________________ (16) on the ground in front of Caroline. The squirrel (*eat*) ________________ (17) a nut. Caroline (watch) ________________ (18) the squirrel. She (*watch, always*) ________________ (19) squirrels when she eats lunch in the park. Some ducks (*swim*) ________________ (20) in the pond in the picture, and some birds (*fly*) ________________ (21) in the sky. A police officer (*ride*) ________________ (22) a horse. He (*ride*) ________________ (23) a horse through the park every day. Near Caroline, a family (*have*) ________________ (24) a picnic. They (*go*) ________________ (25) on a picnic every week.

❑ Exercise 37. Warm-up. (Chart 4-8)

Do you agree or disagree with each sentence? Circle *yes* or *no*.

1. I think about my parents every day. yes no
2. I am thinking about my parents right now. yes no
3. I think that it is difficult to be a good parent. yes no

4-8 *Think About* and *Think That*

THINK + *ABOUT* + A NOUN (a) I *think* *about* *my family* every day. (b) I *am thinking* *about* *grammar* right now.	In (a): Ideas about my family are in my mind every day. In (b): My mind is busy now. Ideas about grammar are in my mind right now.
THINK + *THAT* + A STATEMENT (c) I *think* *that* *Emma is lazy.* (d) Ed *thinks* *that* *I am lazy.* (e) I *think* *that* *the weather is nice.*	In (c): In my opinion, Emma is lazy. I believe that Emma is lazy. People use ***think that*** when they want to say (to state) their beliefs. The present progressive is often used with ***think about***. The present progressive is almost never used with ***think that***. INCORRECT: *I am thinking that Emma is lazy.*
(f) I *think that* Marco is a nice person. (g) I *think* Marco is a nice person.	Examples (f) and (g) have the same meaning. People often omit ***that*** after ***think***, especially in speaking.

❑ **Exercise 38. Grammar and speaking.** (Chart 4-8)

Use ***I think that*** to give your opinion. Share a few of your opinions with the class.

1. English grammar is easy / hard / fun / interesting.

   I think that English grammar is interesting.

2. People in this city are friendly / unfriendly / kind / cold.

   ____

3. The food at (*name of a place*) is delicious / terrible / good / excellent / awful.

   ____

4. Baseball / football / soccer / golf is interesting / boring / confusing / etc.

   ____

❑ **Exercise 39. Writing and speaking.** (Chart 4-8)

Complete the sentences with your own words. Share a few of your completions with the class.

1. I think that the weather today is ____________________
2. I think my classmates are ____________________
3. Right now I'm thinking about ____________________
4. In my opinion, English grammar is ____________________
5. In my opinion, soccer is ____________________

6. I think that my parents are ____

7. I think this school is ____

8. I think about ____ often.

9. I think that ____

10. In my opinion, ____

❑ Exercise 40. Let's talk: game. (Charts 4-5 → 4-8)

Work in small groups. One person will think about an animal or a food. The other students will ask questions and try to guess the answer.

Example: animal
STUDENT A: I'm thinking about an animal
STUDENT B: Is it big?
STUDENT A: No.
STUDENT C: Does it have wings?
STUDENT A: Yes.
STUDENT D: Is it a mosquito?
STUDENT A: Yes!

Another student chooses an animal or food.

❑ Exercise 41. Reading. (Chart 4-5 → 4-8)

Read the paragraph and the statements. Circle "T" for true and "F" for false.

Sleep: How Much Do People Need?

Adults need about eight hours of sleep a night. Some need more and some need less, but this is an average amount. Newborn babies need the most sleep, about 14 to 16 hours every 24 hours. They sleep for about four hours. Then they wake up, eat, and then sleep again. As babies grow, they need a little less sleep, about 10 to 14 hours. Here is an interesting fact. Teenagers also need about 10 to 14 hours of sleep a night. Some people think teenagers sleep a lot because they are lazy. Actually, their bodies are changing, so they need a lot of rest. How much sleep do you get every night? Is it enough?

1. Everyone needs eight hours of sleep a night. T F
2. Newborn babies sleep 14 to 16 hours and then wake up. T F
3. Teenagers need a lot of sleep. T F
4. Teenagers and adults need the same amount of sleep. T F

❑ Exercise 42. Looking at grammar. (Chapter 4)

Choose the correct completion.

1. Lola and Pablo _____ TV right now.
   a. watch   b. watching   (c.) are watching

2. A: _____ you writing to your parents?
   B: No. I'm studying.
   a. Are   b. Do   c. Don't

3. I _____ like to write letters.
   a. no   b. don't   c. am not

4. A: Jack has six telephones in his apartment.
   B: I _____ you. No one needs six telephones in one apartment.
   a. am believe   b. am not believing   c. don't believe

5. When I want to know the time, I _____ a clock.
   a. see   b. look at   c. watch

6. A: Do you know Fatima?
   B: Yes, I do. I _____ she is a very nice person.
   a. am thinking   b. thinking   c. think

7. Where _____ Boris? Upstairs or downstairs?
   a. does   b. is   c. lives

8. Oh, no! Paul _____. He is allergic to cats.
   a. is sneezing   b. doesn't sneeze   c. sneezes

9. A: You look sad.
   B: Yes, I _____ about my family back in my country. I miss them.
   a. think   b. am thinking   c. thinking

❑ Exercise 43. Check your knowledge. (Chapter 4)

Correct the mistakes.

1. It's ~~rainning~~ *raining* today. I ~~no~~ *don't* like the rain.
2. I like New York City. I am thinking that it is a wonderful city.
3. Does Abdul be sleeping right now?
4. Why you are going downtown today?
5. I am liking flowers. They are smelling good.

6. Bill at a restaurant right now. He usually eat at home, but today he eatting dinner at a restaurant.
7. Alex is siting at his desk. He writting a letter.
8. Where do they are sitting today?

❑ Exercise 44. Reading and writing. (Chapter 4)

Part I. Read the paragraph. Look at new vocabulary with your teacher first.

A Sleepless Night

Mila is in bed. It is 3:00 A.M. She is very tired, but she isn't sleeping. She is thinking about medical school. She is worrying about her final exams tomorrow. She needs to pass because she wants to be a doctor. She is tossing and turning in bed. She wants a few more days to study. She is thinking about possible test questions. She is wide-awake. She isn't going back to sleep tonight.

Do you know these words?
medical school
final exams
pass
toss and turn
wide-awake

Part II. Imagine it is 3:00 A.M. You are in bed, and you are wide-awake. You are having a sleepless night. What are you thinking about? Write a paragraph. Use both simple present and present progressive verbs.

Part III. Editing check: Work individually or change papers with a partner. Check (✓) for the following:

1. _____ paragraph indent
2. _____ capital letter at the beginning of each sentence
3. _____ period at the end of each sentence
4. _____ a verb in every sentence
5. _____ use of present progressive for activities right now
6. _____ correct spelling (use a dictionary or spell-check)

Chapter 5

Talking About the Present

❑ **Exercise 1. Warm-up.** (Chart 5-1)
Match the questions to the pictures.

Picture A

It's 11:00.

Picture B

It's Saturday.

Picture C

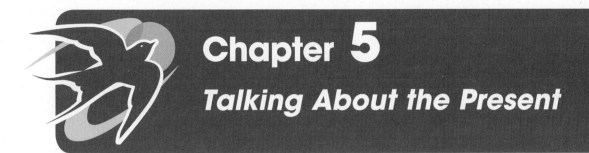

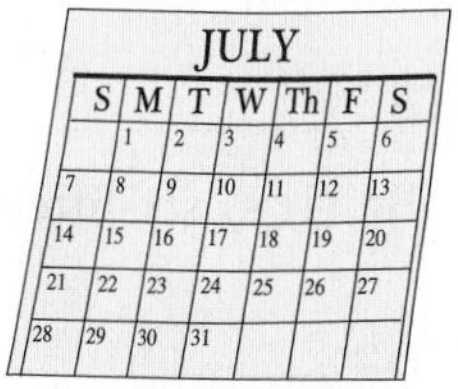

It's July.

1. What month is it?
2. What time is it?
3. What day is it?

5-1 Using *It* to Talk About Time

QUESTION		ANSWER	
(a) What day is it?	→	***It's*** Monday.	In English, people use ***it*** to express (to talk about) time.
(b) What month is it?	→	***It's*** September.	
(c) What year is it?	→	***It's*** (2014).	
(d) What's the date today?	→	***It's*** September 15th.	
	→	***It's*** the 15th of September.	
(e) What time is it?	→	***It's*** 9:00.*	
	→	***It's*** nine.	
	→	***It's*** nine o'clock.	
	→	***It's*** 9:00 A.M.	

*American English uses a colon (two dots) between the hour and the minutes: 9:00 A.M. British English uses one dot: 9.00 A.M.

❑ **Exercise 2. Looking at grammar.** (Chart 5-1)

Make questions. Begin each question with ***What***.

1. A: *What day is it?*
   B: It's Tuesday.
2. A: ______________________
   B: It's March 14th.
3. A: ______________________
   B: (It's) ten-thirty.
4. A: ______________________
   B: (It's) March.
5. A: ______________________
   B: (It's) six-fifteen.
6. A: ______________________
   B: (It's) Wednesday.
7. A: ______________________
   B: (It's) the 1st of April.
8. A: ______________________
   B: (It's) 2014.
9. A: ______________________
   B: It's 7:00 A.M.

Sun	Mon	Tues	Wed	Thurs	Fri	Sat
				1	2	3
4	5	6	7	8	9	10
11	12	13	14	15	16	17
18	19	20	21	22	23	24
25	26	27	28	29	30	31

a calendar page

❑ Exercise 3. Warm-up. (Chart 5-2)

Which answers are true for you? Complete item 3 with the time your English class meets.

1. I go to school
   ____ on Monday.
   ____ on Tuesday.
   ____ on Wednesday.
   ____ on Thursday.
   ____ on Friday.
   ____ on Saturday.
   ____ on Sunday.

2. I have class
   ____ in the morning.
   ____ in the evening.
   ____ at night.

3. I have class from ________ (time) to ________ (time).

5-2 Prepositions of Time

AT	(a) We have class **at** one o'clock. (b) I have an appointment with the doctor **at** 3:00. (c) We sleep **at** night.	**at** + a specific time on the clock **at** + *night*
IN	(d) My birthday is **in** October. (e) I was born **in** 1989. (f) We have class **in** the morning. (g) Bob has class **in** the afternoon. (h) I study **in** the evening.	**in** + a specific month **in** + a specific year **in** + *the morning* **in** + *the afternoon* **in** + *the evening*
ON	(i) I have class **on** Monday(s). (j) I was born **on** October 31. (k) I was born **on** October 31, 1991.	**on** + a specific day of the week **on** + a specific date
FROM . . . TO	(l) We have class **from** 1:00 **to** 2:00.	**from** (a specific time) **to** (a specific time)

❑ Exercise 4. Looking at grammar. (Chart 5-2)

Complete the sentences with prepositions of time.

1. *We have class . . .*

   a. ___*at*___ ten o'clock.

   b. ________ ten ________ eleven.

   c. ________ the morning and ________ the afternoon.

2. *I study . . .*

a. ________ the evening.

b. ________ night.

3. *I was born . . .*

a. ________ May.

b. ________ 1990.

c. ________ May 21.

d. ________ May 21, 1990.

4. a. The post office isn't open ________ Sundays.

b. It's open ________ 8:00 A.M. ________ 5:00 P.M., Monday through Saturday.

c. The post office closes ________ 5:00 P.M.

❑ **Exercise 5. Let's talk: pairwork.** (Chart 5-2)

Complete the sentences with information about your partner. Share some of your partner's answers with the class.

1. When do you eat breakfast?

a. I eat breakfast in ____*the morning*____.

b. I eat breakfast at ________________.

c. I eat breakfast from ________________ to ________________.

2. When do you study?

a. I study at ________________.

b. I study in ________________________.

c. I study on ________________________.

d. I study from ____________ to ____________.

3. Tell about the time of your birth.

a. I was born in ____________________.

b. I was born on ____________________.

c. I was born at ____________.

❑ Exercise 6. Listening and grammar. (Chart 5-2)

CD 1 Track 17

Part I. Listen to each description. Write the name of the person.

Example: You will hear: I was born in June. I go to class in the morning. My name is . . .

You will write: ___Lisa___

June 2, 1992
7:00 A.M.
June 24, 1985
1:00 P.M.
July 7, 1997
7:00 P.M.
July 24, 1990
11:00 A.M.
Lisa
Marta
Shen
Ron

1. ________________
2. ________________
3. ________________
4. ________________

Part II. Use the information in the pictures to complete the sentences.

1. I was born __________ July. I was born __________ July 7. My name is __________.
2. I was born __________ 1985. I was born __________ June 24, 1985. My name is __________.
3. I go to class __________ the morning. I go to class __________ 7:00. My name is __________.
4. Hi, my name is __________. I was born __________ July. I was born __________ July 24. I go to class __________ the morning.

❑ Exercise 7. Warm-up. (Chart 5-3)

Which answers are true for you?

A: In your hometown, how's the weather in the summer?

B: It's sunny / cloudy / rainy / cold / hot / windy.

A: What's the weather like in the winter?

B: It's sunny / cloudy / rainy / cold / hot / windy.

5-3 Using *It* and *What* to Talk About the Weather

(a) ***It's*** sunny today. (b) ***It's*** hot and humid today. (c) ***It's*** a nice day today.	In English, people usually use ***it*** when they talk about the weather.
(d) ***What's the weather like*** in Istanbul in January? (e) ***How's the weather*** in Moscow in the summer? (f) ***What's the temperature*** in Bangkok today?	People commonly ask about the weather by saying *What's the weather like?* OR *How's the weather?* ***What*** is also used to ask about the temperature.

❑ **Exercise 8. Let's talk: pairwork.** (Chart 5-3)

How's the weather today? Choose *yes* or *no*. Share your answers with a partner. Do you and your partner agree? Report some of your answers to the class.

1. hot	yes	no	8. sunny	yes	no
2. warm	yes	no	9. nice	yes	no
3. cool	yes	no	10. clear	yes	no
4. chilly	yes	no	11. partly cloudy	yes	no
5. cold	yes	no	12. humid*	yes	no
6. freezing	yes	no	13. windy	yes	no
7. below freezing	yes	no	14. stormy	yes	no

❑ **Exercise 9. Let's talk: small groups.** (Chart 5-3)

Change the Fahrenheit (F) temperatures to Celsius** (C) by choosing temperatures from the box. Then describe the temperature in words.

38°C 24°C ✓10°C 0°C −18°C

	FAHRENHEIT	CELSIUS	DESCRIPTION
1.	50°F	*10°C*	*cool, chilly*
2.	32°F	______	______
3.	100°F	______	______
4.	75°F	______	______
5.	0°F	______	______

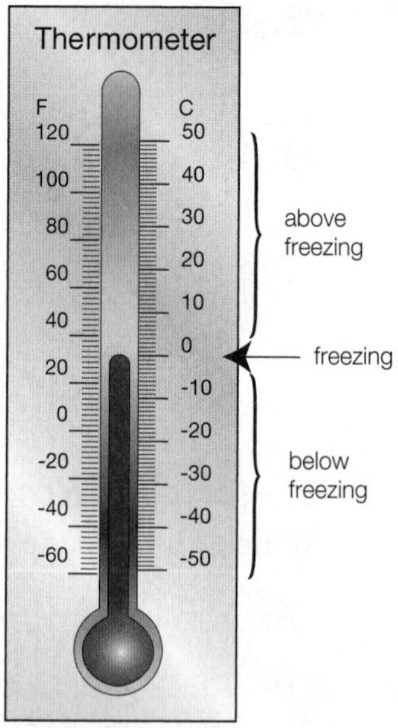

*humid = hot and wet

***Celsius* is also called "Centigrade."

❑ **Exercise 10. Let's talk: small groups.** (Chart 5-3)

Read the chart and follow the instructions.

"Approximate" means "close but not exact." Here is a fast way to get an **approximate** number when you convert from one temperature system to another.*

- To change **Celsius to Fahrenheit**: DOUBLE THE CELSIUS NUMBER AND ADD 30.

Examples: 12°C × 2 = 24 + 30 = 54°F (Exact numbers: 12°C = 53.6°F)
20°C × 2 = 40 + 30 = 70°F (Exact numbers: 20°C = 68°F)
35°C × 2 = 70 + 30 = 100°F (Exact numbers: 35°C = 95°F)

- To change **Fahrenheit to Celsius**: SUBTRACT 30 FROM THE FAHRENHEIT NUMBER AND THEN DIVIDE BY 2.

Examples: 60°F − 30 = 30 ÷ 2 = 15°C. (Exact numbers: 60°F = 15.6°C.)
80°F − 30 = 50 ÷ 2 = 25°C. (Exact numbers: 80°F = 26.7°C.)
90°F − 30 = 60 ÷ 2 = 30°C. (Exact numbers: 90°F = 32.2°C.)

*To get exact numbers, use these formulas: C = 5/9 (°F − 32) OR F = 9/5 (°C) + 32.

Change the temperatures from Celsius to Fahrenheit and from Fahrenheit to Celsius. Calculate the approximate numbers.

1. 22°C *22°C = approximately 74°F (22°C x 2 = 44 + 30 = 74°F)*
2. 2°C ______
3. 30°C ______
4. 16°C ______
5. 25°F ______
6. 70°F ______
7. 100°F ______

❑ Exercise 11. Let's talk: interview. (Chart 5-3)

Interview your classmates about their hometowns. Ask questions about the name of the hometown, its location, its population, its weather, and its average temperature in a particular month (of your choice). Share some of their answers with the class.

Example:

STUDENT A: What's your hometown?
STUDENT B: Athens.
STUDENT A: Where is it?
STUDENT B: In southeastern Greece near the Aegean Sea.
STUDENT A: What's the population of Athens?
STUDENT B: Almost four million.
STUDENT A: What's the weather like in Athens in May?
STUDENT B: It's mild. Sometimes it's a little rainy.
STUDENT A: What's the average temperature in May?
STUDENT B: The average temperature is around 21° Celsius.

Write down the information you get here.

NAME	*Spyros*			
HOMETOWN	*Athens*			
LOCATION	*SE Greece*			
POPULATION	*almost 4 million*			
WEATHER	*mild in May, around 21°C, in the mid-seventies Fahrenheit*			

❑ Exercise 12. Warm-up. (Chart 5-4)

Complete the sentences.

1. There is / isn't a whiteboard in this room.
2. There are / aren't computers in this room.
3. There are __________ students in this room.
   (number)

5-4 *There + Be*

THERE + BE +		SUBJECT +	PLACE	
(a) ***There***	***is***	***a bird***	in the tree.	***There*** + ***be*** is used to say that something exists in a particular place. Notice: The subject follows ***be:*** *there + is + singular noun* *there + are + plural noun*
(b) ***There***	***are***	***four birds***	in the tree.	

(c) ***There's*** a bird in the tree.
(d) ***There're*** four birds in the tree.

CONTRACTIONS:
there + is = there's
there + are = there're

❑ Exercise 13. Looking at grammar. (Chart 5-4)

Complete the sentences with ***is*** or ***are***. Then choose *yes* or *no*. Compare your answers with your classmates' answers.

1. There ____*is*____ a grammar book on my desk. yes no
2. There ____*are*____ many grammar books in this room. yes no
3. There __________ comfortable chairs in this classroom. yes no
4. There __________ a nice view from the classroom window. yes no
5. There __________ interesting places to visit in this area. yes no
6. There __________ a good place to eat near school. yes no
7. There __________ fun activities to do on weekends in this area. yes no
8. There __________ difficult words in this exercise. yes no

❏ Exercise 14. Let's talk: pairwork. (Chart 5-4)

Work with a partner. Complete each sentence with words from the box or your own words. You can look at your book before you speak. When you speak, look at your partner.

a book	a map	a notebook
books	papers	notebooks
tall buildings	a park	restaurants
a bulletin board	a pen	a sink
a calendar	a pencil	stores
chairs	a pencil sharpener	students
a chalkboard	people	a teacher
a clock	a picture	a whiteboard
a coffee shop	pictures	a window
desks	a post office	windows
light switches		

1. PARTNER A: There is . . . on this desk.
   PARTNER B: There are . . . on that desk.
2. PARTNER A: There are . . . on that wall.
   PARTNER B: There is . . . on this wall.
3. PARTNER A: There are . . . in this room.
   PARTNER B: There is also . . . in this room.
4. PARTNER A: There is . . . near our school.
   PARTNER B: There are also . . . near our school.

❏ Exercise 15. Let's talk: small groups. (Chart 5-4)

First, everyone in your group puts two or three objects (e.g., a coin, some keys, a pen, a dictionary) on a table in the classroom. Then take turns describing the items on the table. Begin with ***There is*** and ***There are***.

Example:
STUDENT A: There are three dictionaries on the table.
STUDENT B: There are some keys on the table.
STUDENT C: There is a pencil sharpener on the table.

❏ Exercise 16. Listening. (Chart 5-4)

CD 1 Track 18

Listen to each sentence. Choose the word you hear. *Note:* You will hear contractions for ***There is*** and ***There are***.

Example: You will hear: There're several windows in this room.
You will choose: There's (There're)

1.	There's	There're	5. There's	There're
2.	There's	There're	6. There's	There're
3.	There's	There're	7. There's	There're
4.	There's	There're	8. There's	There're

❑ Exercise 17. Warm-up. (Chart 5-5)

Answer the questions.

1. Is there an elevator in this building? yes no
2. Are there stairs in this building? yes no

5-5 *There + Be:* Yes/No Questions

QUESTION					SHORT ANSWER
	BE +	THERE +	SUBJECT		
(a)	*Is*	*there*	*an apple*	in the refrigerator?	→ Yes, *there is*. → No, *there isn't*.
(b)	*Are*	*there*	*eggs*	in the refrigerator?	→ Yes, *there are*. → No, *there aren't*.

❑ Exercise 18. Let's talk: pairwork. (Chart 5-5)

Work with a partner. Ask questions about the refrigerator in the picture. Use the nouns in the list. Begin with ***Is there*** or ***Are there***.

Example: a piece of cheese
PARTNER A: Is there a piece of cheese in the refrigerator?
PARTNER B: Yes, there is.
PARTNER A: Your turn now.

Example: onions
PARTNER B: Are there onions in the refrigerator?
PARTNER A: No, there aren't.
PARTNER B: Your turn now.

PARTNER A	PARTNER B
1. a carton of eggs	1. strawberries
2. a loaf of bread	2. oranges
3. apples	3. a bottle of orange juice
4. a cube of butter	4. a bowl of rice
5. potatoes	5. a bag of flour
6. vegetables	6. pickles

❑ Exercise 19. Let's talk: small groups. (Chart 5-5)

Take turns asking and answering questions about this city. Begin with ***Is there*** or ***Are there***. If the answer is "I don't know," ask someone else.

Example: a zoo
STUDENT A: Is there a zoo in (*name of this city*)?
STUDENT B: Yes, there is. / No, there isn't.
STUDENT B: (*to Student C*) Is there an airport near (*name of this city*)?
STUDENT C: I don't know.
STUDENT B: (*to Student D*) Is there an airport near (*name of this city*)?
STUDENT D: Yes, there is. / No, there isn't.
Etc.

1. a zoo
2. an airport
3. lakes
4. good restaurants
5. a good Chinese restaurant
6. an art museum
7. an aquarium
8. interesting bookstores
9. a subway system
10. public swimming pools
11. a good public transportation system
12. a movie theater

❑ Exercise 20. Let's talk: class activity. (Chart 5-5)

Solve the puzzle. *Teacher's Note:* See *Let's Talk: Answers*, p. 278, to answer your students' questions.

The Romero family needs to decide where to stay for their summer vacation. They want a hotel with everything in the list below. Your teacher has information about several hotels. Ask her/him questions using the list. Then write *yes* or *no* in the correct column of the chart. Which hotel has everything that the Romeros want?

List:

a swimming pool
a beach
hiking trails
horses to ride
ocean-view rooms

Example:
STUDENT A: Is there a swimming pool at Hotel 1?
TEACHER: Yes, there is.
STUDENT B: Are there hiking trails at Hotel 3?
TEACHER: Yes, there are.

	A SWIMMING POOL	A BEACH	HIKING TRAILS	HORSES	OCEAN-VIEW ROOMS
HOTEL 1	*yes*				
HOTEL 2		*yes*			
HOTEL 3			*yes*		
HOTEL 4				*yes*	
HOTEL 5					*yes*

❑ **Exercise 21. Warm-up.** (Chart 5-6)
Answer the questions.

1. How many students are there at this school?
2. How many people are there in your country?
3. How many people are there on the earth?

5-6 *There + Be:* Asking Questions with *How Many*

QUESTION						SHORT ANSWER
	HOW MANY +	SUBJECT +	ARE +	THERE +	PLACE	
(a)	*How many*	*chapters*	*are*	*there*	in this book? →	Fifteen. (There are 15 chapters in this book.)
(b)	*How many*	*provinces*	*are*	*there*	in Canada? →	Ten. (There are ten provinces in Canada.)
(c)	How many **words** do you see? INCORRECT: *How many word do you see?*					Notice: The noun that follows ***how many*** is plural.

❑ **Exercise 22. Let's talk: class activity.** (Chart 5-6)
Ask and answer questions about this classroom. Use ***How many*** and the given words.

Example: desks
STUDENT A: How many desks are there in this room?
STUDENT B: Thirty-two. OR There are thirty-two desks in this room.
STUDENT A: That's right. OR No, I count thirty-three desks.

1. windows
2. laptops
3. students
4. teachers
5. women
6. men
7. grammar books
8. dictionaries

❑ **Exercise 23. Let's talk: pairwork.** (Chart 5-6)
Work with a partner. Ask questions. Begin with ***How many***.

Example: days in a week
PARTNER A: How many days are there in a week?
PARTNER B: Seven. OR There are seven days in a week.
PARTNER A: Right. There are seven days in a week. Your turn now.

PARTNER A	PARTNER B
1. chapters in this book	1. pages in this book
2. doors in this room	2. people in this room
3. floors in this building	3. letters in the English alphabet (26)
4. states in the United States (50)	4. provinces in Canada (10)
5. countries in North America (3)	5. continents in the world (7)

❑ Exercise 24. Warm-up. (Chart 5-7)

Guess the person. Notice the prepositions in red.

Who am I?

1. I live in London.
2. I live on Downing Street.
3. I live at 10 Downing Street.

5-7 Prepositions of Place

(a) My book is **on** *my desk.*	In (a): *on* = a preposition *my desk* = object of the preposition *on my desk* = a prepositional phrase
(b) Ned lives **in** *Miami.* **in** *Florida.* **in** *the United States.* **in** *North America.*	A person lives ***in*** a city, a state, a country, a continent.
(c) Meg lives **on** *Hill Street.* (d) She lives **at** *4472 Hill Street.*	***on*** a street, avenue, road, etc. ***at*** a street address
(e) My father is **in** *the kitchen*.	In (e): ***in*** is used with rooms: ***in*** *the kitchen,* ***in*** *the classroom,* ***in*** *the hall,* ***in*** *my bedroom, etc.*
(f) Ivan is **at** *work*. (g) Yoko is **at** *school*. (h) Olga is **at** *home*.	***At*** + *work, school, home* expresses activity: In (f): Ivan is working at his office (or other place of work). In (g): Yoko is a student. She is studying. (Or, if she is a teacher, she is teaching.) In (h): Olga is doing things at her home.
(i) Siri is **in** *bed*. (j) Tim is **in** *class*. (k) Mr. Lee is **in** *the hospital*. (l) Paul is **in** *jail/prison*.	**In** + *bed, class, hospital, jail* has these special meanings: In (i): Siri is resting or sleeping *under* the covers. In (j): Tim is studying (or teaching). In (k): Mr. Lee is sick. He is a patient. In (l): Paul is a prisoner. He is not free to leave. NOTE: American English = *in the hospital* British English = *in hospital*

❑ **Exercise 25. Looking at grammar.** (Chart 5-7)
Complete the sentences with ***in, on,*** or ***at.***

Write about Alonso.

1. Alonso lives __________ Canada.
2. He lives __________ Toronto.
3. He lives __________ Lake Street.
4. He lives __________ 5541 Lake Street __________ Toronto, Canada.

Write about Dr. Eng.

5. Dr. Eng lives on ____________________.
6. He lives in ____________________.
7. He lives at ____________________.

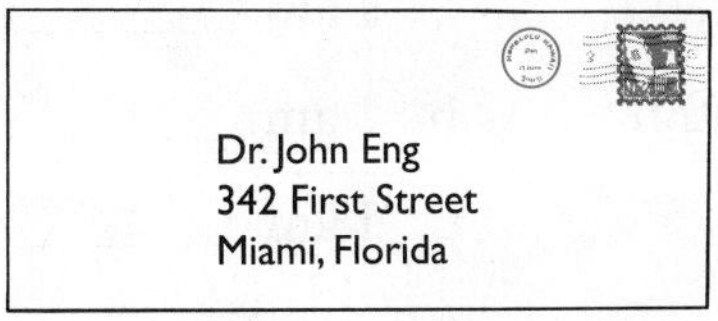

Write about yourself.

8. I live ______________________________.
(name of country)
9. I live ______________________________.
(name of city)
10. I live ______________________________.
(name of street)
11. I live ______________________________.
(street address)

❑ Exercise 26. Game. (Chart 5-7)

Work in teams. Complete the sentences with ***in, on,*** or ***at***. Then guess the person, building, or company. Use words from the box. The team with the most correct answers wins.

Alexandria Pyramids	Facebook	Nike
Apple	Giza Pyramids	president of the U.S.
Boeing	Louvre Museum	prime minister of Canada
Eiffel Tower	Microsoft	vice president of the U.S.

1. I am a building.
   a. I am ________ Paris.
   b. I am ________ Anatole Avenue.
   c. I am ________ 5 Anatole Avenue.
   ANSWER: ____________________

2. I am a person.
   a. I live ________ Ottawa.
   b. I live ________ 24 Sussex Drive.
   c. I live ________ Sussex Drive.
   ANSWER: ____________________

3. I am a building.
   a. I am ________ Pyramid Street.
   b. I am ________ 124 Pyramid Street.
   c. I am ________ Egypt.
   ANSWER: ____________________

4. I am a company.
   a. I am ________ Oregon.
   b. I am ________ Bowerman Drive.
   c. I am ________ One Bowerman Drive.
   ANSWER: ____________________

5. I am a person.
   a. I live ________ Pennsylvania Avenue.
   b. I live ________ 600 Pennsylvania Avenue N.W.
   c. I live ________ the United States.
   ANSWER: ____________________

6. I am a company.
   a. I am ________ Illinois.
   b. I am ________ 100 North Riverside Plaza.
   c. I am ________ Chicago.
   ANSWER: ____________________

❑ Exercise 27. Looking at grammar. (Chart 5-7)

Complete the sentence with ***at*** or ***in***.

Rachel isn't . . .

1. ________ her bedroom.
2. ________ bed.
3. ________ work.
4. ________ prison.
5. ________ home.
6. ________ jail.
7. ________ class.
8. ________ Africa.
9. ________ the hall.
10. ________ the hospital. She's well now.

❑ Exercise 28. Looking at grammar. (Chart 5-7)

Complete the sentences with ***at*** or ***in***.

1. When I was ________ work yesterday, I had an interesting phone call.
2. Poor Anita. She's ________ the hospital again for more surgery.
3. Mr. Gow is a teacher, but he isn't ________ school today. He's sick, so he is ________ home.
4. Last year at this time, Eric was ________ Vietnam. This year he's ________ Spain.
5. There's a fire extinguisher ________ the hall.
6. There are thirty-seven desks ________ our classroom.
7. Rob is ________ jail. He's going to be ________ prison for a long time.
8. Our hotel rooms are on the same floor. I'm ________ 501 and you're ________ 505.
9. Singapore is ________ Asia.
10. The kids are ________ the kitchen. They're making dinner for us!
11. A: Is Jennifer ________ home?

    B: No, she's still ________ class.
12. A: Where's Jack?

    B: He's ________ his room.

    A: What's he doing?

    B: He's ________ bed. He has a headache.

❑ Exercise 29. Warm-up. (Chart 5-8)

Answer the questions.

Right now . . .

1. who is in front of you?
2. who is behind you?
3. who is beside you?
4. who is far away from the teacher?
5. who is in the middle of the room?
6. who is near the door?

5-8 More Prepositions of Place: A List

above	beside	in back of	in the middle of	on
around	between	in the back of	inside	on top of
at	far (away) from	in front of	near	outside
behind	in	in the front of	next to	under
below				

(a) The book is ***beside*** the cup.
(b) The book is ***next to*** the cup.
(c) The book is ***near*** the cup.

(d) The book is ***between*** two cups.

(e) The book is ***far away from*** the cup.

(f) The cup is ***on*** the book.
(g) The cup is ***on top of*** the book.

(h) The cup is ***under*** the book.

(i) The cup is ***above*** the book.

(j) The hand is ***around*** the cup.

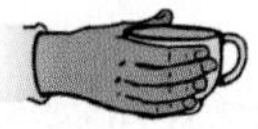

(k) The man is ***in back of*** the bus.
(l) The man is ***behind*** the bus.

(m) The man is ***in the back of*** the bus.

(n) The man is ***in front of*** the bus.
In (k), (l), and (n): the man is ***outside*** the bus.

(o) The man is ***in the front of*** the bus.

(p) The man is ***in the middle of*** the bus.
In (m), (o), and (p): the man is ***inside*** the bus.

❑ **Exercise 30. Looking at grammar.** (Chart 5-8)

Describe the pictures by completing the sentences with prepositional expressions of place.

1.  The apple is ___on / on top of___ the plate.

2. The apple is ________________ the plate. 

3.  The apple is ________________ the plate.

4. The apple is ________________ the glass. 

5.  The apple isn't near the glass. It is ________________ the glass.

6. The apple is ________________ the glass. 

7.  The apple is ________________ two glasses.

8. The hand is ________________ the glass. 

9.  The dog isn't inside the car. The dog is ________________ the car.

10. The dog is in ________________ of the car. 

11.  The dog is in ________________ of the car.

12. The dog is in ________________ of the car. 

13.  The dog is in ________________ of the car.

❑ Exercise 31. Let's talk: pairwork. (Charts 5-4 → 5-8)

Work with a partner. Ask and answer questions about the picture. Use the questions below and the words from the box to help you.

Questions: *Where is the . . . ?* OR *Where are the . . . ?* OR *How many . . . are there?*

Examples:

PARTNER A: Where is the bird?
PARTNER B: The bird is on the table.
PARTNER A: Your turn to ask.

PARTNER B: How many birds are there?
PARTNER A: There is one bird.
PARTNER B: Your turn to ask.

bikes	butterflies	guitar	river
bird	clouds	mountains	train
boat	fish	knife	trees
boots	fishing pole	picnic bench	
bridge	flowers	picnic table	

❑ Exercise 32. Listening. (Chart 5-8)

CD 1
Track 19

Listen to the statements about the picture on p. 144. Choose "T" for true and "F" for false.

Example: You will hear: A bike is in the water.
You will choose: T (F)

1. T F	6. T F	11. T F
2. T F	7. T F	12. T F
3. T F	8. T F	13. T F
4. T F	9. T F	14. T F
5. T F	10. T F	15. T F

❑ Exercise 33. Let's talk: pairwork. (Chart 5-8)

Work with a partner. Choose a small object (a pen, pencil, coin, etc.). Give and follow directions. You can look at your book before you speak. When you speak, look at your partner.

Example: (*a small object such as a coin*)
PARTNER A (*book open*): Put it on top of the desk.
PARTNER B (*book closed*): (*Partner B puts the coin on top of the desk.*)

1. Put it on your head.
2. Put it above your head.
3. Put it between your fingers.
4. Put it near me.
5. Put it far away from me.
6. Put it under your book.
7. Put it below your knee.
8. Put it in the middle of your grammar book.

Change roles.

9. Put it inside your grammar book.
10. Put it next to your grammar book.
11. Put it on top of your grammar book.
12. Put it in front of me.
13. Put it behind me.
14. Put it in back of your back.
15. Put it in the back of your grammar book.
16. Put your hand around it.

❑ Exercise 34. Vocabulary and grammar. (Chapters 4 and 5)

Part I. Work in pairs or as a class. Answer the questions. (Alternate questions if working in pairs.) Use the vocabulary from the box to help you.

burn	a bowl / a bowl of salad	meat / a piece of meat
eat dinner	a candle	a plate
have a steak for dinner	a cup / a cup of coffee	a restaurant
hold a knife and a fork	a fork	a saucer
	a glass / a glass of water	a spoon
	a knife	a steak
	a vase of flowers	a table
		a server

1. What is Jill doing?
2. What do you see on the table?
3. What is Jill holding in her right hand? in her left hand?
4. What is in the bowl?
5. What is on the plate?
6. What is in the cup?
7. What is burning?
8. Is Jill eating breakfast?
9. Is Jill at home? Where is she?
10. What is she cutting?

Part II. Complete the sentences.

1. Jill is sitting ________ a table.
2. There is a candle ________ the table.
3. There is coffee ________ the cup.
4. Jill ________ holding a knife ________ her right hand.
5. She's eating ________ a restaurant.
6. She ________ eating at home.
7. She ________ eating breakfast.

❑ Exercise 35. Vocabulary and grammar. (Chapters 4 and 5)

Part I. Work in pairs or as a class. Answer the questions. (Alternate questions if working in pairs.) Use the vocabulary from the box to help you.

read a book	the circulation desk
study at the library	a librarian
take notes	a shelf (singular)
	shelves (plural)*

1. What is Jon doing?
2. What do you see in the picture?
3. Is Jon at home? Where is he?
4. Is Jon reading a newspaper?
5. Where is the librarian standing?
6. Is Jon right-handed or left-handed?

Part II. Complete the sentences.

1. Jon is studying ________ the library.
2. He is sitting ________ a table.
3. He is sitting ________ a chair.
4. His legs are ________ the table.
5. There are books ________ the shelves.
6. Jon is writing ________ a piece of paper.
7. He's taking notes ________ a piece of paper.
8. He ________ reading a newspaper.
9. The librarian ________ standing ________ the circulation desk.
10. Another student is sitting ____________ Jon.

---

*See Chart 6-6, p. 174, for information about nouns with irregular plural forms.

❑ Exercise 36. Vocabulary and grammar. (Chapters 4 and 5)

Part I. Work in pairs or as a class. Answer the questions. (Alternate questions if working in pairs.) Use the vocabulary from the box to help you.

cash a check	a bank teller	a man (singular)
stand in line	a counter	men (plural)*
	a line	people (plural)*
		a woman (singular)
		women (plural)*

1. What is Megan doing?
2. Is Megan at a store? Where is she?
3. What do you see in the picture?
4. Who is standing behind Megan, a man or a woman?
5. Who is standing at the end of the line, a man or a woman?
6. How many men are there in the picture?
7. How many women are there in the picture?
8. How many people are there in the picture?
9. How many people are standing in line?

Part II. Complete the sentences.

1. Megan is ____________ a bank.
2. Four people ____________ standing in line.
3. Megan is standing ____________ the counter.
4. The bank teller is standing ________________ the counter.
5. A woman ____________ standing ________________ Megan.
6. Megan ________ standing ________ the end ________ the line.
7. A man ________ standing ________ the end ________ the line.
8. A businessman ________ standing ________________ the woman in the skirt and the man with the beard.

*See Chart 6-6, p. 174, for information about nouns with irregular plural forms.

❑ **Exercise 37. Warm-up.** (Chart 5-9)

These sentences have the same meaning. Which speaker sounds more polite to you?

I want some coffee.
I would like some coffee.

5-9 *Would Like*

(a) I'm thirsty. I *want* a glass of water. (b) I'm thirsty. I *would like* a glass of water.	Examples (a) and (b) have the same meaning, but ***would like*** is usually more polite than ***want***. *I would like* is a nice way of saying *I want.*
(c) *I would like* *You would like* *She would like* *He would like* *We would like* *They would like* } a glass of water.	Notice in (c): There is no final **-s** on ***would***. There is no final **-s** on ***like***.
(d) CONTRACTIONS *I'd* = *I would* *you'd* = *you would* *she'd* = *she would* *he'd* = *he would* *we'd* = *we would* *they'd* = *they would*	***Would*** is often contracted with pronouns in both speaking and writing. In speaking, ***would*** is usually contracted with nouns too. WRITTEN: Ray would like to come. SPOKEN: "Ray'd like to come."
WOULD LIKE + INFINITIVE (e) I *would like* *to eat* a sandwich.	Notice in (e): ***would like*** can be followed by an infinitive.
WOULD + SUBJECT + *LIKE* (f) *Would* you *like* some tea?	In a question, ***would*** comes before the subject.
(g) Yes, I *would*. (I would like some tea.)	***Would*** is used alone in short answers to questions with ***would like***. It is not contracted in short answers.

❑ Exercise 38. Grammar. (Chart 5-9)

Change the sentences to ***would like***.

1. **Dan wants** a cup of coffee.

   → ___*Dan would like*___ a cup of coffee.

2. **He wants** some sugar in his coffee.

   → ___*He would like*___ some sugar in his coffee.

3. **Hassan and Eva want** some coffee too.

   → ______________________ some coffee too.

4. **They want** some sugar in their coffee too.

   → ______________________ some sugar in their coffee too.

5. **I want to thank** you for your help.

   → ______________________ you for your help.

6. **My friend wants to thank** you too.

   → ______________________ you too.

7. **My friends want to thank** you too.

   → ______________________ you too.

❑ Exercise 39. Let's talk: class activity. (Chart 5-9)

Your teacher will ask you questions. Answer the questions. Close your book for this activity.

1. Who's hungry right now? (____), are you hungry? What would you like?
2. Who's thirsty? (____), are you thirsty? What would you like?
3. Who's sleepy? What would you like to do?
4. What would you like to do this weekend?
5. What would you like to do after class today?
6. What would you like to have for dinner tonight?
7. What countries would you like to visit?
8. What cities would you like to visit in (*the United States, Canada, etc.*)?
9. What languages would you like to learn?
10. Pretend that you are a host at a party at your home and your classmates are your guests. Ask them what they would like to eat or drink.
11. Think of something fun to do tonight or this weekend. Use *would you like* and invite a classmate to join you.

❑ Exercise 40. Warm-up. (Chart 5-10)

What is the difference in meaning between these sentences?

I like chocolate.

I would like some chocolate.

5-10 *Would Like* vs. *Like*

(a) I *would like to go* to the zoo.	In (a): ***I would like to go to the zoo*** means *I want to go to the zoo.* **Would like** indicates that I want to do something now or in the future.
(b) I *like to go* to the zoo.	In (b): ***I like to go to the zoo*** means *I enjoy the zoo.* **Like** indicates that I always, usually, or often enjoy something.

❑ Exercise 41. Listening. (Chart 5-10)

CD 1 Track 20

Listen to the sentences and choose the verbs you hear. Some sentences have contractions.

Example: You will hear: I'd like some tea.
You will choose: like (’d like)

1. like ’d like
2. like ’d like
3. like ’d like
4. likes ’d like
5. like ’d like
6. likes ’d like
7. like ’d like
8. like ’d like
9. like ’d like
10. like ’d like

❑ Exercise 42. Let's talk: class activity. (Charts 3-7, 5-9, and 5-10)

Discuss possible completions for the sentences. Use your own words.

1. I need to ______________________________ every day.
2. I want to ______________________________ today.
3. I like to ______________________________ every day.
4. I would like to ______________________________ today.
5. I don't like to ______________________________ every day.
6. I don't want to ______________________________ today.
7. Do you like to ______________________________?
8. Would you like to ______________________________?
9. I need to _______________ and _______________ today.
10. _______________ would you like to _______________ this evening?

❑ Exercise 43. Let's talk: pairwork. (Charts 5-9 and 5-10)

Work in pairs. Ask and answer questions. You can look at your book before you speak. When you speak, look at your partner.

Example:

PARTNER A: Do you like apples?
PARTNER B: Yes, I do. OR No, I don't.
PARTNER A: Would you like an apple right now?
PARTNER B: Yes, I would. OR Yes, thank you. OR No, but thank you for asking.
PARTNER A: Your turn now.

PARTNER A	PARTNER B
1. Do you like coffee? Would you like a cup of coffee? 2. Do you like to watch movies? Would you like to go to a movie with me later today? 3. What do you like to do on weekends? What would you like to do this weekend? 4. What do you need to do this evening? What would you like to do this evening?	1. Do you like chocolate? Would you like some chocolate right now? 2. Do you like to go shopping? Would you like to go shopping with me later today? 3. What do you like to do in your free time? What would you like to do in your free time tomorrow? 4. Do you like to travel? What countries would you like to visit?

❑ Exercise 44. Vocabulary and grammar. (Chapters 4 and 5)

Part I. Work in pairs or as a class. Answer the questions. (Alternate questions if working in pairs.) Use the vocabulary from the box to help you.

the date	a bank	first name/given name
sign a check*	cash	middle initial
sign her name	a check	last name/family name/surname
write a check		name and address

1. What is Mary doing?
2. What is Mary's address?
3. What is Mary's full name?
4. What is Mary's middle initial?
5. What is Mary's last name?
6. How much money does Mary want?
7. What is in the upper-left corner of the check?
8. What is in the lower-left corner of the check?
9. What is the name of the bank?

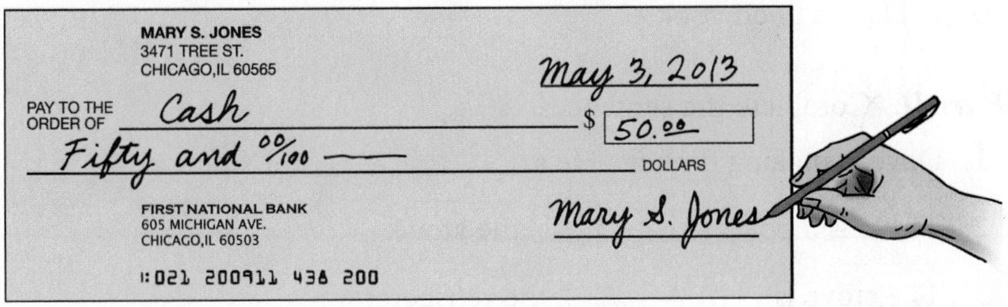

Part II. Complete the sentences.

1. Mary is writing a ______________.
2. She is signing ______________ name.
3. The date on the check is ______________.
4. Mary lives ______________ 3471 Tree Street.
5. Mary lives ______________ Chicago, Illinois.
6. Mary is writing a check for ______________.

**Check* (American English) is spelled *cheque* in British and Canadian English. The pronunciation of *check* and *cheque* is the same.

❑ Exercise 45. Vocabulary and grammar. (Chapters 4 and 5)

Part I. Work in pairs or as a class. Answer the questions. (Alternate questions if working in pairs.) Use the vocabulary from the box to help you.

cook	(in the) kitchen	bread
cook dinner	a list/a grocery list	butter
make dinner	a pepper shaker	coffee
taste (food)	a pot	an egg
	a refrigerator	pepper
	a salt shaker	salt
		a stove
		a clock

1. What is Dave doing?
2. What do you see in the picture?
3. Where is Dave?
4. Is Dave tasting his dinner?
5. Is Dave a good cook?
6. Where is the refrigerator?
7. What is on the refrigerator?
8. Is the food on the stove hot or cold?
9. Is the food in the refrigerator hot or cold?

Part II. Complete the sentences.

1. Dave is making dinner. He's ____________ the kitchen.
2. There is a pot ____________ the stove.
3. The stove is ____________ the refrigerator.
4. There is a grocery list ____________ the refrigerator door.
5. Dave needs ____________ to the grocery store.
6. A salt shaker and a pepper shaker are ____________ the stove.
7. There is hot food ____________ top ____________ the stove.
8. There is cold food ____________ the refrigerator.

❑ Exercise 46. Vocabulary and grammar. (Chapters 4 and 5)

Part I. Work in pairs or as a class. Answer the questions. (Alternate questions if working in pairs.) Use the vocabulary from the box to help you.

sing	a cat	a living room
sit on a sofa/a couch	a dog	a rug
sleep	a fish	a singer
swim	a fishbowl	a TV set/a television set
watch TV/television	a floor	
	a lamp	

1. What are Nate and Lisa doing?
2. What do you see in the picture?
3. Are Nate and Lisa in the kitchen? Where are they?
4. Where is the lamp?
5. Where is the rug?
6. Where is the dog?
7. Where is the cat?
8. Is the cat walking? What is the cat doing?
9. What is the dog doing?
10. What is on top of the TV set?
11. Is the fish watching TV?
12. What is on the TV screen? What are Nate and Lisa watching?

Part II. Complete the sentences.

1. Nate and Lisa ________ watching TV. They like ________ watch TV.
2. They ________ sitting ________ a sofa.
3. They ________ sleeping.
4. There is a rug ________ the floor.
5. A dog ________ sleeping ________ the rug.
6. A cat ________ sleeping ________ the sofa.

❑ Exercise 47. Let's talk: game. (Chapters 4 and 5)

Work in teams. Make sentences about the picture. Every sentence needs to have a preposition. Use the vocabulary from the box to help you. One team member writes the sentences on paper. Your teacher will give you a time limit. The team with the most grammatically correct sentences wins.

draw a picture	a clock	a piece of paper
talk on the phone	a calendar	a telephone book
talk to (someone)	a heart	a wall
talk to each other	a phone/a telephone	
	a picture	
	a picture of a mountain	

Nick Kate

❑ Exercise 48. Looking at grammar. (Chapters 4 and 5)

Choose the correct completion.

1. Jack lives ______ China.
   (a.) in b. at c. on

2. I need ______ a new notebook.
   a. buy b. to buy c. buying

3. ______ a cup of tea?
   a. Would you like b. Do you like c. Are you like

4. There ______ twenty-two desks in this room.
   a. be b. is c. are

5. Pilots sit ______ an airplane.
   a. in front of b. in the front of c. front of

6. I live ______ 6601 Fourth Avenue.
   a. in b. on c. at

7. The students ______ do their homework.
   a. don't want   b. aren't wanting   c. don't want to

8. ______ a TV in Marisa's bedroom?
   a. Are there   b. There   c. Is there

❑ **Exercise 49. Check your knowledge.** (Chapter 5)
Correct the mistakes.

1. Do you want ^*to* go downtown with me?
2. There's many problems in big cities today.
3. I'd like see a movie tonight.
4. We are needing to find a new apartment soon.
5. Mr. Rice woulds likes to have a cup of tea.
6. How many students there are in your class?
7. What day it is today?
8. I am like to leave right now.
9. How the weather in Kenya?
10. The teacher would like to checking our homework now.

❑ **Exercise 50. Looking at grammar.** (Chapters 4 and 5)
Complete the sentences with your own words. Use your own paper.

1. I need ____ because ____.
2. I want ____ because ____.
3. I would like ____.
4. Would you like ____?
5. Do you like ____?
6. There is ____.
7. There are ____.
8. I'm listening to ____, but I also hear ____.
9. I'm looking at ____, but I also see ____.
10. I'm thinking about ____.
11. I think that ____.
12. In my opinion, ____.
13. How many ____ are there ____?
14. Is there ____?
15. Are there ____?

❑ Exercise 51. Reading and writing. (Chapters 4 and 5)

Part I. Read the sample paragraph. Underline the verbs.

A Happy Dream

I am walking alone in a big field of flowers. There are thousands of colorful flowers around me. The air smells very sweet. The sun is shining, and the sky is bright blue. There are some tall trees, and the wind is gently blowing. Birds are singing in the trees. I am feeling very calm. I have no worries. My life is very peaceful. I would like to stay here forever. I don't want to wake up.

Part II. Write about a dream that you remember that describes a place. It can be a happy or a sad dream. If you can't remember a dream, imagine one. Use present verbs.

Include this information:

1. Where are you?
2. What are you doing?
3. Describe the place. What is there around you?
4. How are you feeling?

Part III. Editing check: Work individually or change papers with a partner. Check (✓) for the following:

1. ____ paragraph indent
2. ____ capital letter at the beginning of each sentence
3. ____ period at the end of each sentence
4. ____ a verb in every sentence
5. ____ correct use of prepositions of place
6. ____ use of present progressive for activities right now
7. ____ ***there is*** + singular noun
8. ____ ***there are*** + plural noun
9. ____ correct spelling (use a dictionary or spell-check)

Chapter 6

Nouns and Pronouns

❑ **Exercise 1. Warm-up.** (Chart 6-1)

Work in small groups. Make lists of things that belong to each category. Compare your lists with other groups' lists. All of the words you use in this exercise are called "nouns."

1. Name clothing you see in this room. (*shirt,* etc.)
2. Name kinds of fruit. (*apple,* etc.)
3. Name things you drink. (*coffee,* etc.)
4. Name parts of the body. (*head,* etc.)
5. Name kinds of animals. (*horse,* etc.)
6. Name famous cities in the world* (*Paris, Tokyo,* etc.)
7. Name languages.* (*English,* etc.)
8. Name school subjects. (*history,* etc.)

6-1 Nouns: Subjects and Objects

NOUN (a) Birds | fly. subject verb	A NOUN is used as the SUBJECT of a sentence. A NOUN is used as the OBJECT of a verb.* In (a): ***Birds*** is a NOUN. It is used as the subject of the sentence.
NOUN NOUN (b) Karl | is holding | a pen. subject verb object	In (b): ***pen*** is a NOUN. It has the article ***a*** in front of it; ***a pen*** is used as the object of the verb ***is holding***. Objects are NOUNS, and they come after a verb.

*Some verbs can be followed by an object. These verbs are called transitive verbs (*v.t.* in a dictionary). Some verbs cannot be followed by an object. These verbs are called intransitive verbs (*v.i.* in a dictionary).

*The names of cities and languages begin with capital letters.

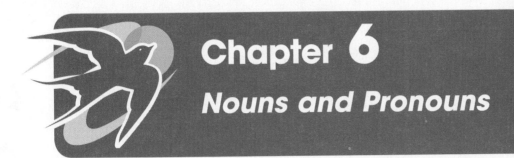

❑ Exercise 2. Looking at grammar. (Chart 6-1)

Check (✓) the words that are nouns.

1. ____ eat	7. ____ flowers
2. _✓_ dog	8. ____ juice
3. ____ nice	9. ____ ears
4. ____ math	10. ____ Paris
5. ____ write	11. ____ great
6. ____ have	12. ____ English

❑ Exercise 3. Looking at grammar. (Chart 6-1)

For each sentence, write the object or write "no object."

	NOUN
1. Cats catch mice. What do cats catch?	object = _mice_
2. Cats purr. What do cats do?	object = _no object_
3. Mice like cheese. What do mice like?	object = ________
4. Mice don't like people. Who don't mice like?	object = ________
5. Cats and mice have whiskers. What do cats and mice have?	object = ________
6. Cats sleep a lot. What do cats do?	object = ________
7. Cats scratch furniture. What do cats scratch?	object = ________

❑ Exercise 4. Looking at grammar. (Chart 6-1)

Check (✓) the sentences that have objects. Underline the objects.

1. a. _✓_ I am writing an email.
   b. _✓_ I am writing an email right now.
   c. ____ I am writing right now.

2. a. ____ Students memorize vocabulary.
   b. ____ Some students memorize every day.
   c. ____ Some students memorize vocabulary every day.

3. a. ____ The printer needs paper.
   b. ____ The printer needs ink and paper.
   c. ____ The printer has problems.

4. a. ____ The company is hiring.
   b. ____ The company is hiring workers.
   c. ____ The company is hiring today.

5. a. ____ Babies cry.
   b. ____ Babies cry frequently.
   c. ____ Babies cry loudly.

❑ **Exercise 5. Warm-up.** (Chart 6-2)

Complete each sentence with a preposition that describes the picture. Are the words in the box nouns, verbs, or adjectives?

above	across	in	on	under

1. The man is ____________ the ground.
2. The man is ____________ the plane.
3. The plane is ____________ the sky.

6-2 Nouns as Objects of Prepositions

NOUN			NOUN
(a) ***Birds***	fly	in	the ***sky***.
subject	verb	prep.	object of prep.

A NOUN is also used as the OBJECT OF A PREPOSITION.

In (a): ***in*** is a PREPOSITION (prep.). The noun ***sky*** (with the article *the* in front) is the OBJECT of the preposition ***in***.

In the sky is a PREPOSITIONAL PHRASE. (*phrase* = a group of words)

NOUN		NOUN		NOUN
(b) ***Karl***	is holding	a ***pen***	in	his ***hand***.
subject	verb	object	prep.	object of prep.

In (b): notice that the prepositional phrase comes after the noun it refers to.

INCORRECT: Karl is holding in his hand a pen.

SOME COMMON PREPOSITIONS

about	between	for	near	to
across	by	from	of	under
at	during	in	on	with

❑ Exercise 6. Looking at grammar. (Chart 6-2)

Check (✓) the phrases that have prepositions. Underline the noun that is the object of each preposition.

1. ____ right now
2. ____ at noon
3. ____ on the counter
4. ____ in my closet
5. ____ some salt and pepper
6. ____ two days a week
7. ____ under the chair
8. ____ with a broom

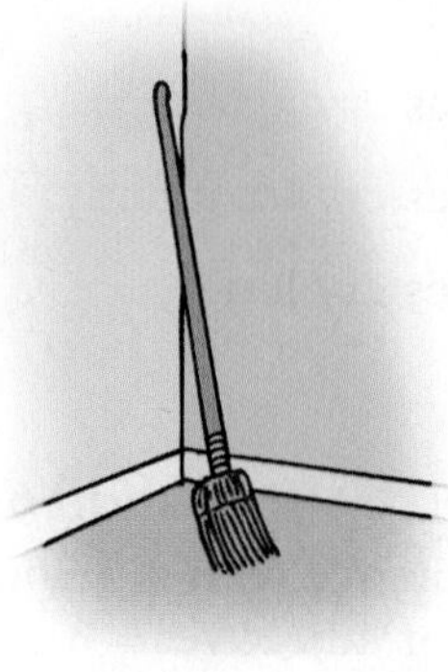

a broom

❑ Exercise 7. Looking at grammar. (Chart 6-2)

Underline the prepositions. Circle the object of each preposition.

1. a. A tutor helps Sari with her (homework.)
   b. A tutor helps Sari on Tuesday afternoons.
   c. A tutor helps Sari in the library.
2. a. The teacher erases the board.
   b. The teacher erases the board after class.
   c. The teacher erases the board with an eraser.
3. a. Elin cleans windows.
   b. Elin cleans in the afternoons.
   c. Elin cleans five days a week.
4. a. I do my homework in the library.
   b. I do my homework every weekend.
   c. I do my homework with my friends.
5. a. Birds fly during the day.
   b. Birds live in nests.
   c. Birds sit on eggs.

❑ **Exercise 8. Looking at grammar.** (Charts 6-1 and 6-2)

Write the noun(s) for each sentence. Describe the grammatical structure of the sentences as shown in the examples.

Examples: Alicia studies chemistry. Noun(s): Alicia, chemistry

Alicia	studies	chemistry.	(none)	(none)
subject	verb	object of verb	preposition	object of prep.

The kids are playing in the park. Noun(s): kids, park

The kids	are playing	(none)	in	the park.
subject	verb	object of verb	preposition	object of prep.

1. Kids like candy. Noun(s): ______________

subject	verb	object of verb	preposition	object of prep.

2. Dayo lives in Africa. Noun(s): ______________

subject	verb	object of verb	preposition	object of prep.

3. The sun is shining. Noun(s): ______________

subject	verb	object of verb	preposition	object of prep.

4. Lev is reading books about movies and filmmaking. Noun(s): ______________

subject	verb	object of verb	preposition	object of prep.

5. Dara doesn't eat chicken or beef. Noun(s): ______________

subject	verb	object of verb	preposition	object of prep.

6. Monkeys and birds eat fruit and insects. Noun(s): ______________

subject	verb	object of verb	preposition	object of prep.

❑ Exercise 9. Warm-up. (Chart 6-3)

Do you agree or disagree with each sentence? Circle *yes* or *no.*

1. I cook delicious meals. yes no
2. I like raw vegetables. yes no
3. Fresh fruit is expensive. yes no

6-3 Adjectives with Nouns

(a) I don't like ***cold** weather.* adj. + noun (b) Alex is a ***happy** child.* adj. + noun (c) The ***hungry** boy* has a ***fresh** apple.* adj. + noun adj. + noun	An ADJECTIVE (adj.) describes a noun. In grammar, we say that adjectives modify nouns. The word *modify* means "change a little." Adjectives give a little different meaning to a noun: *cold weather, hot weather, nice weather, bad weather.* Adjectives come in front of nouns.
(d) The *weather* *is* ***cold**.* noun + *be* + adj.	Reminder: An adjective can also follow ***be**;* the adjective describes the subject of the sentence. (See Chart 1-7, p. 16.)

COMMON ADJECTIVES

beautiful - ugly	good - bad	angry	hungry
big - little	happy - sad	bright	important
big - small	large - small	busy	intelligent
boring - interesting	long - short	delicious	interesting
cheap - expensive	noisy - quiet	exciting	kind
clean - dirty	old - new	famous	lazy
cold - hot	old - young	favorite	nervous
dangerous - safe	poor - rich	free	nice
dry - wet	sour - sweet	fresh	ripe
easy - hard	strong - weak	healthy	serious
easy - difficult		honest	wonderful

❑ Exercise 10. Looking at grammar. (Chart 6-3)

Circle the nouns. Underline the adjectives. Draw an arrow from each adjective to the noun it describes.

1. Jake has an expensive bike.
2. My sister has a beautiful house.
3. We often eat at an Italian restaurant.
4. Valentina sings her favorite songs in the shower.
5. Olga likes American hamburgers.
6. You like sour apples, but I like sweet fruit.

❑ Exercise 11. Let's talk: small groups. (Chart 6-3)

Work in small groups. Take turns adding adjectives to the sentences. Use any adjectives that make sense. Think of at least three possible adjectives to complete each sentence.

1. I don't like ___*cold / hot / wet / rainy / bad / etc.*___ weather.
2. Do you like ________________ food?
3. I admire ________________ people.
4. ________________ people make me angry.
5. Pollution is a/an ________________ big problem.
6. I had a/an ________________ experience yesterday.
7. I don't like ________________ cities.
8. I had a/an ________________ dinner last night.

❑ Exercise 12. Let's talk: small groups. (Chart 6-3)

Part I. Complete each sentence with the name of a country and the adjective that goes with it.

1. Food from ___*China*___ is ___*Chinese*___ food.
2. Food from ___*Mexico*___ is ________________ food.
3. Food from ________________ is ________________ food
4. Food from ________________ is ________________ food.
5. Food from ________________ is ________________ food.
6. Food from ________________ is ________________ food.
7. Food from ________________ is ________________ food.
8. Food from ________________ is ________________ food.

Part II. What is the favorite ethnic food in your group? Give an example of this kind of food. Then find out the most popular ethnic food in other groups.

Example: Favorite ethnic food?
GROUP A: Italian
Example: An example of Italian food?
GROUP A: spaghetti

Favorite ethnic food in our group: ________________

An example of this kind of food: ________________

Part III. Working as a class, make a list of adjectives of nationality.

❑ Exercise 13. Warm-up. (Chart 6-4)

Choose all the correct completions for each sentence.

he	him	it
she	her	

1. I understand ______________________.
2. You don't understand ______________________.
3. ______________________ understands us.

6-4 Subject Pronouns and Object Pronouns

SUBJECT PRONOUNS	OBJECT PRONOUNS	SUBJECT — OBJECT
(a) *I* speak English.	Bob knows *me*.	**I — me**
(b) *You* speak English.	Bob knows *you*.	**you — you**
(c) *She* speaks English.	Bob knows *her*.	**she — her**
(d) *He* speaks English.	Bob knows *him*.	**he — him**
(e) *It* starts at 8:00.	Bob knows *it*.	**it — it**
(f) *We* speak English.	Bob talks to *us*.	**we — us**
(g) *You* speak English.	Bob talks to *you*.	**you — you**
(h) *They* speak English.	Bob talks to *them*.	**they — them**
(i) I know *Tony*. *He* is a friendly person. (j) I like *Tony*. I know *him* well.		A pronoun has the same meaning as a noun. In (i): ***He*** has the same meaning as ***Tony***. In (j): ***Him*** has the same meaning as ***Tony***. In grammar, we say that a pronoun "refers to" a noun. The pronouns ***he*** and ***him*** refer to the noun ***Tony***.
(k) I have *a red book*. *It* is on my desk.		Sometimes a pronoun refers to a *noun phrase*. In (k): ***It*** refers to the whole phrase ***a red book***.

❑ Exercise 14. Looking at grammar. (Chart 6-4)

Complete the sentences with the correct subject and object pronouns.

1. Jack loves Janey. ___He___ loves ___her___ very much.
2. Janey loves Jack. __________ loves __________ very much.
3. Janey and Jack love their daughter, Mia. __________ love __________ very much.

4. Janey and Jack love their son, Todd. ____________ love ____________ very much.
5. Todd loves his little sister, Mia. ____________ loves ____________ very much.
6. Janey loves her children. ____________ loves ____________ very much.
7. Jack loves his children. ____________ loves ____________ very much.
8. Janey and Jack love Todd and Mia. ____________ love ____________ very much.

❑ Exercise 15. Looking at grammar. (Chart 6-4)

Choose the correct answers.

1. Rita has a book. (She) / It bought her / (it) last week.
2. I know the new students, but Franco doesn't know him / them yet.
3. Where are my keys? Are they / them in your purse?
4. Ary is in Canada. She / Her is studying at a university.
5. Bert lives in my dorm. I eat breakfast with he / him every morning.
6. Sandra is my neighbor. I talk to she / her every day. She / Her and I / me have interesting conversations.
7. I have two pictures on my bedroom wall. I like it / them. It / They are beautiful.
8. Zola and I have a dinner invitation. Mr. and Mrs. Soto want we / us to come to dinner at their house.
9. Min has a new car. He / It is a convertible.
10. My husband and I have a new car. We / Us got it / him last month.

❑ Exercise 16. Let's talk: interview. (Chart 6-4)

Interview your classmates. Find someone who can answer *yes* to a question. Then ask the follow-up question using the appropriate object pronoun.

Example:
STUDENT A: Do you send emails?
STUDENT B: No, I don't.
STUDENT A: (*Ask another student.*) Do you send emails?
STUDENT C: Yes, I do.
Follow-up question:
STUDENT A: When do you send **them**?
STUDENT C: I send **them** all day.

1. Do you do your homework?
   When do you . . . ?
2. Do you visit friends?
   When do you . . . ?
3. Do you read newspapers or magazines?
   When do you . . . ?

4. Do you talk to (*name of classmate*)?
   When do you . . . ?

5. Do you watch TV?
   When do you . . . ?

6. Do you buy groceries?
   When do you . . . ?

7. Do you wear boots?
   When do you . . . ?

8. Do you use a laptop computer?
   When do you . . . ?

❑ Exercise 17. Looking at grammar. (Chart 6-4)

Complete the sentences with the correct pronouns.

1. A: Do you know Zuri and Obi?

   B: Yes, ____I____ do. I live near ____them____.

2. A: Is the chemical formula for water H_3O?

   B: No, __________ isn't. __________ is H_2O.

3. A: Do Julia and you want to come to the movie with us?

   B: Yes, __________ would. Julia and __________ would like to go to the movie with __________.

4. A: Do Mr. and Mrs. Kelly live in the city?

   B: No, __________ don't. __________ live in the suburbs. I visited __________ last month.

5. A: Do you know how to spell "Mississippi"?

   B: Sure! I can spell __________. __________ is easy to spell.

6. A: Is Paul Peterson in your class?

   B: Yes, __________ is. I sit next to __________.

❑ Exercise 18. Listening. (Chart 6-4)

CD 1
Track 21

Listen to the sentences. Notice that the "h" in ***her*** and ***him*** is often dropped in spoken English. The "th" in ***them*** can also be dropped. ***Him*** and ***them*** may sound the same.

1. Renata knows Oscar. She knows him very well.
2. Where does Shelley live? Do you have her address?
3. There's Vince. Let's go talk to him.
4. There are Dave and Lois. Let's go talk to them.

5. I'm looking online for JoAnne's phone number. What's her last name again?
6. I need to see our airline tickets. Do you have them?

❑ Exercise 19. Listening. (Charts 1-5 and 6-4)

Listen to each conversation and write the words you hear.

CD 1 Track 22

Example: You will hear: How is Mr. Park doing?
You will write: How ___is___ Mr. Park doing?

You will hear: Great! I see him every week at the office.
You will write: Great! I see ___him___ every week at the office.

1. A: Mika and ____________ downtown this afternoon. Do you want to come ____________?
   B: I don't think so, but thanks anyway. Chris and ____________ to the library. ____________ study for our test.

2. A: Hi, Abby. How do you like your new apartment?
   B: ____________ great. I have a new roommate too. She's very nice.
   A: What's ____________ name?
   B: Rita Lopez. Do you ____________?
   A: No, but I know ____________ brother. He's in my math class.

3. A: Do you see Mike and George very much?
   B: Yes, I see ____________ often. We play video games at my house.
   A: Who usually wins?
   B: Mike. We never beat ____________!

❑ Exercise 20. Warm-up. (Chart 6-5)

How many? Choose the correct number.

1. cup	one	two or more
2. class	one	two or more
3. countries	one	two or more
4. knives	one	two or more
5. radio	one	two or more

6-5 Nouns: Singular and Plural Forms

SINGULAR	PLURAL	
(a) *one pen* *one apple* *one cup* *one elephant*	*two pen**s*** *three apple**s*** *four cup**s*** *five elephant**s***	To make the plural form of most nouns, add **-s**.
(b) *baby* *city*	*bab**ies*** *cit**ies***	End of noun: *consonant* + **-y** Plural form: change ***y*** to ***i***, add **-es**
(c) *boy* *key*	*boy**s*** *key**s***	End of noun: *vowel* + **-y** Plural form: add **-s**
(d) *wife* *thief*	*wi**ves*** *thie**ves***	End of noun: **-fe** or **-f** Plural form: change ***f*** to ***v***, add **-s** or **-es**
(e) *dish* *match* *class* *box*	*dish**es*** *match**es*** *class**es*** *box**es***	End of noun: **-sh, -ch, -ss, -x** Plural form: add **-es** Pronunciation: /əz/
(f) *tomato* *potato* *zoo* *radio*	*tomato**es*** *potato**es*** *zoo**s*** *radio**s***	End of noun: *consonant* + **-o** Plural form: add **-es** End of noun: *vowel* + **-o** Plural form: add **-s**

❑ Exercise 21. Looking at grammar. (Chart 6-5)

Complete the sentences. Use the plural form of the words in the boxes. Use each word only once.

Part I.

baby	city	cowboy	key	party
✓ boy	country	dictionary	lady	tray

1. Mr. and Mrs. Novak have one daughter and two sons. They have one girl and two ______boys______.
2. The students in my class come from many ____________________.
3. Women give birth to ____________________.
4. My money and my ____________________ are in my pocket.
5. I know the names of many ____________________ in the United States and Canada.
6. I like to go to ____________________ because I like to meet and talk to people.
7. People carry their food on ____________________ in a cafeteria.
8. We always check our ____________________ when we write compositions.
9. Good evening, ____________________ and gentlemen.
10. ____________________ ride horses.

Part II.

knife leaf life thief wife

11. It is fall. The ____________________ are falling from the trees.
12. Sue and Ann are married. They have husbands. They are ________________.
13. We all have some problems in our ________________.
14. Police officers catch ____________________.
15. Please put the ____________________, forks, and spoons on the table.

Part III.

bush	glass	sandwich	tomato
class	match	sex	zoo
dish	potato	tax	

16. Steve drinks eight ____________________ of water every day.
17. There are two ________________: male and female.
18. Please put the ____________________ and the silverware on the table.
19. All citizens pay money to the government every year. They pay their __________.
20. I can see trees and ________________ outside the window.
21. I want to light the candles. I need some ____________________.
22. When I make a salad, I use lettuce and ____________________.
23. Sometimes Pam has a hamburger and French-fried ____________________ for dinner.
24. Some animals live all of their lives in ________________.
25. Mehmet is a student. He likes his ________________.
26. We often eat ________________________ for lunch.

❑ Exercise 22. Listening. (Chart 6-5)

Choose the word you hear.

CD 1 Track 23

1. toy	(toys)	6. box	boxes
2. table	tables	7. package	packages
3. face	faces	8. chair	chairs
4. hat	hats	9. edge	edges
5. office	offices	10. top	tops

❑ Exercise 23. Listening. (Chart 6-5)

Listen to each sentence. Circle the word you hear.

CD 1
Track 24

1.	desk	(desks)	6.	exercise	exercises
2.	place	places	7.	piece	pieces
3.	sandwich	sandwiches	8.	rose	roses
4.	sentence	sentences	9.	bush	bushes
5.	apple	apples	10.	college	colleges

a rose

a rose bush

❑ Exercise 24. Grammar and speaking. (Chart 6-5)

Write the correct ending. Write **Ø** if no ending is necessary. Then decide if you agree or disagree with the sentence. Share some of your answers with a partner or the class. Remember: ***a*** = ***one***.

1.	I like banana __s__, strawberr~~y~~ __ies__, and peach __es__.	yes	no
2.	I eat a banana____ every day.	yes	no
3.	My favorite animals are elephant____.	yes	no
4.	A baby elephant____ is cute.	yes	no
5.	Baby____ are cute.	yes	no
6.	The grammar exercise____ in this book are easy.	yes	no
7.	A ride on a motorcycle____ is fun.	yes	no
8.	A ride on an airplane____ is comfortable.	yes	no
9.	This exercise____ is easy.	yes	no
10.	Cockroach____ are ugly, and they scare me.	yes	no

a cockroach

❑ Exercise 25. Warm-up. (Chart 6-6)

Write ***a*** before the singular nouns.

1. a. ____ child
   b. ____ children

2. a. ____ teeth
   b. ____ tooth

3. a. ____ foot
   b. ____ feet

6-6 Nouns: Irregular Plural Forms

SINGULAR	PLURAL	EXAMPLES
(a) *child*	**children**	Mr. Smith has one *child*. Mr. Cook has two **children**.
(b) *foot*	**feet**	I have a right *foot* and a left *foot*. I have two **feet**.
(c) *man*	**men**	I see a *man* on the street. I see two **men** on the street.
(d) *mouse*	**mice**	My cat sees a *mouse*. Cats like to catch **mice**.
(e) *tooth*	**teeth**	My *tooth* hurts. My **teeth** are white.
(f) *woman*	**women**	There's one *woman* in our class. There are ten **women** in your class.
(g) *sheep*	**sheep**	Annie drew a picture of one *sheep*. Tommy drew a picture of two **sheep**. 
(h) *fish*	**fish**	Bob has an aquarium. He has one *fish*. Sue has an aquarium. She has seven **fish**. 
(i) *(none)**	**people**	There are fifteen **people** in this room. (Notice: *People* does not have a final **-s**.)

* ***People*** is always plural. It has no singular form.

❑ Exercise 26. Looking at grammar. (Chart 6-6)

Complete the sentences with the correct form of the noun in each picture.

1

2

3
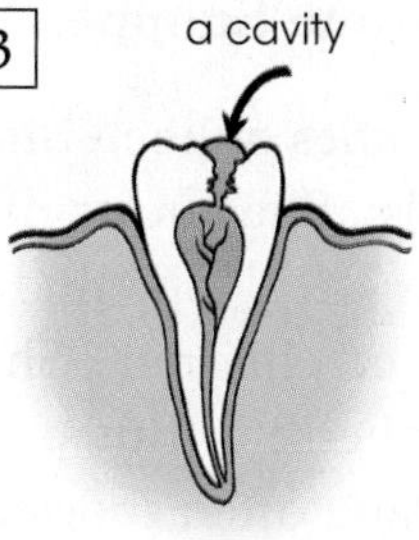

4

5

6

7

8

1. The dancer is standing on one ______________. After a dance, her __________ are sore.
2. There are three ______________ in the bowl. One ______________ is blowing bubbles.
3. The dentist is checking my ________________. One ________________ has a cavity.
4. Janine has four ________________. I have one ______________.
5. Sometimes, I have trouble sleeping, so I count ______________. One ______________, two ______________, . . . one hundred ______________. Oh, no, I'm still awake!
6. This ________________ is strong. This ______________ is weak.
7. Are ______________ stronger than ________________, or are ________________ stronger than ______________?
8. There is a __________ in my bedroom wall. There are __________ under my house.

❑ Exercise 27. Reading and grammar. (Charts 6-5 and 6-6)

Part I. Read the story. Look at new vocabulary with your teacher first.

An Online Shopper

Do you know these words?
malls
sales
purchases
free shipping

Tara likes to buy clothes online. She lives far away from stores and shopping malls. She knows many good online sites. She frequently checks for sales. She finds shirts, pants, and jackets for her husband and children. She buys skirts, dresses, warm coats, and hats for herself. But she doesn't get shoes online. She has big feet and often shoes don't fit. Sometimes she returns her purchases. For Tara, the best websites have free shipping for returns.

Part II. Add plural endings to the nouns. Write **Ø** for "no ending."

1. Tara shops at online site____.
2. She lives far away from mall____.
3. She checks website____ for sale____.
4. She like to buy clothes for her husband____ and child____.
5. She buys jacket____, skirt____, shirt____, dress____, and coat____.
6. She doesn't buy shoe____ online because she has big f____.
7. Tara likes website____ with free shipping for return____.

❑ Exercise 28. Looking at grammar. (Charts 6-1 → 6-6)

A *complete sentence* is a group of words that has a subject and a verb. An *incomplete sentence* is a group of words that does not have a subject and a verb.

If the words are a complete sentence, change the first letter to a capital letter and add final punctuation (a period or a question mark). If the words are an incomplete sentence, write "NC" to mean "not complete."

1. ~~m~~onkeys like bananas. (M)
2. in my garden → *NC*
3. ~~d~~o you like sour apples? (D)
4. this class ends at two o'clock
5. teaches English
6. my mother works
7. in an office

8. my mother works in an office

9. does your brother have a job

10. does not work

11. my sister lives in an apartment

12. has a roommate

13. the apartment has two bedrooms

14. a small kitchen and a big living room

15. on the third floor

❑ **Exercise 29. Looking at grammar.** (Charts 6-1 → 6-6)
Choose the correct completion.

1. My sister and I live together. Our parents often call or visit ____.
   (a.) us b. them c. we d. they

2. Dan has a broken leg. I visit ____ every day.
   a. he b. him c. them d. it

3. Maya and I are good friends. ____ spend a lot of time together.
   a. They b. You c. We d. She

4. Our kids enjoy the zoo. We often take ____ to the zoo.
   a. it b. they c. them d. him

5. Cristina drives an old car. She takes good care of ____.
   a. her b. them c. it d. him

6. Mark and ____ don't know Mr. Sung.
   a. I b. me c. us d. them

7. Ms. Vargas is a lawyer in Chicago. Do you know ____?
   a. them b. it c. him d. her

8. Ahmed lives near Yoko and ____.
   a. I b. me c. he d. she

9. My sister and a friend are visiting me. ____ are visiting here for two days.
   a. She b. They c. We d. Them

10. Do ____ have the correct time?
    a. you b. them c. him d. her

❑ **Exercise 30. Warm-up.** (Chart 6-7)
Complete the sentences.

Who does this book belong to?

1. STUDENT A:	It's his book	OR	It's his.
2. STUDENT B:	It's her book.	OR	It's hers.
3. STUDENT C:	It's your book.	OR	It's yours.
4. STUDENT D:	It's our book.	OR	It's ________.
5. STUDENT E:	It's their book.	OR	It's ________.

Do you know this exception?

6. It's my book. OR It's ________.

6-7 Possessive Pronouns: *Mine, Yours, His, Hers, Ours, Theirs*

	POSSESSIVE ADJECTIVE	POSSESSIVE PRONOUN	
(a) This book belongs to me. It is ***my*** book. It is ***mine***.	**my**	**mine**	A POSSESSIVE ADJECTIVE is used in front of a noun: ***my*** book.
(b) That book belongs to you. It is ***your*** book. It is ***yours***.	**your** **her** **his**	**yours** **hers** **his**	A POSSESSIVE PRONOUN is used alone, without a noun following it, as in (c).
(c) That book is ***mine***. INCORRECT: *That is mine book.*	**our** **their**	**ours** **theirs**	

❑ **Exercise 31. Looking at grammar.** (Chart 6-7)
Write or say the correct possessive pronoun.

1. It's your money. It's ________.
2. It's our money. It's ________.
3. It's her money. It's ________.
4. It's their money. It's ________.
5. It's his money. It's ________.
6. It's my money. It's ________.
7. The money belongs to Matt. It's ________.
8. The money belongs to Elena. It's ________.
9. The money belongs to Matt and Elena. It's ________.
10. The money belongs to Stuart and me. It's ________.

❑ **Exercise 32. Looking at grammar.** (Charts 2-5, 6-2, 6-4, and 6-7)
Complete the sentences. Use object pronouns, possessive adjectives, and possessive pronouns.

1. ***I*** own this book.
   a. This book belongs to ___me___.
   b. This is ___my___ book.
   c. This book is ___mine___.

2. ***They*** own these books.
   a. These books belong to ____________.
   b. These are ____________ books.
   c. These books are ____________.

3. ***You*** own that book.
   a. That book belongs to ____________.
   b. That is ____________ book.
   c. That book is ____________.

4. ***She*** owns this pen.
   a. This pen belongs to ____________.
   b. This is ____________ pen.
   c. This pen is ____________.

5. ***He*** owns that pen.
   a. That pen belongs to ____________.
   b. That is ____________ pen.
   c. That pen is ____________.

6. ***We*** own those books.
   a. Those books belong to ____________.
   b. Those are ____________ books.
   c. Those books are ____________.

❑ Exercise 33. Looking at grammar. (Charts 2-5 and 6-7)

Write the correct completion.

1. Is this ___*your*___ pen?
   your / yours
2. Please give this dictionary to Oksana. It's ____________.
   her / hers
3. A: Don't forget ____________ hat. Here.
   your / yours

   B: No, that's not ____________ hat. ____________ is green.
   my / mine — My / Mine
4. A: Please take this bouquet of flowers as a gift from me. Here. They're ____________.
   your / yours

   B: Thank you. You're very thoughtful.
5. A: That car belongs to Mr. and Mrs. Townsend.

   B: No, that's not ____________. ____________ car is new.
   their / theirs — Their / Theirs
6. A: Malik and I really like ____________ new apartment. It has lots of space.
   our / ours

   How do you like ____________?
   your / yours

   B: ____________ is small, but it's comfortable.
   Our / Ours
7. A: Excuse me. Is this ____________ umbrella?
   your / yours

   B: I don't have an umbrella. Ask Jay. Maybe it's ____________.
   he / his
8. A: This isn't ____________ phone.
   my / mine

   B: Are you sure?

   A: Yes, I have a flip phone. This one belongs to Carla. ____________ is a smartphone.
   Her / Hers

❑ Exercise 34. Warm-up. (Chart 6-8)

Choose all the grammatically correct sentences.

1. His bedroom is messy.
2. The boy his bedroom is messy.
3. The boy bedroom is messy.
4. The boy's bedroom is messy.

6-8 Possessive Nouns

	SINGULAR NOUN	POSSESSIVE FORM	
(a) My *friend* has a car. My ***friend's car*** is blue.	***friend***	***friend's***	To show that a person possesses something, add an apostrophe (') and **-s** to a singular noun. POSSESSIVE NOUN, SINGULAR: *noun* + *apostrophe* (') + **-s**
(b) The *student* has a book. The ***student's book*** is red.	***student***	***student's***	
	PLURAL NOUN	POSSESSIVE FORM	
(c) The *students* have books. The ***students' books*** are red.	***students***	***students'***	Add an apostrophe (') at the end of a plural noun (after the **-s**). POSSESSIVE NOUN, PLURAL: *noun* + **-s** + *apostrophe* (')
(d) My *friends* have a car. My ***friends' car*** is blue.	***friends***	***friends'***	

❑ **Exercise 35. Looking at grammar.** (Chart 6-8)
Complete the sentences with the correct nouns.

1. Rebecca's dress is very colorful.

   The ___*dress*___ belongs to ___*Rebecca*___.

2. Dave's car was expensive.

   The ________ belongs to ________.

3. Where is Samir's room?

   The ________ belongs to ________.

4. Is the doctor's office crowded?

   The ________ belongs to ________.

❑ **Exercise 36. Looking at grammar.** (Chart 6-8)
Choose the correct answer for each boldfaced noun.

1. My **teacher's** office is large.	one teacher	more than one
2. My **teachers'** office is large.	one teacher	more than one
3. The **nurses'** uniform is green.	one nurse	more than one
4. The **nurse's** uniform is green.	one nurse	more than one
5. My **friends'** work is interesting.	one friend	more than one
6. The **dentist's** schedule is busy.	one dentist	more than one

❑ Exercise 37. Looking at grammar. (Chart 6-8)

Complete the sentences with your classmates' names.

1. ______________________ hair is short and straight.
2. ______________________ grammar book is on her desk.
3. ______________________ last name is ______________________.
4. I don't know ______________________ address.
5. ______________________ eyes are brown.
6. ______________________ shirt is blue.
7. ______________________ backpack is on the floor.
8. I need to borrow ______________________ pen.

❑ Exercise 38. Game. (Chart 6-8)

Work in teams. Complete the sentences with words from the box. You may use a word more than one time. The team with the most correct answers wins.

brother	father	son
children	mother	wife
daughter	sister	

Family relationships

1. My uncle is my father's ________________.
2. My grandmother is my mother's ________________.
3. My brother-in-law is my husband's ________________.
4. My sister's ________________ are my nieces and nephews.
5. My niece is my brother's ________________.
6. My nephew is my sister's ________________.
7. My aunt's ________________ is my mother.
8. My wife's ________________ is my mother-in-law.
9. My brother's ________________ is my sister-in-law.
10. My father's ________________ and ________________ are my grandparents.

❑ **Exercise 39. Looking at grammar.** (Charts 2-5, 6-7, and 6-8)

Complete the sentences. Use the correct possessive form of the given words.

1. I a. This bookbag is ___mine___.
   Ava b. That bookbag is ___Ava's___.
   I c. ___My___ bookbag is red.
   she d. ___Hers___ is green.

2. we a. These books are ________.
   they b. Those books are ________.
   we c. ________ books are on the table.
   they d. ________ are on the desk.

3. Don a. This raincoat is ________.
   Kate b. That raincoat is ________.
   he c. ________ is light brown.
   she d. ________ is light blue.

4. I a. This notebook is ________.
   you b. That one is ________.
   I c. ________ has ________ name on it.
   you d. ________ has ________ name on it.

5. Ray a. ________ apartment is on Pine Street.
   we b. ________ is on Main Street.
   he c. ________ apartment has three rooms.
   we d. ________ has four rooms.

6. I a. This is ________ pen.
   you b. That one is ________.
   I c. ________ is in ________ pocket.
   you d. ________ is on ________ desk.

7. we a. ________________ car is a Chevrolet.
   they b. ________________ is a Volkswagen.
   we c. ________________ gets 17 miles to the gallon.
   they d. ________________ car gets 30 miles to the gallon.

8. Gabi a. These books are ________________.
   Evan b. Those are ________________.
   she c. ________________ are on ________________ desk.
   he d. ________________ are on ________________ desk.

❑ Exercise 40. Listening. (Chart 6-8)

Listen to each sentence and choose the word you hear.

CD 1 Track 25

Example: You will hear: Your dad's job sounds interesting.
You will choose: dad (dad's)

1.	Mack	Mack's	5.	friend	friend's
2.	Mack	Mack's	6.	friend	friend's
3.	teacher	teacher's	7.	manager	manager's
4.	teacher	teacher's	8.	cousin	cousin's

❑ Exercise 41. Looking at grammar. (Chart 6-8)

Add apostrophes where necessary.

1. ~~Brians~~ *Brian's* last name is Wolf.
2. Stefan likes to work late at night. → (*no change*)
3. My teachers give a lot of homework.
4. My teachers names are Ms. Cordova and Mr. Durisova.
5. My teachers first name is Ellen.
6. The teacher collected all the students test papers at the end of the class.
7. Nicole is a girls name.
8. Erica and Natalie are girls names.
9. Do you know Monicas brother?
10. Ryans friends visited him last night.

❑ Exercise 42. Warm-up. (Chart 6-9)
Choose the correct answer.

1. Who is that?
   a. It's Tom.
   b. It's Tom's.

2. Whose is that?
   a. It's Tom.
   b. It's Tom's.

6-9 Questions with *Whose*

(a) ***Whose book*** is this? → ***Mine.*** → It's ***mine***. → It's ***my*** book. (b) ***Whose books*** are these? → ***Rita's.*** → They're ***Rita's***. → They're ***Rita's*** books.	***Whose*** asks about possession. ***Whose*** is often used with a noun (e.g., *whose book*), as in (a) and (b).
(c) ***Whose*** is this? (*The speaker is pointing to one book.*) (d) ***Whose*** are these? (*The speaker is pointing to some books.*)	***Whose*** can be used without a noun if the meaning is clear, as in (c) and (d).
(e) ***Who's*** your teacher?  	In (e): ***Who's* = *who is*** ***Whose*** and ***who's*** have the same pronunciation.

❑ Exercise 43. Looking at grammar. (Chart 6-9)
Choose the correct answer.

1. Whose birthday is today?
   a. Audrey's.
   b. Audrey.

2. Who is on the phone?
   a. Audrey's.
   b. Audrey.

3. Who is working at the bakery?
   a. Allen.
   b. Allen's.

4. Whose bakery is the best?
   a. Allen.
   b. Allen's.

5. Who's going to join us for lunch?
   a. Toshi's.
   b. Toshi.

6. Whose dirty socks are on the floor?
   a. Julian's.
   b. Julian.

❑ Exercise 44. Looking at grammar. (Chart 6-9)

Complete the sentences with ***Whose*** or ***Who's***.

1. ____________ your roommate this year?
2. ____________ pen is this?
3. ____________ on the phone?
4. ____________ that?
5. ____________ is that?
6. ____________ making so much noise?

❑ Exercise 45. Listening. (Chart 6-9)

Listen to each sentence. Choose ***Whose*** or ***Who's***.

CD 1
Track 26

1. Whose Who's
2. Whose Who's
3. Whose Who's
4. Whose Who's
5. Whose Who's
6. Whose Who's
7. Whose Who's
8. Whose Who's
9. Whose Who's
10. Whose Who's

❑ Exercise 46. Looking at grammar. (Charts 2-6, 2-7, and 6-9)

Write the correct completion.

1. Whose watch ___is___ (is / are) ___this___ (this / these)?
2. Whose glasses ____________ (is / are) ____________ (that / those)?
3. Whose hat ____________ (is / are) ____________ (that / those)?
4. Whose shoe ____________ (is / are) ____________ (this / these)?
5. Whose keys ____________ (is / are) ____________ (this / these)?

❑ Exercise 47. Let's talk: pairwork. (Chart 6-9)

Work with a partner. Touch or point to something in the classroom that belongs to someone and ask a question with ***Whose***.

Example:
PARTNER A: (*points to a book*) Whose book is this?
PARTNER B: It's mine. / Mine. / It's my book.
PARTNER A: Your turn.

❑ Exercise 48. Warm-up. (Chart 6-10)

Choose the answer that describes the picture. Only one answer is correct.

a. Woman's Restroom

b. Women's Restroom

6-10 Possessive: Irregular Plural Nouns

(a) The ***children's*** *toys* are on the floor. (b) That store sells ***men's*** *clothing.* (c) That store sells ***women's*** *clothing.* (d) I like to know about other ***people's*** *lives.*	Irregular plural nouns (*children, men, women, people*) have an irregular plural possessive form. The apostrophe (') comes <u>before</u> the final **-s**. REGULAR PLURAL POSSESSIVE NOUN: *the **students'** books* IRREGULAR PLURAL POSSESSIVE NOUN: *the **women's** books*

❑ Exercise 49. Looking at grammar. (Charts 6-8 and 6-10)

Complete each section with the possessive form of the given noun.

These books belong to . . .

1. Maggie. They're ___*Maggie's*___ books.
2. my friend. They're _______________ books.
3. my friends. They're _______________ books.
4. the child. They're _______________ books.
5. the children. They're _______________ books.
6. the woman. They're _______________ books.
7. the women. They're _______________ books.

❑ Exercise 50. Looking at grammar. (Charts 6-8 and 6-10)

Complete each sentence with the possessive form of the given noun.

1. children — That store sells ___*children's*___ books.
2. women — Vanessa and Angelina are ________________ names.
3. person — A biography is the story of a ________________ life.
4. people — Biographies are the stories of ________________ lives.
5. students — ________________ lives are busy.
6. brother — Do you know my ________________ wife?
7. wife — Vanya fixed his ________________ old sewing machine.

8. dog — My ________________ name is Fido.
9. dogs — My ________________ names are Fido and Rover.
10. men — Are Jim and Tom ________________ names?
11. man, woman — Chris can be a ________________ nickname or a ________________ nickname.
12. children — Our ________________ school is near our house.

❑ Exercise 51. Looking at grammar. (Charts 6-8 and 6-10)

Choose the correct completion.

1. The ____ work hard.
   (a.) students — b. student's — c. students'
2. My ____ name is Honey.
   a. cats — b. cat's — c. cats'
3. My ____ are traveling in Spain.
   a. cousins — b. cousin's — c. cousins'
4. My ____ is meeting them in two weeks.
   a. uncle — b. uncle's — c. uncles'
5. The three ____ coats are in the closet.
   a. boys — b. boy's — c. boys'

6. The ____ is riding his bike.
   a. boys b. boy c. boys'

7. We have three ____ and one girl in my family.
   a. boys b. boy's c. boys'

8. Two of my ____ live near me.
   a. friends b. friend's c. friends'

9. My ____ names are Frank and Martin.
   a. friend b. friend's c. friends'

10. My best ____ name is Andy.
   a. friends b. friend's c. friends'

❑ **Exercise 52. Check your knowledge.** (Chapter 6)
Correct the mistakes.

1. Jamil a car has. → *Jamil has a car.*
2. Babys cry.
3. Kurt helps Justin and I.
4. Our teacher gives tests difficult.
5. Charlie is cutting with a lawnmower the grass.
6. Do you know Yuko roommate?
7. My roommate desk is always a mess.
8. There are nineteen peoples in my class.
9. Veronica and Victor have three childrens.
10. Excuse me. Where is the men room?
11. There is twenty classroom in this building.
12. Mr. Torro is our teacher. Me like he very much.
13. Does that store sell children toys?
14. Whose is book on the chair?
15. It is mine book.

a lawnmower

❑ Exercise 53. Grammar and writing. (Chapter 6)

Part I. Read the paragraph. Look at the boldface words. Write "S" if the word is singular and "P" if it is plural.

S

My favorite **store** is City Market. It is a grocery store. I like this store because it has many kinds of **groceries**. I can buy interesting **ingredients** there. I often cook **dishes** from my **country**. City Market has a big **selection** of rice and fresh **vegetables**. I like to buy fresh, not frozen, vegetables and meat, but the meat at City Market is expensive, so I don't buy much. The store is near my **house**, and I can walk to it. The **people** are friendly and helpful.

Part II. Where do you like to shop? It can be a grocery store, clothes store, online store, etc. Complete the sentences. Combine the sentences into a paragraph. Add a few extra details to make your writing more interesting. Begin with ***My favorite store is . . . .***

1. My favorite store is ____ .
2. I like this store because it ____ .
3. I often/sometimes buy ____ .
4. I don't like to buy ____ .
5. The store is ____ .

Part III. Work individually or change papers with a partner. Check (✓) for the following:

1. ____ indented paragraph
2. ____ capital letter at the beginning of each sentence
3. ____ period at the end of each sentence
4. ____ a verb in every sentence
5. ____ correct use of ***-s/-es/-ies*** endings for plural nouns
6. ____ correct use of irregular plural forms
7. ____ correct spelling (use a dictionary or spell-check)

Chapter 7
Count and Noncount Nouns

❑ **Exercise 1. Warm-up.** (Chart 7-1)
Which of the following can you count? There is only one possibility.

1. ____ sugar bowl
2. ____ sugar

7-1 Nouns: Count and Noncount

	SINGULAR	PLURAL	
COUNT NOUN	*a book* *one book*	*books* *two books* *some books* *a lot of books*	**A COUNT NOUN** SINGULAR: ***a*** + *noun* / ***one*** + *noun* PLURAL: *noun* + **-*s***
NONCOUNT NOUN	*mail* *some mail* *a lot of mail*	(no plural form)	**A NONCOUNT NOUN** SINGULAR: Do not use ***a***. Do not use ***one***. PLURAL: A noncount noun does not have a plural form.

COMMON NONCOUNT NOUNS

advice	mail	bread	pepper
furniture	money	cheese	rice
help	music	coffee	salt
homework	traffic	food	soup
information	vocabulary	fruit	sugar
jewelry	weather	meat	tea
luck	work	milk	water

❑ Exercise 2. Looking at grammar. (Chart 7-1)

Look at the *italicized* words. Underline the noun. Is it count or noncount?

1. He is sitting on *a chair.*	(count)	noncount
2. He is sitting on *old furniture.*	count	(noncount)
3. She has *a coin.*	count	noncount
4. She has *some money.*	count	noncount
5. The street is full of *heavy traffic.*	count	noncount
6. There are *a lot of cars* in the street.	count	noncount
7. I know *a fact* about bees.	count	noncount
8. I have *some information* about bees.	count	noncount
9. The teacher gives us *a lot of homework.*	count	noncount
10. We have *an easy assignment.*	count	noncount
11. I like *classical music.*	count	noncount
12. Would you like *some coffee?*	count	noncount
13. Our school has *a big library.*	count	noncount
14. We are learning *new vocabulary* every day.	count	noncount
15. I need *some advice.*	count	noncount
16. Peter has *a good job.*	count	noncount
17. He likes *his work.*	count	noncount
18. Margo wears *a lot of bracelets.*	count	noncount

❑ Exercise 3. Vocabulary and grammar. (Chart 7-1)

Describe the pictures. Add ***-s*** to the ends of the words if necessary or write **Ø** (no ending).

PICTURE	DESCRIPTION
	1. one ring __Ø__
	2. two ring __s__

PICTURE	DESCRIPTION
	3. three ring___s___
	4. some jewelry___Ø___
	5. two letter____
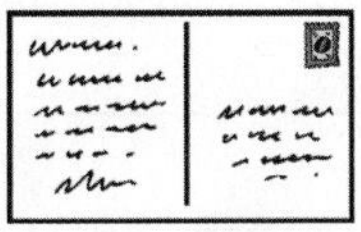	6. one postcard____
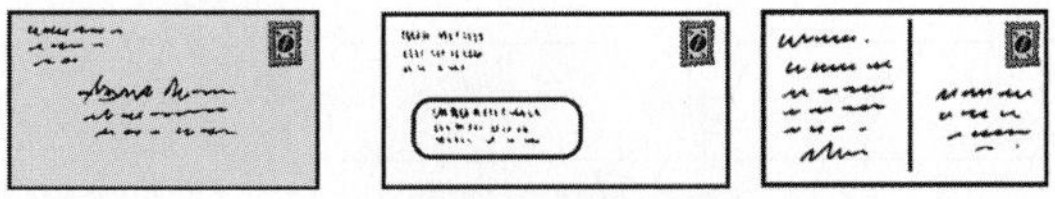	7. some mail____
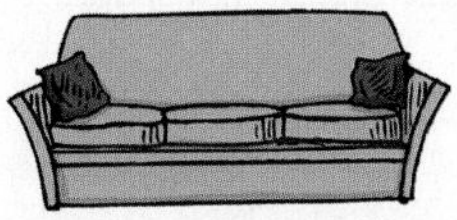	8. one couch____
	9. two table____
	10. some chair____
	11. some furniture____
	12. a. a lot of car____ b. a lot of traffic____
	13. a. a lot of money____ b. a lot of coin____

❑ Exercise 4. Looking at grammar: small groups. (Chart 7-1)

Work in small groups. List the noncount nouns. Find the count nouns that are close in meaning. Use ***a/an*** with the count nouns.

advice	desk	jewelry	music
assignment	fact	job	song
bracelet	furniture	✓ letter	suggestion
cloud	homework	✓ mail	weather
coin	information	money	work

	NONCOUNT	COUNT
1.	*mail*	*a letter*
2.	______________	______________
3.	______________	______________
4.	______________	______________
5.	______________	______________
6.	______________	______________
7.	______________	______________
8.	______________	______________
9.	______________	______________
10.	______________	______________

❑ Exercise 5. Looking at grammar. (Chart 7-1)

Complete the nouns with ***-s*** or **Ø** (no article).

1. a house____, one house____, two house____, a lot of house____, some house____
2. a car____, one car____, four car____, a lot of car____
3. water____, some water____, a lot of water____
4. a computer____, three computer____, some computer____, a lot of computer____

❑ Exercise 6. Game. (Chart 7-1)

Work in teams. Complete the sentences with as many nouns as possible. Write the names of things you see in the classroom. The team with the most grammatically correct nouns wins.

I see . . .

1. a	3. five	5. a lot of
2. two	4. some	6. many

❑ **Exercise 7. Game.** (Chapter 6 and Chart 7-1)

Work in groups or individually. The object of the game is to fill in each list with nouns that belong to the category of that list. If possible, write one noun that begins with each letter of the alphabet. When you finish your lists, count the nouns you have. That is your score. Who has the highest score?

	LIST 1 Things in nature	**LIST 2** Things you eat and drink	**LIST 3** Animals and insects	**LIST 4** Things for sale at (*name of a local store*)
A	*air*			
B	*bushes*			
C				
D				
E	*earth*			
F	*fish*			
G	*grass*			
H				
I	*ice*			
J				
K				
L	*leaves*			
M				
N				
O	*ocean*			
P	*plants*			
Q				
R	*rain*			
S	*stars*			
T	*trees*			
U				
V				
W	*water*			
X				
Y				
Z				
	Score: *13*	Score: ______	Score: ______	Score: ______

❑ Exercise 8. Warm-up (Chart 7-2)

Are the words in red correct or incorrect?

1. I work in an office.
2. It is in a hotel.
3. I take an elevator to the top floor.
4. I have an amazing view.

7-2 Using *A* vs. *An*

(a) ***A** dog* is ***an** animal.*	***A*** and ***an*** are used in front of singular count nouns. In (a): ***dog*** and ***animal*** are singular count nouns.
(b) I work in ***an** office.* (c) Mr. Tang is ***an** old man.*	Use ***an*** in front of words that begin with the vowels ***a, e, i,*** and ***o:*** *an apartment, an elephant, an idea, an ocean.* In (c): Notice that ***an*** is used because the adjective (*old*) begins with a vowel and comes in front of a singular count noun (*man*).
(d) I have ***an** uncle.* COMPARE (e) He works at ***a** university.*	Use ***an*** if a word that begins with "u" has a vowel sound: *an uncle, an ugly picture.* Use ***a*** if a word that begins with "u" has a /yu/ sound: *a university, a usual event.*
(f) I need ***an** hour* to finish my work. COMPARE (g) I live in ***a** house.* He lives in ***a** hotel.*	In some words that begin with "h," the "h" is not pronounced. Instead, the word begins with a vowel sound and ***an*** is used: *an hour, an honor.* In most words that begin with "h," the "h" is pronounced. Use ***a*** if the "h" is pronounced.

❑ Exercise 9. Looking at grammar. (Chart 7-2)

Complete the sentences with ***a*** or ***an***.

1. Lars is eating ________ apple.
2. Tia is eating ________ banana.
3. Alice works in ________ office.
4. I have ________ idea.
5. I have ________ good idea.
6. Ada is taking ________ easy class.
7. Cuba is ________ island near the United States.
8. ________ hour has sixty minutes.

9. ________ healthy person gets regular exercise.

10. Elsa is ________ honest worker.

11. Markus needs ________ math tutor.

12. Bashir has ________ exciting job. He is ________ pilot. He flies helicopters.

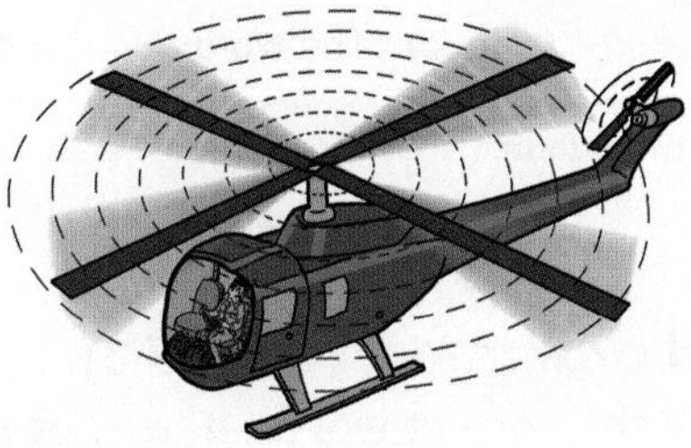

❑ Exercise 10. Listening. (Chart 7-2)

Listen to each sentence. Choose the word you hear.

CD 1 Track 27

Example: You will hear: I come from a small town.
You will choose: (a) an

1.	a	an	6.	a	an
2.	a	an	7.	a	an
3.	a	an	8.	a	an
4.	a	an	9.	a	an
5.	a	an	10.	a	an

❑ Exercise 11. Warm-up (Chart 7-3)

Answer the questions about the nouns in the box.

a bike	some cars	some motorcycles
some pollution	some traffic	a truck

1. Which nouns are count? ______________________________
2. Which nouns are noncount? ______________________________
3. Which nouns are singular count? ______________________________
4. Which nouns are plural count? ______________________________

Can you make a rule about when to use ***some?***

7-3 Using *A/An* vs. *Some*

(a) I have ***a*** *pen.*	***A/An*** is used in front of SINGULAR COUNT nouns. In (a): The word ***pen*** is a singular count noun.
(b) I have ***some*** *pens.*	***Some*** is used in front of PLURAL COUNT nouns. In (b): The word ***pens*** is a plural count noun.
(c) I have ***some*** *rice.*	***Some*** is used in front of NONCOUNT nouns.* In (c): The word ***rice*** is a noncount noun.

* Reminder: Noncount nouns do not have a plural form. Noncount nouns are grammatically singular.

❑ Exercise 12. Looking at grammar. (Chart 7-3)

Look at each noun and circle the correct word: ***a, an,*** or ***some***. Then decide if the noun is singular count, plural count, or noncount.

					SINGULAR COUNT	PLURAL COUNT	NONCOUNT
1.	a	an	(some)	letters		✓	
2.	a	an	(some)	mail			✓
3.	(a)	an	some	letter	✓		
4.	a	an	some	table			
5.	a	an	some	tables			
6.	a	an	some	furniture			
7.	a	an	some	car			
8.	a	an	some	automobiles			
9.	a	an	some	buses			
10.	a	an	some	traffic			
11.	a	an	some	advice			
12.	a	an	some	egg			
13.	a	an	some	eggs			
14.	a	an	some	hour			
15.	a	an	some	minutes			

❑ Exercise 13. Looking at grammar. (Chart 7-3)

Write each word from the box in the correct column.

✓ answer	computer	evening	ideas	uncle	word
✓ boy	day	idea	mail	vocabulary	words

a	***an***	***some***
boy	answer	

❑ Exercise 14. Looking at grammar. (Chart 7-3)

Complete each sentence with ***a, an,*** or ***some.*** Is each noun singular count or noncount?

I have . . .

1.	some fruit.	singular count	(noncount)
2.	______ apple.	singular count	noncount
3.	______ money.	singular count	noncount
4.	______ euro.	singular count	noncount
5.	______ sandwich.	singular count	noncount
6.	______ flour.	singular count	noncount
7.	______ soup.	singular count	noncount
8.	______ letter.	singular count	noncount
9.	______ information.	singular count	noncount
10.	______ water.	singular count	noncount
11.	______ word.	singular count	noncount
12.	______ homework.	singular count	noncount
13.	______ problem.	singular count	noncount
14.	______ answer.	singular count	noncount

❑ Exercise 15. Let's talk: small groups. (Chart 7-3)

Work in small groups. Complete the lists with nouns. You may use adjectives with the nouns. Share some of your answers with the class.

1. things you usually see in an apartment
   a. a ______________________
   b. an ______________________
   c. some ______________________ (*plural noun*)
   d. some ______________________ (*noncount noun*)
2. things you usually see in a classroom
   a. a ______________________
   b. an ______________________
   c. some ______________________ (*plural noun*)
   d. some ______________________ (*noncount noun*)
3. things you usually see outdoors
   a. a ______________________
   b. an ______________________
   c. some ______________________ (*plural noun*)
   d. some ______________________ (*noncount noun*)

❑ Exercise 16. Looking at grammar. (Chart 7-3)

Complete the sentences with ***a/an*** or ***some***.

1. Marisol is wearing ____*some*____ silver jewelry. She's wearing ____*a*____ necklace and ____*some*____ earrings.
2. Amir and I are busy. I have ____________ homework to do. He has ____________ work to do.
3. Asha has ____________ job. She is ____________ teacher.
4. We have ____________ table, ____________ couch, and ____________ chairs in our living room.
5. We have ____________ furniture in our living room.
6. Natalie is listening to ____________ music.

7. I'm hungry. I would like ____________ orange.

8. The kids are hungry. They would like ____________ fruit. They would also like ____________ cheese.

9. I need ____________ information about the bus schedule.

10. I have a problem. I need ____________ advice.

❑ Exercise 17. Let's talk: pairwork. (Chart 7-3)

Work with a partner. Use ***a, an,*** or ***some*** with the given word. Partner A: Your book is open to this page. Partner B: Your book is open to *Let's Talk: Answers,* p. 278.

Example: desks
PARTNER A: a desks
PARTNER B: Again?
PARTNER A: some desks
PARTNER B: Right.

1. apple
2. apples
3. children
4. old man
5. men
6. word
7. music
8. rice
9. hour
10. island

Change roles.
Partner B: Your book is open to this page. Partner A: Your book is open to p. 278.

11. animal
12. animals
13. people
14. fruit
15. egg
16. university
17. uncle
18. bananas
19. bread
20. vocabulary

❑ Exercise 18. Looking at grammar. (Chart 7-3)

Use the given word to complete the sentence. Add ***-s*** to a count noun (or give the irregular plural form). Do not add ***-s*** to a noncount noun.

1. money	I need some ___*money*___.	
2. key	I see some ___*keys*___ on the table.	
3. man	Some ___*men*___ are standing in the street.	
4. flour	I need to buy some ____________.	
5. flower	Andy wants to buy some ____________ for his mom.	

6.	information	I need some ______________________.
7.	jewelry	Fred is looking for some ______________ for his wife.
8.	child	Some ________________________ are playing in the park.
9.	homework	I can't go to the movie because I have some ______________ to do.
10.	advice	Could you please give me some ________________?
11.	suggestion	I have some ____________________________ for you.
12.	help	I need some ____________________ with my homework.
13.	sandwich	We're hungry. We want to make some ______________________.
14.	animal	I see some ____________________ in the picture.

15.	banana	The monkeys are hungry. They would like some ______________.
16.	water	I'm thirsty. I would like some __________________.
17.	weather	We're having some hot ______________________ right now.
18.	picture	I have some ____________________ of my family in my wallet.
19.	rice, bean	I usually have some ____________________ and ____________________ for dinner.

❑ **Exercise 19. Reading and grammar.** (Chart 7-3)

Part I. Read the story. Look at new vocabulary with your teacher first.

some ice cream

a coupon

Do you know these words?

on sale
brand
20% off

A Coupon Shopper

Beth likes to shop with coupons. Coupons help her save **some** money. She usually gets coupons from newspapers, online, or in **some** stores. Today she is shopping for paper products like toilet paper and tissue. She has **a** coupon for free toilet paper. It says "Buy one package—get one free." She also wants **some** rice and butter. She doesn't have **a** coupon for rice, but her favorite rice is on sale. She has **a** coupon for butter, but it is still expensive with the coupon. She is looking for a cheaper brand. She also has **some** "20% off" coupons for frozen food. Ice cream sounds good. She loves ice cream, and she thinks **a** 20% coupon is good. Beth is happy because she is saving **some** money today.

Part II. Write the noun in the story that follows each word in **bold**. Can you say why ***a*** or ***some*** is used for each noun?

1. some ___money___
2. some ____________
3. a ____________
4. some ____________
5. a ____________
6. a ____________
7. some ____________
8. a ____________
9. some ____________

Part III. Answer the questions.

1. What do people generally buy with coupons?
2. Do people buy things they don't need when they shop with coupons?
3. Do you use coupons? Why or why not?

❑ **Exercise 20. Warm-up.** (Chart 7-4)
Answer the questions. Answers may vary.

1. What do you drink every day?
   a. _____ coffee
   b. _____ milk
   c. _____ tea
   d. _____ water
   e. _____ juice

2. What do you put your drink(s) in?
   a. _____ a cup
   b. _____ a glass

3. Which phrases sound OK to you?
   a. _____ a cup of coffee
   b. _____ a glass of water
   c. _____ a glass of coffee
   d. _____ a glass of tea
   e. _____ a cup of water
   f. _____ a cup of juice

7-4 Measurements with Noncount Nouns

(a) I'd like *some water.* (b) I'd like *a glass of water.* (c) I'd like *a cup of coffee.* (d) I'd like *a piece of fruit.*	Units of measure are used with noncount nouns to express a specific quantity. Examples: *a glass of, a cup of, a piece of.* In (a): ***some water*** = an unspecific quantity In (b): ***a glass of water*** = a specific quantity

COMMON EXPRESSIONS OF MEASURE

a bag of rice	a bunch of bananas	a jar of pickles
a bar of soap	a can of corn*	a loaf of bread
a bottle of olive oil	a carton of milk	a piece of cheese
a bowl of cereal	a glass of water	a sheet of paper
a box of candy	a head of lettuce	a tube of toothpaste

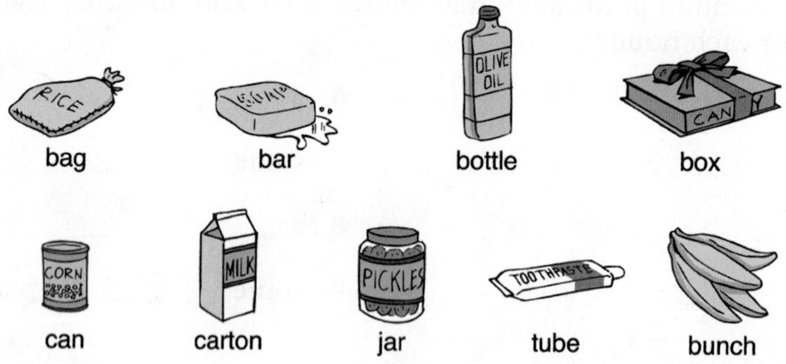

* In British English: *a tin of corn*

❑ **Exercise 21. Vocabulary and grammar.** (Chart 7-4)

Complete the sentences. Use ***a piece of, a cup of, a glass of, a bowl of.***

I'm hungry and thirsty. I'd like . . .

1. ___*a cup of*___ coffee.
2. ________ bread.
3. ________ water.
4. ________ tea.
5. ________ cheese.
6. ________ soup.
7. ________ meat.
8. ________ wine.
9. ________ fruit.
10. ________ rice.

❑ **Exercise 22. Let's talk: pairwork.** (Chart 7-4)

Work with a partner. Look at the list of food and drinks. Check (✓) what you eat and drink every day. Add your own words to the list. Then tell your partner the usual quantity you have every day. Use ***a piece of, two pieces of, a cup of, three cups of, a glass of, a bowl of,*** or ***one, two, a, some,*** etc., in your answers. Share a few of your partner's answers with the class.

Example:

_✓_ egg
____ banana
____ coffee
_✓_ fruit
___*ice cream*___
___*orange juice*___

PARTNER A: I have one egg every day.
I usually eat two pieces of fruit.
I like a bowl of ice cream at night.
I drink a glass of orange juice every morning.

List of food and drinks:

____ egg
____ soup
____ fruit
____ bread
____ banana
____ apples
____ rice
____ ice cream
____ water
____ chicken
____ cheese
____ tea

____
____
____
____
____
____

❑ Exercise 23. Looking at grammar. (Chart 7-4)

Complete the sentences with nouns.

1. I'm going to the store. I need to buy a carton of ___orange juice / milk / etc.___
2. I also need a tube of ________________ and two bars of ________________.
3. I need to find a can of ________________ and a jar of ________________.
4. I need to get a loaf of ________________ and a box of ________________.
5. I would like a head of ________________ if it looks fresh.
6. Finally, I would like a couple of bottles of ____________ and a jar of ____________.

❑ Exercise 24. Game. (Chart 7-4)

Work in teams. Make a list of everything in the picture by completing the sentence ***I see . . . .*** Try to use numbers (e.g., ***three** spoons*) or other units of measure (e.g., ***a box of** candy*). Use ***a*** for singular count nouns (e.g., ***a** fly*). Your teacher will give you a time limit. The team with the most correct answers wins.

Example: I see three spoons, a box of candy, a fly, etc.

❑ Exercise 25. Let's talk: pairwork. (Chart 7-4)

Work with a partner. Pretend that you are moving into a new apartment together. What do you need? First, make a list. Then write the things you need and indicate quantity (***two, some, a lot of,*** etc.). List twenty to thirty things. Begin with ***We need.***

Example:
PARTNER A: a couch and two beds
PARTNER B: a can opener
PARTNER A: pots and pans
PARTNER B: bookcases
PARTNER A: paint
Etc.

Possible answer: We need one couch and two beds, one can opener, some pots and pans, a lot of bookcases, one can of paint, etc.

❑ Exercise 26. Let's talk: pairwork. (Chart 7-4)

Work with a partner. Complete the sentences with ***a***, ***an***, or ***some*** and the nouns. Partner A: Your book is open to this page. Partner B: Your book is open to *Let's Talk: Answers*, p. 278. Help your partner with the correct responses if necessary.

1. *I'm hungry. I'd like . . .*
   a. food.
   b. apple.
   c. sandwich.
   d. bowl of soup.

2. *I'm thirsty. I'd like . . .*
   a. glass of milk.
   b. water.
   c. cup of tea.

3. *I'm sick. I need . . .*
   a. medicine.
   b. ambulance.

4. *I'm cold. I need . . .*
   a. coat.
   b. hat.
   c. warm clothes.*
   d. heat.

5. *I'm tired. I need . . .*
   a. sleep.
   b. break.
   c. relaxing vacation.

Change roles.
Partner B: Your book is open to this page. Partner A: Your book is open to p. 278.

6. *I'm hungry. I'd like . . .*
   a. snack.
   b. fruit.
   c. orange.
   d. piece of chicken.

7. *I'm thirsty. I'd like . . .*
   a. juice.
   b. bottle of water.
   c. glass of iced tea.

8. *I'm sick. I need . . .*
   a. doctor.
   b. help.

9. *I'm cold. I need . . .*
   a. boots.
   b. blanket.
   c. hot bath.
   d. gloves.

10. *I'm tired. I need . . .*
    a. strong coffee.
    b. break.
    c. vacation.
    d. nap.

❑ Exercise 27. Warm-up. (Chart 7-5)

Which answers are true for you?

1. Do you eat much fruit?
   a. Yes, I eat a lot. b. I eat a little. c. No, I don't like fruit.

2. Do you eat many bananas?
   a. Yes, I eat a lot. b. I eat a few. c. No, I don't like bananas.

bananas

**Clothes* is always plural. The word *clothes* does not have a singular form.

7-5 Using *Many, Much, A Few, A Little*

(a) I don't get *many letters*. (b) I don't get *much mail*. (c) Jan gets *a few letters*. (d) Ken gets *a little mail*.	***Many*** is used with PLURAL COUNT nouns. ***Much*** is used with NONCOUNT nouns. ***A few*** is used with PLURAL COUNT nouns. ***A little*** is used with NONCOUNT nouns.

❑ Exercise 28. Looking at grammar. (Chart 7-5)

Complete the questions with ***many*** or ***much***. Then give true answers. (If the answer is "zero," use "any" in the response.)

Example: How ___much___ tea do you drink in a day?
Possible answers: I drink three cups. I drink one cup. I don't drink any tea. Etc.

1. How ___much___ money do you have in your wallet?
2. How ___many___ roommates do you have?
3. How __________ languages do you speak?
4. How __________ homework does your teacher usually assign?
5. How __________ tea do you drink in a day?
6. How __________ coffee do you drink in a day?
7. How __________ sentences are there in this exercise?
8. How __________ moons does the Earth have?

❑ Exercise 29. Grammar and speaking: pairwork. (Chart 7-5)

Complete the sentences with ***many*** or ***much***. Then work with a partner. Ask about each item. Circle the answer your partner gives. Who has more items in their kitchen?

In your kitchen, do you have . . .

1.	___much___ sugar?	Yes, I do.	No, I don't.
2.	__________ paper bags?	Yes, I do.	No, I don't.
3.	__________ flour?	Yes, I do.	No, I don't.
4.	__________ salt?	Yes, I do.	No, I don't.
5.	__________ spices?	Yes, I do.	No, I don't.
6.	__________ olive oil?	Yes, I do.	No, I don't.
7.	__________ butter?	Yes, I do.	No, I don't.
8.	__________ dishwashing liquid?	Yes, I do.	No, I don't.

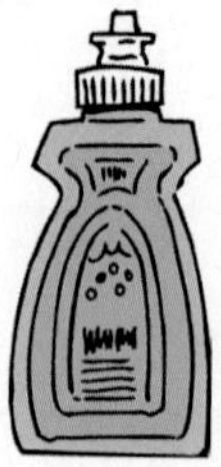

9. ______________ cans of soup? Yes, I do. No, I don't.

10. ______________ rolls of paper towels? Yes, I do. No, I don't.

❑ Exercise 30. Looking at grammar. (Chart 7-5)

Read the paragraph. Write ***a little*** or ***a few*** before each noun.

Andrew is having a party, but he has a problem. He doesn't like to cook. His cabinets and refrigerator are almost empty. His friends are very surprised. When they get to his house, they find out he has only . . . .

1. ______________ eggs.	6. ______________ vegetables.
2. ______________ juice.	7. ______________ butter.
3. ______________ potatoes.	8. ______________ ketchup.
4. ______________ fruit.	9. ______________ pieces of chicken.
5. ______________ meat.	10. ______________ cans of soup.

❑ Exercise 31. Looking at grammar. (Chart 7-5)

Part I. Change ***a lot of*** to ***many*** or ***much***.

1. Daniel has a lot of problems. → *Daniel has many problems.*
2. I don't have a lot of money.
3. I don't put a lot of sugar in my coffee.
4. I have a lot of questions to ask you.
5. Pietro and Mia have a small apartment. They don't have a lot of furniture.
6. Lara is lazy. She doesn't do a lot of work.
7. I don't drink a lot of coffee.
8. Do you send a lot of text messages?

Part II. Change ***some*** to ***a few*** or ***a little***.

1. I need some paper. → *I need a little paper.*
2. I usually add some salt to my food.
3. I have some questions to ask you.
4. Robert needs some help. He has some problems. He needs some advice.
5. I need to buy some clothes.
6. I have some homework to do tonight.
7. When I'm hungry in the evening, I usually eat some dark chocolate.
8. We usually do some speaking exercises in class every day.

❑ **Exercise 32. Let's talk: pairwork.** (Chart 7-5)

Work with a partner. Take turns asking and answering questions. Use the words from your list. Remember, you can look at your book before you speak. When you speak, look at your partner. Use this model.

Partner A: How **much/many** ______ would you like?
Partner B: I'd like **a little/a few**, please. Thanks.

Example: chicken
PARTNER A: How **much chicken** would you like?
PARTNER B: I'd like **a little**, please. Thanks.
PARTNER A: Your turn now.

Example: pencil
PARTNER B: How **many pencils** would you like?
PARTNER A: I'd like **a few**, please.
PARTNER B: Your turn now.

PARTNER A	PARTNER B
1. pen	1. salt
2. tea	2. banana
3. book	3. soup
4. apple	4. coffee
5. money	5. toy
6. help	6. cheese

❑ **Exercise 33. Let's talk: small groups.** (Charts 7-1, 7-3, and 7-5)

Work in small groups. Imagine you are all famous chefs. Create a dessert using the ingredients below. Give your recipe a name (it can be funny or strange). Tell the class about your dessert. Begin with ***We need a little / a few / a lot of / two / some.*** OR ***We don't need any.***

1. ____ salt
2. ____ flour
3. ____ honey
4. ____ sugar
5. ____ nuts
6. ____ coconut
7. ____ pieces of chocolate
8. ____ baking soda
9. ____ baking powder
10. ____ eggs
11. ____ cream
12. ____ butter

other ingredients: ______________________

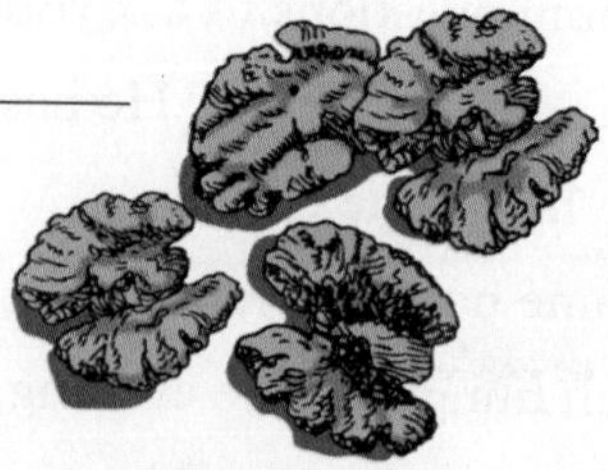

walnuts

❑ Exercise 34. Warm-up. (Chart 7-6)

Read the two conversations. In which conversation are Speaker A and Speaker B thinking about the same bedroom?

1. A: Where are the kids?
   B: I think they're hiding in a bedroom.
2. A: Where's Raymond?
   B: He's in the bedroom.

7-6 Using *The*

(a) A: Where's Max? B: He's in ***the*** *kitchen.* (b) A: I have two pieces of fruit for us, an apple and a banana. What would you like? B: I'd like ***the*** *apple,* please. (c) A: It's a nice summer day today. ***The*** *sky* is blue. ***The*** *sun* is hot. B: Yes, I really like summer.	A speaker uses ***the*** when the speaker and the listener have the same thing or person in mind. ***The*** shows that a noun is specific (not general). In (a): Both A and B have the same kitchen in mind. In (b): When B says "the apple," both A and B have the same apple in mind. In (c): Both A and B are thinking of the same sky (there is only one sky for them to think of) and the same sun (there is only one sun for them to think of).
(d) Nick has ***a*** *pen* and ***a*** *pencil.* ***The*** *pen* is blue. ***The*** *pencil* is yellow. (e) Nick has ***some*** *pens and pencils.* ***The*** *pens* are blue. ***The*** *pencils* are yellow. (f) Nick has ***some*** *rice* and ***some*** *cheese.* ***The*** *rice* is white. ***The*** *cheese* is yellow.	***The*** is used with • singular count nouns, as in (d). • plural count nouns, as in (e). • noncount nouns, as in (f). In other words, ***the*** is used with each of the three kinds of nouns. Notice in the examples: The speaker is using ***the*** for the second mention of a noun. When the speaker mentions a noun for a second time, both the speaker and listener are now thinking about the same thing. First mention: I have ***a*** *pen.* Second mention: ***The*** *pen* is blue.

❑ Exercise 35. Looking at grammar. (Chart 7-6)

Complete the sentences with ***the*** where necessary.

1. Elizabeth is standing outside. It is midnight.

   a. She's looking up at ________ sky.
   b. She sees ________ moon.
   c. She doesn't see ________ sun.
   d. ________ stars are very bright.
   e. ________ planets are difficult to find.

2. Rick and Lucy are looking for an apartment to rent. Right now they are standing in an old apartment. The kitchen has a lot of problems.

   a. ________ refrigerator is broken.

   b. ________ faucet doesn't turn on.

   c. ________ ceiling has a leak.

   d. ________ window doesn't open.

   e. ________ floor has a hole in it.

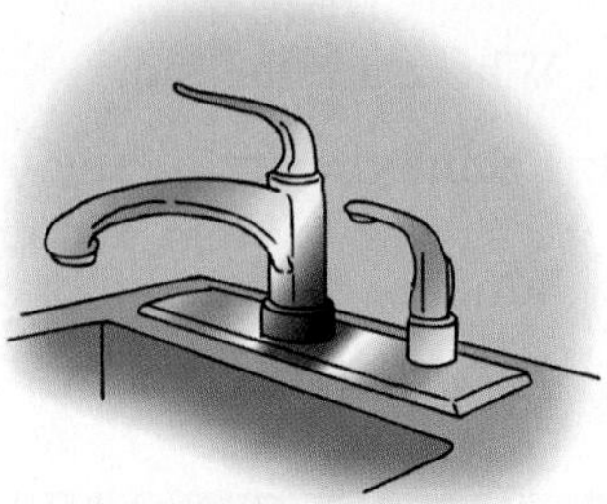
a faucet

❑ Exercise 36. Looking at grammar. (Chart 7-6)

Complete the sentences with ***the*** or ***a/an***.

1. I have ___*a*___ notebook and ________ grammar book. ________ notebook is brown. ________ grammar book is red.

2. Right now Maurice is sitting in class. He's sitting between ________ woman and ________ man. ________ woman is Graciela. ________ man is Mustafa.

3. Hana is wearing ________ ring and ________ necklace. ________ ring is on her left hand.

4. Brad and Angela are waiting for their plane to leave. Brad is reading ________ magazine. Angela is reading ________ newspaper online. When Angela finishes ________ newspaper and Brad finishes ________ magazine, they will trade.

5. In the picture below, there are four figures: ________ circle, ________ triangle, ________ square, and ________ rectangle. ________ circle is next to ________ triangle. ________ square is between ________ triangle and ________ rectangle.

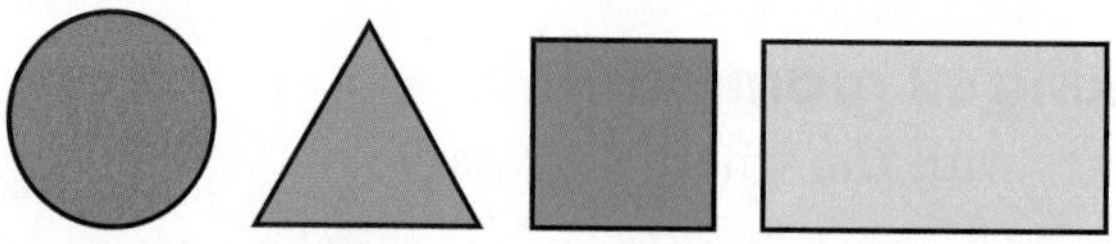

6. I gave my friend ________ card and ________ flower for her birthday. ________ card wished her "Happy Birthday." She liked both ________ card and ________ flower.

❑ Exercise 37. Let's talk: pairwork. (Chart 7-6)

Work with a partner. Read the conversation aloud using ***the*** or ***a/an***. After you finish speaking, write the answers.

A: Look at the picture below. What do you see?

B: I see ______(1) chair, ______(2) table, ______(3) window, and ______(4) plant.

A: Where is ______(5) chair?

B: ______(6) chair is under ______(7) window.

A: Where is ______(8) plant?

B: ______(9) plant is beside ______(10) chair.

Change roles.

A: Do you see any people?

B: Yes. I see ______(11) man and ______(12) woman. ______(13) man is standing. ______(14) woman is sitting down.

A: Do you see any animals?

B: Yes. I see ______(15) dog, ______(16) cat, and ______(17) bird in ______(18) cage.

A: What is ______(19) dog doing?

B: It's sleeping.

A: How about ______(20) cat?

B: ______(21) cat is watching ______(22) bird.

❑ Exercise 38. Looking at grammar. (Chart 7-6)

Complete the sentences with ***the*** or ***a/an***.

1. A: I need to go shopping. I need to buy ________ coat.

   B: I'll go with you. I need to get ________ umbrella.

2. A: Hi! Come in.

   B: Hi! ________ weather is terrible today! My umbrella is all wet.

   A: I'll take your umbrella and put it in ________ kitchen so it can dry.

3. A: Gloria has ________ great job. She builds websites. Her company gives her ________ new computer every year.

   B: Wow! She's lucky.

4. A: How much longer do you need to use ________ computer?

   B: Just five more minutes, and then you can have it.

5. A: I need ________ stamp for this letter. Do you have one?

   B: Right here.

6. A: Would you like ________ egg for breakfast?

   B: No thanks. I'll just have ________ glass of juice and some toast.

7. A: Do you see my pen? I can't find it.

   B: There it is. It's on ________ floor.

   A: Oh. I see it. Thanks.

8. A: Could you answer ________ phone? Thanks.

   B: Hello?

❑ Exercise 39. Game. (Chart 7-6)

Work in teams. Answer the questions. One person on each team writes the answers. You have five minutes. The team with the most grammatically correct answers wins.

1. What's on the floor?

   Some desks, a piece of gum, some dirt, a garbage can, etc.
2. What's on the ceiling?
3. What's out in the hallway?
4. What's outside the window?
5. What's on the board (chalkboard, whiteboard, or bulletin board)?

❏ **Exercise 40. Warm-up.** (Chart 7-7)
Which sentence (a. or b.) is true for each statement?

1. Bananas are expensive right now.
   a. Only some bananas are expensive.
   b. Bananas in general are expensive.

2. The bananas are green.
   a. A specific group of bananas is green.
   b. Bananas in general are green.

7-7 Using Ø (No Article) to Make Generalizations

(a) **Ø** *Apples* are good for you. (b) **Ø** *Students* use **Ø** *pens* and **Ø** *pencils.* (c) I like to listen to **Ø** *music.* (d) **Ø** *Rice* is good for you.	No article (symbolized by **Ø**) is used to make generalizations with • plural count nouns, as in (a) and (b), and • noncount nouns, as in (c) and (d).
(e) Tim and Jan ate some fruit. ***The*** *apples* were very good, but ***the*** *bananas* were too old.	COMPARE: In (a), the word ***apples*** is general. It refers to all apples, any apples. No article (**Ø**) is used. In (e), the word ***apples*** is specific, so ***the*** is used in front of it. It refers to the specific apples that Tim and Jan ate.
(f) We went to a concert last night. ***The*** *music* was very good.	COMPARE: In (c), ***music*** is general. In (f), ***the music*** is specific.

❏ **Exercise 41. Looking at grammar.** (Chart 7-7)
Decide if the words in **bold** are general or specific.

1. The **eggs** are delicious.	general	specific
2. Are **eggs** healthy?	general	specific
3. Please pass the **salt**.	general	specific
4. I love **salt**!	general	specific
5. **Apples** have vitamin C.	general	specific
6. The **apples** have brown spots.	general	specific

❏ **Exercise 42. Looking at grammar.** (Chart 7-7)
Complete the sentences with ***the*** or **Ø** (no article).

1. Oranges are orange, and ___*Ø*___ bananas are yellow.
2. Everybody needs ________ food to live.
3. We ate at a good restaurant last night. ________ food was excellent.
4. ________ salt tastes salty, and ________ pepper tastes hot.

5. ________ coffee has caffeine.

6. ________ coffee in the pot is fresh.

7. ________ pages in this book are full of grammar exercises.

8. ________ books have ________ pages.

9. I like ________ fruit. I also like ________ vegetables.

vegetables

❑ Exercise 43. Listening. (Charts 7-6 and 7-7)

Listen to each sentence. Decide if the given noun has a general or a specific meaning.

CD 1 Track 28

1. vegetables	(general)	specific
2. cats	general	specific
3. teacher	general	specific
4. bananas	general	specific
5. cars	general	specific
6. car	general	specific
7. computers	general	specific
8. park	general	specific

❑ Exercise 44. Let's talk. (Charts 7-3, 7-6, and 7-7)

Work in small groups or as a class. Choose the sentence that is closest in meaning to the given situation. Discuss the differences.

1. Mark is at an electronics store. There are five tablets. He buys one.
   a. He buys a tablet.
   b. He buys the tablet.

2. Pat is at a music store. There is only one guitar on the shelf. She buys it.
   a. She buys a guitar.
   b. She buys the guitar.

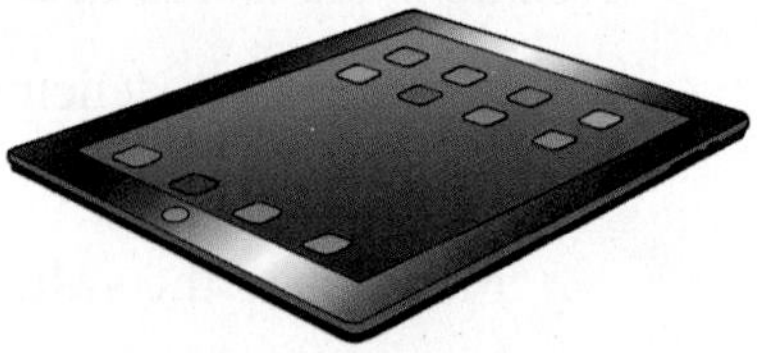
a tablet computer

3. Martha is at the library. There is one book about Nelson Mandela.
   a. She checks out the book about Nelson Mandela.
   b. She checks out a book about Nelson Mandela.

4. Misako walks outside and looks up at the sky.
   a. She sees the sun.
   b. She sees a sun.

5. Horses are my favorite animals.
   a. I love the horses.
   b. I love horses.

6. There are fifty cars in a parking lot. Ten cars are white.
   a. The cars in the parking lot are white.
   b. Some cars in the parking lot are white.

❑ **Exercise 45. Listening.** (Charts 7-1 → 7-7)

Listen to the sentences and write the words you hear. Use ***a, an,*** or ***the.***

CD 1 Track 29

1. A: Do you have ___a___ pen?

   B: There's one on ________ counter in ________ kitchen.

2. A: Where are ________ keys to ________ car?

   B: I'm not sure. You can use mine.

3. A: Shh. I hear ________ noise.

   B: It's just ________ bird outside, probably ________ woodpecker. Don't worry.

4. A: Henry Jackson teaches at ________ university.

   B: I know. He's ________ English professor.

   A: He's also the head of ________ department.

5. A: Hurry! We're late.

   B: No, we're not. It's five o'clock, and we have ________ hour.

   A: No, we don't. It's six! Look at ________ clock.

   B: Oops. I need ________ new battery for my watch.

❑ **Exercise 46. Warm-up.** (Chart 7-8)

Which words can complete each sentence?

1. I have some fruit / some oranges / any oranges.
2. I don't have some fruit / any fruit / any oranges.
3. Do you have some fruit / some oranges / any fruit / any oranges?

7-8 Using *Some* and *Any*

AFFIRMATIVE	(a) Vera has **some** *money*.	Use ***some*** in affirmative statements.
NEGATIVE	(b) Vera doesn't have **any** *money*.	Use ***any*** in negative statements.
QUESTION	(c) Does Vera have **any** *money*? (d) Does Vera have **some** *money*?	Use either ***some*** or ***any*** in a question.
(e) I don't have **any** *money*. (noncount noun) (f) I don't have **any** *matches*. (plural count noun)		***Any*** is used with noncount nouns and plural count nouns.

❑ Exercise 47. Looking at grammar. (Chart 7-8)

Complete the sentences with ***some*** or ***any***.

1. Harry has ___*some*___ money.
2. I don't have ___*any*___ money.
3. Do you have ___*some / any*___ money?
4. Do you need ____________ help?
5. No, thank you. I don't need ____________ help.
6. Kalil needs ____________ help.
7. Diana usually doesn't get ____________ mail.
8. We don't have ____________ fruit in the apartment. We don't have ____________ apples, ____________ bananas, or ____________ oranges.
9. The house is empty. There aren't ____________ people in the house.
10. I need ____________ paper. Do you have ____________ paper?
11. Heidi can't write a letter because she doesn't have ____________ paper.
12. Sasha is getting along fine. He doesn't have ____________ problems.
13. I need to go to the grocery store. I need to buy ____________ food. Do you need to buy ____________ groceries?
14. I'm not busy tonight. I don't have ____________ homework to do.
15. I don't have ____________ money in my wallet.
16. There are ____________ beautiful flowers in my garden this year.

❑ Exercise 48. Let's talk: interview. (Chart 7-8)

Walk around the room. Interview your classmates. Use this model.

Student A: Do you have some/any ____?
Student B: Yes, I have some ____. OR No, I don't have any ____.

1. pencils with erasers
2. notebook paper
3. money in your pocket
4. children
5. stepchildren
6. pets
7. worries
8. advice for me

Now share some of your answers with the rest of the class.

❑ Exercise 49. Let's talk: small groups. (Chart 7-8)

Work in small groups. You are at a mall. You have a gift card for your group. The amount is equal to the cost of a new computer. What do you want to buy for your group? What don't you want to buy? Add two more suggestions to the list.

camera	music CD	socks	video game
DVD	perfume	software	winter jacket
hat	pet	suitcase	______________
jewelry	shoe	summer clothes	______________

1. We want to buy some / a lot of / two . . . .
2. We don't want to buy any . . . .

❑ Exercise 50. Looking at grammar. (Chapters 6 and 7)

Complete the sentences with these words. If necessary, use the plural form.

bush	glass	✓ match	strawberry
centimeter	homework	page	thief
dish	inch	paper	tray
edge	information	piece	valley
fish	knife	sex	weather
foot	leaf	size	woman

1. I want to light a candle. I need some ______*matches*______.
2. ____________________ fall from the trees in autumn.
3. The application asked for my name, address, and ____________________: male or female.
4. Some ____________________, forks, and spoons are on the table.
5. I want to take the bus downtown, but I don't know the bus schedule. I need some ____________________ about the bus schedule.
6. I need to write a composition. I have a pen, but I need some ____________________.
7. Plates and bowls are called ____________________.
8. Married ____________________ are called wives.
9. There are a lot of trees and ____________________ in the park.
10. Ike is studying. He has a lot of ____________________ to do.
11. My dictionary has 437 ____________________.
12. This puzzle has 200 ____________________.

13. A piece of paper has four ____________________.

14. Mountains are high, and ____________________ are low.

15. When the temperature is around 35°C (77°F), I'm comfortable. But I don't like very hot ____________________.

16. ____________________ steal things: money, jewelry, cars, etc.

17. ____________________ are small, red, sweet, and delicious.

18. People carry their food on ____________________ at a cafeteria.

19. Sweaters in a store usually come in four ____________________: small, medium, large, and extra large.

20. In some countries, people usually use cups for their tea. In other countries, they use ____________________ for their tea.

21. Toshiro has five ____________________ in his aquarium.

22. There are 100 ____________________ in a meter.

23. There are 12 ____________________ in a foot.*

24. There are 3 ____________________ in a yard.*

❑ **Exercise 51. Check your knowledge.** (Chapter 7)
Correct the mistakes.

1. I need ~~an~~ *some* advice from you.
2. I don't like hot weathers.
3. I usually have a egg for breakfast.
4. Sun rises every morning.
5. The students in this class do a lot of homeworks every day.
6. How many language do you know?
7. I don't have many money.
8. Alexander and Carmen don't have some children.
9. A pictures are beautiful. You're a good photographer.

---

*1 inch = 2.54 centimeters; 1 foot = 30.48 centimeters; 1 yard = 0.91 meters

10. There isn't a traffic early in the morning.

11. I can't find any bowl for my soup.

❑ Exercise 52. Let's talk. (Chapter 7)

Imagine that a new shopping center is coming to your neighborhood. It will have a drugstore, a bank, and a grocery store. Decide what additional stores you want. Your teacher will help you with any vocabulary you don't know.

Part I. Choose any six businesses from the list and write their names in any of the five available spaces on Blueprint #1 on this page.

✓ a bank	✓ a grocery store	a post office
a bookstore	an ice-cream shop	a shoe store
a camera shop	an Internet café	a sports equipment store
✓ a drugstore	a laundromat	a vegetarian food store
a drycleaner's	a movie theater	a video rental store
an exercise gym	a music store	
a fast-food restaurant	a pet supply store	

Blueprint #1
(your business locations)

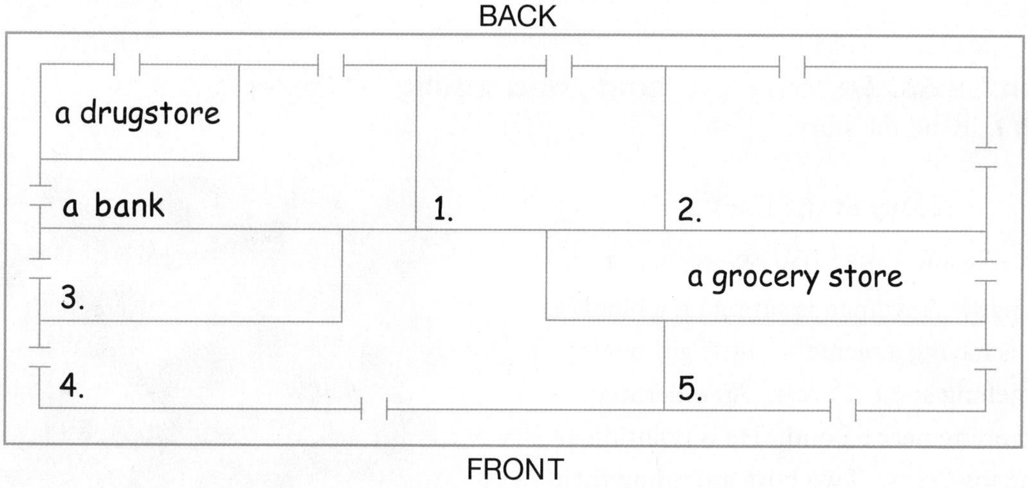

Part II. Work with a partner, but do not look at each other's blueprints. Ask your partner about the location of his/her new businesses. Write your partner's answers on your copy of Blueprint #2 on p. 222. Use this pattern:

Partner A: Is there **a/an** . . . ?
Partner B: Yes, there is. / No, there isn't.
Partner A: Where is **the** . . . ?
Partner B: It's next to / beside / in back of / in front of **the** . . . .

Example:
PARTNER A: Is there **an** exercise gym?
PARTNER B: No, there isn't.
PARTNER A: Is there **a** bank?
PARTNER B: Yes, there is.
PARTNER A: Where is **the** bank?
PARTNER B: It's in front of **the** drugstore.

Blueprint #2
(your partner's business locations)

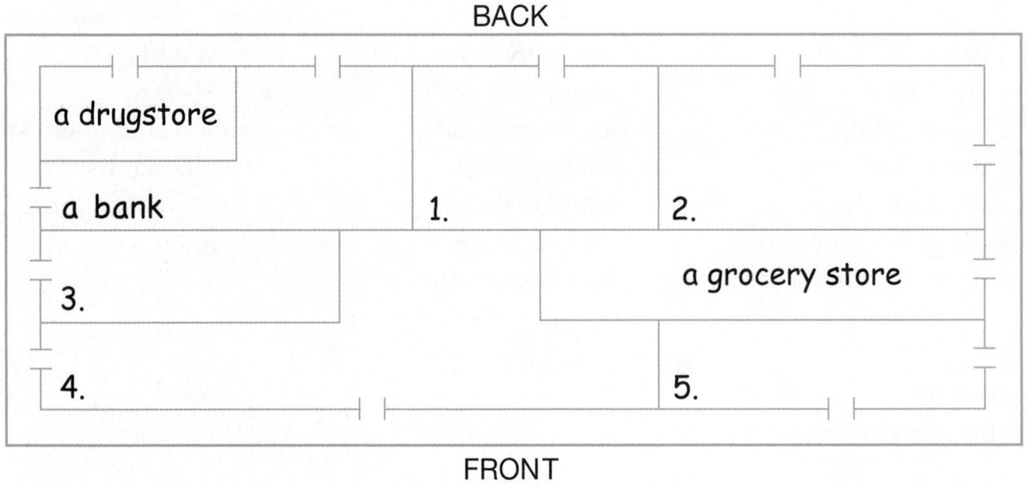

❑ **Exercise 53. Reading, grammar, and writing.** (Chapter 7)
Part I. Read the story.

A Day at the Park

It is a beautiful day. Some people are at a park. A woman is sitting on a blanket. She is having a picnic. A little girl nearby is smelling some flowers. An older man is standing near a pond. He is pointing at some toy boats. Two boys are riding their bikes. A man and a woman are sitting on a bench. The woman is knitting. The man is feeding some birds. Some ducks are swimming, and a cat wants to catch them. The cat is hungry.

Part II. Write ***a, an,*** or ***some*** in front of each word according to the paragraph. Is the article usage clear to you?

1. ___________ beautiful day
2. ___________ people
3. ___________ park
4. ___________ woman
5. ___________ blanket
6. ___________ picnic
7. ___________ little girl
8. ___________ flowers
9. ___________ older man
10. ___________ pond
11. ___________ toy boats
12. ___________ man and ___________ woman
13. ___________ bench
14. ___________ woman
15. ___________ man
16. ___________ birds
17. ___________ ducks
18. ___________ cat
19. ___________ cat

Part III. Describe the picture. Begin with ***It is a*** ________ ***day***. Make sure to use ***a, an,*** and ***some***.

Part IV. Editing check: Work individually or change papers with a partner. Check (✓) for the following:

1. ____ indented paragraph
2. ____ capital letter at the beginning of each sentence
3. ____ period at the end of each sentence
4. ____ a verb in every sentence
5. ____ correct use of ***a, an, some***
6. ____ ***-s/-es*** endings for plural nouns
7. ____ correct spelling (use a dictionary or spell-check)

Chapter 8

Expressing Past Time, Part 1

❑ **Exercise 1. Warm-up.** (Chart 8-1)
Read the statements and choose the answers.

1. I am tired now. yes no
2. I was tired two hours ago. yes no
3. Some students are absent today. yes no
4. Some students were absent yesterday. yes no

8-1 Using *Be*: Past Time

PRESENT TIME	PAST TIME
(a) I ***am*** in class ***today***.	(d) I ***was*** in class ***yesterday***.
(b) Alison ***is*** sick ***today***.	(e) Alison ***was*** sick ***yesterday***.
(c) My friends ***are*** at home ***today***.	(f) My friends ***were*** at home ***yesterday***.

SIMPLE PAST TENSE OF *BE*

SINGULAR	PLURAL
I was	**we were**
you were (one person)	**you were** (more than one person)
she was	**they were**
he was	
it was	

I, she, he, it } + *was*

we, you, they } + *were*

❑ **Exercise 2. Looking at grammar.** (Chart 8-1)
Complete the sentences with ***was*** or ***were***.

TODAY	YESTERDAY
1. You are at school.	You *were* at home.
2. We are at school.	We ________ at home.
3. He is at school.	He ________ at home.

4. You and I are at school. You and I ____________ at home.
5. She is at school. She ____________ at home.
6. They are at school. They ____________ at home.
7. Brian and James are at school. Brian and James ____________ at home.
8. My parents are at school. My parents ____________ at home.
9. I am at school. I ____________ at home.
10. The teacher is at school. The teacher ____________ at home.

❑ **Exercise 3. Looking at grammar.** (Chart 8-1)

Change the sentences to past time.

1. Bashar is in class today. → *He was in class yesterday too.*
2. I'm in class today. → *I was in class yesterday too.*
3. Martina is at the library today.
4. We're in class today.
5. You're busy today.
6. I'm happy today.
7. The classroom is hot today.
8. Elise is in her office today.
9. Tony is in his office today.
10. Noor and Eli are in their offices today.

❑ **Exercise 4. Let's talk.** (Chart 8-1)

Part I. Think about yourself as a three-year-old child. Check (✓) the words that describe you best.

____ quiet	____ loud	____ afraid
____ shy	____ smart	____ friendly
____ funny	____ curious	____ a troublemaker

Part II. Work with a partner. Tell your partner about yourself. Begin with ***I was . . . .***

❑ **Exercise 5. Warm-up.** (Chart 8-2)
Choose the correct verb to make true sentences.

The weather

1. Last month, it was / was not nice.
2. The weekends were / were not sunny.
3. Yesterday, it was / was not hot.

8-2 Simple Past Tense of *Be*: Negative

(a) I *was not* in class yesterday. (b) I *wasn't* in class yesterday.	NEGATIVE CONTRACTIONS ***was*** + ***not*** = ***wasn't*** ***were*** + ***not*** = ***weren't***
(c) They *were not* at home last night. (d) They *weren't* at home last night.	I, she, he, it } + wasn't we, you, they } + weren't

❑ **Exercise 6. Looking at grammar.** (Chart 8-2)
Complete the sentences with ***wasn't*** or ***weren't***.

Joe and JoAnn went on a trip. They were very happy because . . .

1. the airplane ride ___wasn't___ long.
2. the trains __________ slow.
3. the hotel __________ expensive.
4. the restaurants __________ expensive.
5. the tourist areas __________ crowded.
6. the language __________ difficult.
7. the weather __________ cold.

❑ **Exercise 7. Grammar and speaking.** (Chart 8-2)
Use the given words to make true sentences. Share some of your answers with the class.

Yesterday at noon, I was/wasn't . . .

1. hungry.
2. tired.
3. at home.
4. at school.
5. with my family.
6. sick.
7. in the hospital.
8. on an airplane.
9. outdoors.
10. at the movies.

❑ **Exercise 8. Listening.** (Charts 8-1 and 8-2)

Listen to the sentences. Choose the verbs you hear.

CD 1 Track 30

Example: You will hear: I was at school all day yesterday.
You will choose: (was) wasn't

1. was wasn't
2. was wasn't
3. was wasn't
4. was wasn't
5. was wasn't
6. was wasn't
7. were weren't
8. were weren't
9. were weren't
10. were weren't

❑ **Exercise 9. Warm-up: pairwork.** (Chart 8-3)

Work with a partner. Ask these questions.

Last night at midnight,

1. were you asleep?
2. were you on the phone?
3. was it quiet at your home?

8-3 Past of *Be:* Questions

YES/NO QUESTIONS					SHORT ANSWER	(LONG ANSWER)
(a)	*Were* (*be*) +	*you* (subject)	in class yesterday?	→ →	*Yes, I was.* *No, I wasn't.*	(I was in class yesterday.) (I wasn't in class yesterday.)
(b)	*Was* (*be*) +	*Carlos* (subject)	tired last night?	→	*Yes, he was.* *No, he wasn't.*	(He was tired last night.) (He wasn't tired last night.)
INFORMATION QUESTIONS					**SHORT ANSWER**	**(LONG ANSWER)**
(c)	*Where were you* *Where* + (*be*) + (subject)		yesterday?	→	*In class.*	(I was in class yesterday.)
(d)	*When was Emily* *When* + (*be*) + (subject)		sick?	→	*Last week.*	(She was sick last week.)

❑ **Exercise 10. Looking at grammar.** (Chart 8-3)
Make questions and give short answers. Use the words from the box.

at the airport	in Iceland
at the dentist	in the hospital
✓ at the library	

1. (*you \ at home \ last night*)
   A: ___*Were you at home last night?*___
   B: No, ___*I wasn't.*___
   A: Where ___*were you?*___
   B: I ___*was at the library.*___

2. (*Mr. Gupta \ at work \ last week*)
   A: ______________________________
   B: No, ______________
   A: Where ______________________________
   B: He ______________________________

3. (*Oscar and Anya \ at the train station \ at midnight*)
   A: ______________________________
   B: No, ______________
   A: Where ______________________________
   B: They ______________________________

4. (*Gabriella \ at the gym \ yesterday afternoon*)
   A: ______________________________
   B: No, ______________
   A: Where ______________________________
   B: She ______________________________

5. (*you and your family \ in Canada \ last year*)

A: ________________________________

B: No, ________________

A: Where ________________________

B: We __________________________

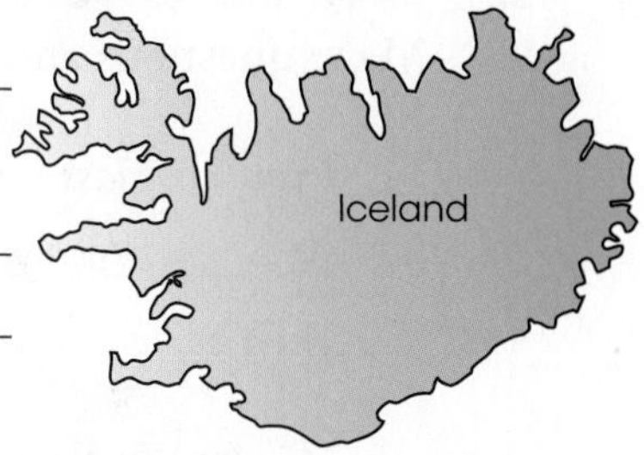

❑ Exercise 11. Let's talk: class activity. (Chart 8-3)

Think about your first day in this class. Check (✓) the words that describe your feelings that day. Then answer your teacher's questions.

Example: happy

TEACHER: Were you happy the first day of class?
STUDENT A: Yes, I was happy.
STUDENT B: No, I wasn't happy.
TEACHER: (*to Student C*) Tell me about (*Student A*) and (*Student B*).
STUDENT C: (*Student A*) was happy. (*Student B*) wasn't happy.

1. ____ excited
2. ____ scared/afraid
3. ____ nervous
4. ____ relaxed (not nervous)
5. ____ quiet
6. ____ talkative

❑ Exercise 12. Let's talk: pairwork. (Chart 8-3)

Work with a partner. Take turns making questions orally. After you finish, write the verbs.

SITUATION: You went on a roller coaster ride with a friend yesterday.

1. ___*Was*___ it fun?
2. ____________ it scary?
3. ____________ you afraid?
4. ____________ the ride long?
5. ____________ you sick afterwards?
6. ____________ your friend sick?
7. ____________ you nervous?
8. ____________ your friend nervous?
9. ____________ the ride safe?
10. ____________ you tired?

❑ Exercise 13. Looking at grammar. (Chapter 2 and Chart 8-3)

Make questions and give short answers.

1. (*you \ in class \ yesterday*)

   A: *Were you in class yesterday?*

   B: Yes, *I was.*

2. (*Claire \ in class \ today*)

   A: *Is Claire in class today?*

   B: No, *she isn't.* She's absent.

3. (*you \ tired \ last night*)

   A: ______________________________

   B: Yes, ______________ I went to bed early.

4. (*you \ hungry \ right now*)

   A: ______________________________

   B: No, ______________, but I'm thirsty.

5. (*the weather \ hot in New York City \ last summer*)

   A: ______________________________

   B: Yes, ______________ It was very hot.

6. (*the weather \ cold in Alaska \ in the winter*)

   A: ______________________________

   B: Yes, ______________ It's very cold.

7. (*Astrid and Mohammed \ here \ yesterday afternoon*)

   A: ______________________________

   B: Yes, ______________

8. (*the students \ in this class \ intelligent*)

   A: ______________________________

   B: Of course ______________ They are very intelligent!

9. (*Mr. Tok \ absent \ today*)

   A: ______________________________

   B: Yes, ______________

   A: Where ______________________________

   B: ______________________________

10. (*Tony and Benito \ at the party \ last night*)

A: ____

B: No, ____________________

A: Where ____

B: ____

11. (*Amy \ out of town \ last week*)

A: ____

B: Yes, ____________________

A: Where ____

B: ____

12. (*Mr. and Mrs. Sanchez \ in town \ this week*)

A: ____

B: No, ____________________ They're out of town.

A: Oh? Where ____

B: ____

❑ Exercise 14. Let's talk: find someone who . . . . (Charts 8-2 and 8-3)

Interview your classmates about their days in elementary school. Make questions with ***was/were***. Find people who can answer *yes* to your questions. Write down their names.

Example: you \ shy
STUDENT A: Were you shy?
STUDENT B: No, I wasn't.
STUDENT A: (*to Student C*) Were you shy?
STUDENT C: Yes, I was.

	FIRST NAME		FIRST NAME
1. you \ shy		7. you \ noisy	
2. you \ outgoing*		8. you \ athletic	
3. you \ talkative		9. you \ active	
4. you \ happy		10. you \ well-behaved	
5. you \ hardworking		11. you \ a serious student	
6. you \ quiet		12. you \ artistic	

**outgoing* = not shy

❑ Exercise 15. Warm-up. (Chart 8-4)

Check (✓) your activities this morning. What do you notice about the verb endings?

Earlier today, I . . .

1. ____ washed my face.
2. ____ brushed my teeth.
3. ____ combed my hair.
4. ____ shaved.

8-4 Simple Past Tense: Using *-ed*

SIMPLE PRESENT	(a) I	*walk*	to school	*every day*.		*verb* + ***-ed*** = simple past tense
SIMPLE PAST*	(b) I	*walked*	to school	*yesterday*.		
SIMPLE PRESENT	(c) Ann	*walks*	to school	*every day*.		I, you, she, he, it, we, they } + walked (verb + ***-ed***)
SIMPLE PAST	(d) Ann	*walked*	to school	*yesterday*.		

*For pronunciation of the simple past tense, see Appendix Chart A5-3, p. 270.

❑ Exercise 16. Looking at grammar. (Chart 8-4)

Complete the sentences orally. Use the simple past. Then write the answers.

1. Every day I walk to work. Yesterday I ______*walked*______ to work.
2. Every day I work. Yesterday I ____________________.
3. Every day Nabeel shaves. Yesterday Nabeel ____________________.
4. Every night Paula watches TV. Last night she ____________________ TV.
5. Every day you exercise. Last night you ____________________.
6. Every day people smile. Yesterday they ____________________.
7. Every week it rains. Last week it ____________________.
8. Every day we ask questions. Yesterday we ____________________ questions.
9. Every day I talk on the phone. Yesterday I ____________________ on the phone.
10. Every day Tomo listens to music. Yesterday he ____________________ to music.

❑ Exercise 17. Let's talk: pairwork. (Chart 8-4)

Work with a partner. Check (✓) all your activities yesterday. Tell your partner about them. Begin with ***Yesterday I . . . .*** Share a few of your partner's answers with the class.

1. ____ ask the teacher a question
2. ____ cook dinner
3. ____ wash some clothes
4. ____ listen to music on the radio
5. ____ use a computer
6. ____ stay home in the evening
7. ____ walk in a park
8. ____ watch TV
9. ____ work at my desk
10. ____ wait for a bus
11. ____ smile at several people
12. ____ talk on a cell phone
13. ____ dream in English
14. ____ dream in my language

❑ Exercise 18. Looking at grammar. (Chart 8-4)

Complete the sentences. Use the simple present or the simple past of the verbs from the box.

ask	erase	smile	walk
cook	✓ rain	stay	watch
dream	shave	wait	work

1. It often ___*rains*___ in the morning. It ___*rained*___ yesterday.
2. I ____________ to school every morning. I ____________ to school yesterday morning.
3. Sara often ____________ questions. She ____________ a question in class yesterday.
4. I ____________ a movie on television last night. I usually ____________ TV in the evening because I want to improve my English.
5. Mario ____________ his own dinner yesterday evening. He ____________ his own dinner every evening.
6. I usually ____________ home at night because I have to study. I ____________ home last night.
7. I have a job at the library. I ____________ at the library every evening. I ____________ there yesterday evening.

8. When I am asleep, I often ____________________. I ____________________ about my family last night.*

9. Linda usually ____________________ for the bus at a bus stop in front of her apartment building. She ____________________ for the bus there yesterday morning.

10. The teacher ____________________ some words from the board a couple of minutes ago. He used his hand instead of an eraser.

11. Our teacher is a warm, friendly person. She often ____________________ when she talks to us.

12. Rick doesn't have a beard anymore. He ____________________ it five days ago. Now he ____________________ every morning.

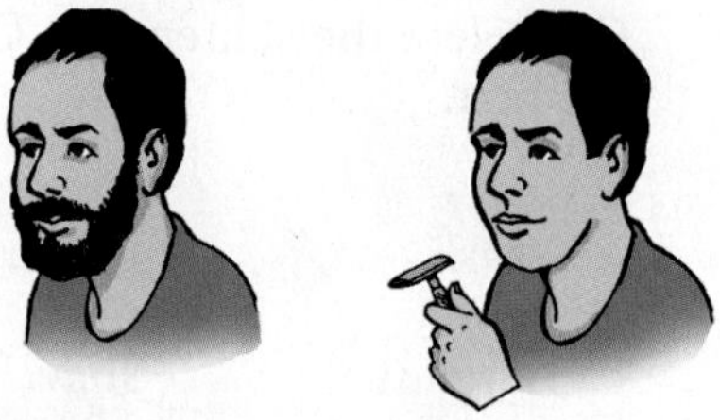

❑ Exercise 19. Vocabulary and listening. (Chapter 3 and Chart 8-4)

CD 1
Track 31

The simple past tense ending can be difficult to hear. Listen to each sentence and choose the verb you hear. Look at new vocabulary with your teacher first.

Example: You will hear: Jeremy loves soccer.

You will choose: love (loves) loved

A soccer coach

1.	work	works	worked
2.	play	plays	played
3.	play	plays	played
4.	score	scores	scored
5.	help	helps	helped
6.	learn	learns	learned
7.	watch	watches	watched
8.	like	likes	liked
9.	work	works	worked
10.	work	works	worked

Do you know these words?
coach
tournament
score
goals

*The past of *dream* can be *dreamed* or *dreamt*.

❑ **Exercise 20. Warm-up.** (Chart 8-5)
Choose the correct time words to make true sentences.

1. I was at home yesterday morning / one hour ago / yesterday evening.
2. I watched TV last weekend / last night / yesterday afternoon.
3. I talked to someone in my family last month / last week / an hour ago.

8-5 Past Time Words: *Yesterday, Last,* and *Ago*

PRESENT		PAST	
today	→	yesterday	Note the changes in time expressions from present to past.
this morning	→	yesterday morning	
this afternoon	→	yesterday afternoon	
this evening	→	yesterday evening	
tonight	→	last night	
this week	→	last week	

REFERENCE LIST: TIME EXPRESSIONS

YESTERDAY	*LAST*	*AGO*
(a) Bob was here . . . ***yesterday***. ***yesterday morning***. ***yesterday afternoon***. ***yesterday evening***.	(b) Sue was here . . . ***last night***. ***last week***. ***last weekend***. ***last month***. ***last year***. ***last spring***. ***last summer***. ***last fall***. ***last winter***. ***last Monday***. ***last Tuesday***. ***last Wednesday***. **etc.**	(c) Tom was here . . . ***five minutes ago***. ***two hours ago***. ***three days ago***. **a (one) *week ago***. ***six months ago***. **a (one) *year ago***.

NOTICE
In (a): ***yesterday*** is used with *morning, afternoon,* and *evening.*
In (b): ***last*** is used with *night,* with long periods of time (*week, month, year*), with seasons (*spring, summer,* etc.), and with days of the week.
In (c): ***ago*** means "in the past." It follows specific lengths of time (e.g., *two minutes + ago, five years + ago*).

❑ Exercise 21. Looking at grammar. (Chart 8-5)

Complete the sentences with ***yesterday*** or ***last***.

1. *I worked in the university bookstore . . .*

   a. ___last___ Friday.

   b. ______________ week.

   c. ______________ fall.

   d. ______________ month.

   e. ______________ year.

   f. ______________ summer.

2. *I visited my cousins . . .*

   a. ______________ night.

   b. ______________ evening.

   c. ______________ morning.

   d. ______________ afternoon.

   e. ______________ Sunday.

   f. ______________ spring.

❑ Exercise 22. Looking at grammar. (Chart 8-5)

Complete the sentences. Use a past time expression and ***wasn't*** or ***weren't***.

1. I'm at home tonight, but ___I wasn't at home last night.___
2. I am here today, but ______________
3. Kaya is busy today, but ______________
4. Mack and Carly are at work this afternoon, but ______________
5. Ben is at the library tonight, but ______________
6. You're here today, but ______________
7. Dr. Ruckman is in her office this morning, but ______________
8. It's cold this week, but ______________
9. We're tired this evening, but ______________

❑ Exercise 23. Looking at grammar. (Chart 8-5)

Use the information in the calendar to complete the sentences about Ken's activities. Use a time expression from Chart 8-5.

JUNE

Sunday	Monday	Tuesday	Wednesday	Thursday	Friday	Saturday
						1
2	3	4	5	6 3:00 p.m. doctor/Dad	7	8
9	10	11	12	13 London	14	15
16 Paris	17 home	18 dance class/Ava	19 10:00 a.m. dentist movie/Sam	20 TODAY	21	22
23	24	25	26	27	28	29
30						

Today is the 20th.

1. *Three days ago*, Ken *was* at home.
2. ________, he ________ in Paris.
3. ________, he ________ in London.
4. ________, he ________ at the dentist.
5. ________, Ken and his dad ________ at the doctor.
6. ________, Ken and Sam ________ at a movie.
7. ________, Ken and Ava ________ at a dance class.

❑ Exercise 24. Looking at grammar. (Chart 8-5)

Complete the sentences with your own words. Use ***ago***.

1. I'm in class now, but I was at home *ten minutes ago / two hours ago / etc.*
2. I'm in class today, but I was absent from class ______________________
3. I'm in this country now, but I was in my country ______________________
4. I was in (*name of a city*) ______________________
5. I was in elementary school ______________________
6. I arrived in this city ______________________
7. There is a nice park in this city. I was at the park ______________________
8. We finished Exercise 16 ______________________
9. I was home in bed ______________________
10. It rained in this city ______________________

❑ Exercise 25. Listening. (Chart 8-5)

Part I. Write the date.

CD 1 Track 32

Today's date is ______________________ .

Listen to the questions. Write the dates.

1. ______________________
2. ______________________
3. ______________________
4. ______________________
5. ______________________
6. ______________________
7. ______________________

Part II. Write the time.

Right now the time is ______________________ .

Listen to the questions. Write the times.

1. ______________________
2. ______________________
3. ______________________

❑ **Exercise 26. Warm-up.** (Chart 8-6)

Read the information about Jerry. Complete the sentences. Change the verbs in red to present time.

Last Night

Last night, Jerry ate dinner at 7:00. Then he did his homework for two hours. At 10:00, he went to bed.

Every Night

Every night, Jerry _______(1)_______ dinner at 7:00. Then he _______(2)_______ his homework for two hours. At 10:00, he _______(3)_______ to bed.

8-6 Simple Past Tense: Irregular Verbs (Group 1)

Some verbs do not have ***-ed*** forms. Their past forms are irregular.

PRESENT		SIMPLE PAST	
come	–	came	(a) I ***come*** to class ***every day***.
do	–	did	(b) I ***came*** to class ***yesterday***.
eat	–	ate	(c) I ***do*** my homework ***every day***.
get	–	got	(d) I ***did*** my homework ***yesterday***.
go	–	went	(e) Meg ***eats*** breakfast ***every morning***.
have	–	had	(f) Meg ***ate*** breakfast ***yesterday morning***.
put	–	put	
see	–	saw	
sit	–	sat	
sleep	–	slept	
stand	–	stood	
write	–	wrote	

❑ **Exercise 27. Vocabulary and speaking.** (Chart 8-6)

Practice using irregular verbs. Close your book for this activity.

Example: ***come–came***

TEACHER: come–came. I come to class every day. I came to class yesterday.
What did I do yesterday?

STUDENTS: (*repeat*) come–came. You came to class yesterday.

1. ***do–did*** We do exercises in class every day. We did exercises yesterday. What did we do yesterday?
2. ***eat–ate*** I eat lunch at 12:00 every day. Yesterday I ate lunch at 12:00. What did I do at 12:00 yesterday?

3. ***get–got*** I get up early every day. I got up early yesterday. What did I do yesterday? Did you get up early yesterday? What time did you get up?
4. ***go–went*** I go downtown every day. I went downtown yesterday. What did I do yesterday? Did you go downtown? Where did you go?
5. ***have–had*** I have breakfast every morning. I had breakfast yesterday morning. I had toast and fruit. What did I have yesterday morning? What did you have for breakfast yesterday morning?
6. ***put–put*** I like hats. I put on a hat every day. I put on a hat yesterday. What did I do yesterday?
7. ***see–saw*** I see my best friend every day. Yesterday I saw my best friend. What did I do yesterday? Did you see your best friend? Who did you see?
8. ***sit–sat*** I usually sit at my desk in the mornings. I sat at my desk yesterday morning. What did I do yesterday morning?
9. ***sleep–slept*** Sometimes I sleep for a long time at night. I slept for 10 hours last night. What did I do last night? Did you sleep for 10 hours last night? How many hours did you sleep last night?
10. ***stand–stood*** I stand at the bus stop every day. I stood at the bus stop yesterday. What did I do yesterday?
11. ***write–wrote*** I usually write in my journal every day. I wrote in my journal yesterday. What did I do yesterday? Did you write in your journal? What did you write about?

❑ **Exercise 28. Let's talk: pairwork.** (Chart 8-6)

Work with a partner. Take turns changing the sentences from the present to the past.

Example: I have class every day.
PARTNER A: I have class every day. I had class yesterday. Your turn now.

Example: Orlando gets mail from home every week.
PARTNER B: Orlando gets mail from home every week. Orlando got mail from home last week. Your turn now.

PARTNER A	PARTNER B
1. Lara gets some mail every day.	1. We have lunch every day.
2. They go to work every day.	2. I write emails to my parents every week.
3. The students stand in line at the cafeteria every day.	3. Jin comes to class late every day.
	4. I do my homework every day.
4. I see my friends every day.	5. I eat breakfast every morning.
5. Hamid sits in the front row every day.	6. Carlos puts his books in his briefcase every day.
6. I sleep for eight hours every night.	

❑ **Exercise 29. Looking at grammar.** (Charts 8-4 and 8-6)

Complete the sentences. Change the words in parentheses to the simple present, the present progressive, or the simple past. Pay attention to the spelling.

1. I (*get*) ______got______ up at eight o'clock yesterday morning.
2. Ellie (*talk*) ____________________ to Barack on the phone last night.
3. Ellie (*talk*) ____________________ to Barack on the phone right now.
4. Ellie (*talk*) ____________________ to Barack on the phone every day.
5. Jim and I (*eat*) ____________________ lunch in the cafeteria two hours ago.
6. We (*eat*) ____________________ lunch in the cafeteria every day.

7. I (*go*) ____________________ to bed early last night.
8. My roommate (*study*) ____________________ Spanish last year.
9. Kate (*write*) ____________________ an email to her parents yesterday.
10. Kate (*write*) ____________________ an email to her parents every week.
11. Kate is in her room right now. She (*sit*) ____________________ at her desk.
12. Hanna (*do*) ____________________ her homework last night.
13. Yesterday I (*see*) ____________________ Fumiko at the library.
14. I (*have*) ____________________ a dream last night. I (*dream*) ____________________ about my friends. I (*sleep*) ____________________ for eight hours.
15. A strange thing (*happen*) ____________________ to me yesterday. I couldn't remember my own telephone number.

16. My wife (*come*) ____________________ home around five every day.

17. Yesterday, she (*come*) ____________________ home at 5:15.

18. Our teacher (*stand*) ____________________ in the middle of the room right now.

19. Our teacher (*stand*) ____________________ in the front of the room yesterday.

20. Devon (*put*) ____________________ the butter in the refrigerator yesterday.

21. He (*put*) ____________________ the milk in the refrigerator every day.

22. Antonio usually (*sit*) ____________________ in the back of the room, but yesterday he (*sit*) ____________________ in the front row. Today, he (*be*) ____________________ absent. He (*be*) ____________________ absent two days ago too.

❑ Exercise 30. Listening. (Chart 8-6)

CD 1
Track 33

Listen to the beginning of each sentence. Choose the correct completion(s). There may be more than one correct answer.

Example: You will hear: He did . . .

You will choose: (a.) his homework. (b.) a good job. c. absent.

1. a. a chair.	b. some rice.	c. some numbers.
2. a. on the floor.	b. a man.	c. together.
3. a. late.	b. yesterday.	c. car.
4. a. an answer.	b. pretty.	c. a book.
5. a. a good grade.	b. last month.	c. a new truck.
6. a. a watch.	b. next to my parents.	c. at the bus stop.

❑ Exercise 31. Warm-up. (Chart 8-7)

Choose the verbs to make true sentences.

When my grandparents were in high school, they . . .

1. had / didn't have computers.
2. ate / didn't eat fast food.

8-7 Simple Past Tense: Negative

	SUBJECT +	*DID* +	*NOT* +	MAIN VERB		
(a)	I	*did*	*not*	*walk*	to school yesterday.	I, you, she, he, it, we, they + ***did not*** + main verb*
(b)	You	*did*	*not*	*walk*	to school yesterday.	
(c)	Tim	*did*	*not*	*eat*	lunch yesterday.	
(d)	They	*did*	*not*	*come*	to class yesterday.	

INCORRECT: *I did not walked to school yesterday.*

INCORRECT: *Tim did not ate lunch yesterday.*

Notice: The base form of the main verb is used with ***did not***.

(e) I ***didn't walk*** to school yesterday.

(f) Tim ***didn't eat*** lunch yesterday.

NEGATIVE CONTRACTION
did + ***not*** = ***didn't***

*EXCEPTION: ***did*** is NOT used when the main verb is ***be***. See Charts 8-2 and 8-3.
CORRECT: Dan *wasn't* here yesterday.
INCORRECT: *Dan didn't be here yesterday.*

❑ **Exercise 32. Looking at grammar.** (Chart 8-7)
Complete the sentences. Use ***not***.

TWO DAYS AGO	YESTERDAY
1. I got to school late.	I ___didn't get___ to school late.
2. You got to school late.	You ________________ school late.
3. She got to school late.	She ________________ to school late.
4. They stayed home.	They ________________ home.
5. We stayed home.	We ________________ home.
6. She did her homework.	She ________________ her homework.
7. You did your homework.	You ________________ your homework.
8. We did our homework.	We ________________ our homework.
9. I was sick.	I ________________ sick.
10. They were sick.	They ________________ sick.

❑ Exercise 33. Let's talk: pairwork. (Chart 8-7)

Work with a partner. Take turns using ***I don't . . . every day*** and ***I didn't . . . yesterday***.

Example: walk to school
PARTNER A: I don't walk to school every day. I didn't walk to school yesterday. Your turn now.

Example: listen to the radio
PARTNER B: I don't listen to the radio every day. I didn't listen to the radio yesterday. Your turn now.

PARTNER A	PARTNER B
1. eat breakfast	1. go to the library
2. watch TV	2. visit my friends
3. go shopping	3. see (*name of a person*)
4. read a newspaper	4. do my homework
5. study	5. get on the Internet

❑ Exercise 34. Looking at grammar. (Chart 8-7)

Complete the sentences. Change the words in parentheses to the simple present, present progressive, or simple past.

1. Jasmin (*come, not*) ___didn't come___ to the meeting yesterday. She (*stay*) ___stayed___ in her office.

2. I (*go*) _______________ to a movie last night, but I (*enjoy, not*) _______________ it. It (*be, not*) _______________ very good.

3. Kay (*read*) _______________ a magazine right now. She (*watch, not*) _______________ TV. She (*like, not*) _______________ to watch TV during the day.

4. A: (*Be*) _______________ you sick yesterday?
   B: No, but my daughter (*feel, not*) _______________ good, so I stayed home with her. She's fine now.

5. Toshi is a busy student. Sometimes he (*eat, not*) _______________ lunch because he (*have, not*) _______________ enough time between classes. Yesterday he (*have, not*) _______________ time for lunch. He (*get*) _______________ hungry during his afternoon class.

❑ **Exercise 35. Let's talk: game.** (Chart 8-7)

Work in groups of six to eight students. Tell your group things you didn't do yesterday. Repeat the information from the other students in your group. The last person in the group repeats all the sentences.

Example: go
STUDENT A: I didn't go to the zoo yesterday.
STUDENT B: (*Student A*) didn't go to the zoo yesterday. I didn't have lunch in Beijing yesterday.
STUDENT C: (*Student A*) didn't go to the zoo yesterday. (*Student B*) didn't have lunch in Beijing yesterday. I didn't swim in the Pacific Ocean yesterday.
Etc.

Suggestions:

drive to	wake up	wear	talk to
walk to	swim	buy	use
eat	sing	study	fly to

❑ **Exercise 36. Reading and grammar.** (Chart 8-7)

Read the story about Matt's morning. Then read the sentences that follow. If a sentence is true, do not change it. If it is not true, write a negative statement.

My Early Morning

Yesterday, my alarm clock didn't go off. I jumped out of bed and looked at the clock. I was late for work. I hurried to the kitchen and quickly prepared breakfast. I had some juice and toast. After breakfast, I put the dishes in the sink. I didn't have time to wash them. Then I quickly got dressed. Soon, I was ready. I walked to the bus. At the bus stop, I didn't recognize anyone. Then I looked at my watch. I was two hours early! I was half asleep when I jumped out of bed earlier and misread* the time on my clock.

1. Matt's alarm clock went off. *Matt's alarm clock didn't go off.*
2. He got out of bed quickly. *(no change)*
3. He cooked a big breakfast. ____________
4. He washed the dishes. ____________
5. He got dressed in a hurry. ____________
6. He saw his friends at the bus stop. ____________
7. He was late for work. ____________
8. It was time for work. ____________

**misread* = read incorrectly

❑ Exercise 37. Warm-up. (Chart 8-8)

Answer the questions.

1. a. Do you wake up early every day?
   b. Did you wake up early today?

2. a. Do you eat breakfast every morning?
   b. Did you eat breakfast this morning?

8-8 Simple Past Tense: Yes/No Questions

	DID + SUBJECT + MAIN VERB					SHORT ANSWER	(LONG ANSWER)
(a)	*Did*	*Tess*	*walk*	to school?	→	*Yes, she did.*	(She walked to school.)
					→	*No, she didn't.*	(She didn't walk to school.)
(b)	*Did*	*you*	*come*	to class?	→	*Yes, I did.*	(I came to class.)
					→	*No, I didn't.*	(I didn't come to class.)

❑ Exercise 38. Let's talk: class activity. (Chart 8-8)

Answer the simple past tense questions. Close your book for this activity.

Example:

TEACHER: Did you work late last night?
STUDENT A: No, I didn't.
TEACHER: (*Student A*), ask another student the same question.
STUDENT A: Did you work late last night?
STUDENT B: Yes, I did.
TEACHER: (*Student B*), ask another student the same question.

Continue to the next question after three to five students have answered.

1. Did you walk home yesterday?
2. Did you come to class late today?
3. Did you wake up early today?
4. Did you eat meat for breakfast?
5. Did you drink coffee this morning?
6. Did you exercise today?
7. Did you play video games yesterday?
8. Did you text someone before 7:00 A.M.?
9. Did you make your bed this morning?
10. Did you wash the dishes this morning?

❏ Exercise 39. Looking at grammar. (Chart 8-8)

Make questions and give short answers.

1. A: *Did you walk downtown yesterday?*

   B: *Yes, I did.* (I walked downtown yesterday.)

2. A: *Did it rain last week?*

   B: *No, it didn't.* (It didn't rain last week.)

3. A: ______________________________

   B: ______________ (I ate lunch at the cafeteria.)

4. A: ______________________________

   B: ______________ (Mr. Kwan didn't go out of town last week.)

5. A: ______________________________

   B: ______________ (I had a cup of tea this morning.)

6. A: ______________________________

   B: ______________ (Ricardo and I went to a dance last night.)

7. A: ______________________________

   B: ______________ (Galina studied English in high school.)

8. A: ______________________________

   B: ______________ (Kirsten and Ali didn't do their homework.)

9. A: ______________________________

   B: ______________ (I saw Gina at dinner last night.)

10. A: ______________________________

    B: ______________ (I didn't dream in English last night.)

❏ Exercise 40. Listening. (Chart 8-8)

Listen to the questions. Write the words you hear.

CD 1 Track 34

Example: You will hear: Did you have your test already?

You will write: ___Did you___ have your test already?

1. __________ do well on the test?
2. __________ finish the assignment?
3. __________ make sense?
4. __________ answer your question?
5. __________ need more help?
6. __________ understand the homework?
7. __________ explain the project?
8. __________ complete the project?
9. __________ do well?
10. __________ pass the class?

❏ Exercise 41. Let's talk: find someone who . . . . (Chart 8-8)

Interview your classmates. Make simple past questions with the given words. Find people who can answer *yes* and write their names.

Example: eat ice cream \ yesterday?
STUDENT A: Did you eat ice cream yesterday?
STUDENT B: No, I didn't. I didn't eat ice cream yesterday.
STUDENT A: (*Ask another student.*) Did you eat ice cream yesterday?
STUDENT C: Yes, I did. I ate ice cream yesterday. (*Write Student C's name.*)

ACTIVITY	FIRST NAME
1. eat rice \ yesterday?	
2. do homework \ last night?	
3. get an email \ yesterday?	
4. go shopping \ yesterday?	
5. sleep well \ last night?	
6. a. have coffee for breakfast \ this morning? b. put sugar in your coffee \ this morning?	
7. see a good movie \ last week?	
8. write in English \ today?	
9. sit on the floor \ yesterday?	
10. stand in line for something \ last week?	

❑ Exercise 42. Listening. (Chart 8-8)

CD 1 Track 35

In spoken English, speakers sometimes change or drop sounds. In questions, ***did*** and the pronoun that follows it can change.

Part I. Listen to the examples.

1. **Did you** ("dih-juh") see the news this morning?
2. A: Jim called.
   B: **Did he** ("dih-de") leave a message?
3. A: Julia called.
   B: **Did she** ("dih-she") leave a message?
4. **Did it** ("dih-dit") rain yesterday?
5. A: The kids are watching TV.
   B: **Did they** ("dih-they") finish their homework?
6. My keys aren't here. **Did I** ("dih-di") leave them in the car?

Part II. You will hear questions with ***did*** + *a pronoun.* Write the full forms.

Examples: You will hear: "Dih-dit" rain yesterday?
You will write: ___*Did it*___ rain yesterday?

You will hear: "Dih-juh" come to class yesterday?
You will write: ___*Did you*___ come to class yesterday?

1. ______________ finish the homework assignment?
2. ______________ take a long time?
3. ______________ hear my question?
4. ______________ hear my question?
5. ______________ speak loud enough?
6. ______________ understand the information?
7. ______________ understand the information?
8. ______________ want more help?
9. ______________ explain it okay?
10. ______________ do a good job?

❑ **Exercise 43. Reading and grammar.** (Chart 8-8)

Read the story. Then write the questions the doctor asked Kevin and give Kevin's answers.

Kevin's Unhealthy Habits

Kevin didn't feel well. He went to see Dr. Benson. Dr. Benson checked him and asked him about his lifestyle. Kevin had several unhealthy habits: he slept very little, he didn't exercise, he ate unhealthy foods, and he smoked. He needed to change these habits. Kevin listened to the doctor, but he didn't change any habits. He went back to the doctor a month later. The doctor asked him several questions.

1. Dr. Benson: *you \ continue*

   ___Did you continue___ to smoke last month? Kevin: ___Yes, I did.___

2. Dr. Benson: *you \ change*

   ______________ your eating habits? Kevin: ______________

3. Dr. Benson: *you \ exercise*

   ______________? Kevin: ______________

4. Dr. Benson: *you \ sleep*

   ______________ more? Kevin: ______________

5. Dr. Benson: *you \ think*

   ______________ my advice was a joke? Kevin: ______________

❑ **Exercise 44. Warm-up.** (Chart 8-9)
Which sentences are true for you?

1. ____ I sometimes drink water with dinner.
2. ____ I drank water with dinner last night.
3. ____ I think about my family every day.
4. ____ I thought about my family at midnight last night.

8-9 Simple Past Tense: Irregular Verbs (Group 2)

bring – brought	drive – drove	run – ran
buy – bought	read – read*	teach – taught
catch – caught	ride – rode	think – thought
drink – drank		

*The simple past form of *read* is pronounced the same as the color *red*.

❑ **Exercise 45. Vocabulary and speaking.** (Chart 8-9)
Practice using irregular verbs. Close your book for this activity.

Example: ***teach–taught***
TEACHER: teach–taught. I teach class every day. I taught class yesterday. What did I do yesterday?
STUDENTS: (*repeat*) teach–taught. You taught class yesterday.

1. ***bring–brought*** I bring my book to class every day. I brought my book to class yesterday. What did I do yesterday?
2. ***buy–bought*** I buy apps for my phone. Yesterday, I bought an app for my phone. What did I do yesterday?
3. ***catch–caught*** On weekends, I go fishing. Sometimes, I catch fish. I caught a fish last week. Sometimes I catch a cold. Last week, I caught a bad cold. What did I do last week?
4. ***think–thought*** I often think about my family. I thought about my family yesterday. What did I do yesterday?
5. **REVIEW:** What did I bring to class yesterday? What did you bring yesterday? What did I buy yesterday? What did I catch last week? What did I think about yesterday? What did you think about yesterday?
6. ***run–ran*** Sometimes I'm late for class, so I run. Yesterday I was late, so I ran. What did I do yesterday?
7. ***read–read*** I like to read books. I read every day. Yesterday I read a book. What did I do yesterday? What did you read yesterday?
8. ***drink–drank*** I usually drink a cup of coffee in the morning. I drank a cup of coffee this morning. What did I do this morning? Did you drink a cup of coffee this morning? What do you usually drink in the morning? Do you drink the same thing every morning?

9. ***drive–drove*** I usually drive my car to school. I drove my car to school this morning. What did I do this morning? Who has a car? Did you drive to school this morning?

10. ***ride–rode*** Sometimes I ride the bus to school. I rode the bus yesterday morning. What did I do yesterday morning? Who rode the bus to school this morning?

11. **REVIEW:** I was late for class yesterday morning, so what did I do? What did I read yesterday? What did you read yesterday? Did you read a newspaper this morning? What did I drink this morning? What did you drink this morning? I have a car. Did I drive to school this morning? Did you? Did you ride the bus?

❑ Exercise 46. Looking at grammar. (Chart 8-9)

Complete each sentence with the correct form of the word in parentheses.

1. A: Why are you out of breath?

   B: I (*run*) _______________ to class because I was late.

2. A: I (*ride*) _______________ the bus to school yesterday. How did you get to school?

   B: I (*drive*) _______________ my car.

3. A: Did you decide to change schools?

   B: I (*think*) _______________ about it, but then I decided to stay here.

4. A: (*you, go*) _______________ shopping yesterday?

   B: Yes. I (*buy*) _______________ a new pair of shoes.

5. A: (*you, study*) _______________ last night?

   B: No, I didn't. I was tired. I (*read*) _______________ the news online and then (*go*) _______________ to bed early.

6. A: Do you like milk?

   B: No. I (*drink*) _______________ milk when I (*be*) _______________ a child, but I don't like milk now.

7. A: Did you leave your dictionary at home?

   B: No. I (*bring*) _______________ it to class with me.

8. Yesterday Sasha (*teach*) _______________ us how to say "thank you" in Japanese. Kim (*teach*) _______________ us how to say "I love you" in Korean.

9. A: Did you enjoy your fishing trip?

   B: I had a wonderful time! I (*catch*) _______________ a lot of fish.

❏ Exercise 47. Let's talk: pairwork. (Chart 8-9)

Work with a partner. Take turns asking and answering simple past tense questions.

Example: think
PARTNER A: Did you think about me last night?
PARTNER B: Yes, I did. I thought about you last night. OR
No, I didn't. I didn't think about you last night.

PARTNER A	PARTNER B
1. drive 2. ride 3. catch 4. teach 5. bring	1. think 2. drink 3. read 4. buy 5. run

❏ Exercise 48. Listening. (Chart 8-9)

Listen to the beginning of each sentence. Choose the correct completion(s). There may be more than one correct answer.

CD 1
Track 36

Example: You will hear: He drank . . .
You will choose: (a.) some tea. b. bread. (c.) water.

1. a. last week.	b. a fish.	c. happy.
2. a. very fast	b. a house.	c. to the store.
3. a. books.	b. the kids.	c. the newspaper.
4. a. a story.	b. a bike.	c. a horse.
5. a. good.	b. some food.	c. a doctor.
6. a. people.	b. into town.	c. home.

❏ Exercise 49. Writing. (Charts 8-1 → 8-9)

Use the expressions from the list to write sentences about yourself. When did you do these things in the past? Use the simple past tense and past time expressions (*yesterday, two days ago, last week, etc.*) in all of your sentences. Use your own paper.

Example: go downtown with (*someone*)
Possible sentence: I went downtown with Marco two days ago.

1. arrive in (*this city*)
2. eat at a restaurant
3. buy (*something*)
4. have a cold
5. be in elementary school
6. drink a cup of coffee
7. talk to (*someone*) on the phone
8. study arithmetic
9. read a newspaper
10. play (soccer, a pinball machine, etc.)
11. see (*someone* or *something*)
12. think about (*someone* or *something*)
13. be born

❑ **Exercise 50. Warm-up.** (Chart 8-10)
Which sentences are true for you?

1. ____ I sing in the shower every morning.
2. ____ I sang in the shower yesterday morning.
3. ____ I sometimes speak English in my dreams.
4. ____ I spoke English in my last dream.

8-10 Simple Past Tense: Irregular Verbs (Group 3)

break – broke	meet – met	sing – sang
fly – flew	pay – paid	speak – spoke
hear – heard	ring – rang	take – took
leave – left	send – sent	wake up – woke up

❑ **Exercise 51. Vocabulary and speaking.** (Chart 8-10)
Practice using irregular verbs. Close your book for this activity.

Example: **break–broke**
TEACHER: break–broke. Sometimes a person breaks an arm or a leg. I broke my arm five years ago. What happened five years ago?
STUDENTS: (*repeat*) break–broke. You broke your arm.
TEACHER: (*to Student A*) Did you ever* break a bone?
STUDENT A: Yes. I broke my leg ten years ago.

1. ***fly–flew*** Sometimes I fly home in an airplane. I flew home in an airplane last month. What did I do last month? Did you fly to this city? When?
2. ***hear–heard*** I hear birds singing every morning. I heard birds singing yesterday. What did I hear yesterday? What did you hear when you woke up this morning?
3. ***pay–paid*** I pay the rent every month. I paid the rent last month. What did I do last month? Did you pay your rent last month?
4. ***send–sent*** I send my mom a gift every year on her birthday. I sent my mom a gift last year on her birthday. What did I do last year? When did you send a gift to someone?
5. ***leave–left*** I leave for school at 8:00 every morning. I left for school yesterday at 8:00 A.M. What did I do at 8:00 A.M. yesterday? What time did you leave for class this morning?
6. ***meet–met*** I sometimes meet friends for lunch. Last month I met some friends for lunch. What did I do last month? Do you sometimes meet friends for lunch?
7. ***take–took*** I take my younger brother to the movies every month. I took my younger brother to the movies last month. What did I do last month? Who has a younger brother or sister? Where and when did you take him/her someplace?

**ever* = at any time

8. ***wake–woke*** I usually wake up at six. This morning I woke up at six-thirty. What time did I wake up this morning? What time did you wake up this morning?

9. ***speak–spoke*** I speak to many students every day. Before class today, I spoke to (. . .). Who did I speak to? Who did you speak to before class today?

10. ***ring–rang*** I didn't turn my cell phone off when I went to bed last night. This morning, it rang at six-thirty and woke me up. What happened at six-thirty this morning? Who had a phone call this morning? What time did the phone ring?

11. ***sing–sang*** I sing in the shower every morning. I sang in the shower yesterday. What did I do yesterday? Do you ever sing in the shower? When was the last time?

12. ***break–broke*** Sometimes I break things. This morning I dropped a glass on the floor, and it broke. What happened this morning? When did you break something?

❑ Exercise 52. Looking at grammar. (Chart 8-10)

Complete the conversations. Use the correct form of the verbs from the box.

break	leave	ring	speak
fly	meet	send	take
hear	pay	sing	wake

1. A: What happened to your finger?

   B: I _______________ it in a soccer game.

2. A: Who did you talk to at the director's office?

   B: I _______________ to the secretary.

3. A: When did Jessica leave for Europe?

   B: She _______________ for Europe five days ago.

4. A: Did you write Ted an email?

   B: No, but I _______________ him a text.

5. A: Do you know Meg Adams?

   B: Yes. I _______________ her a couple of weeks ago.

6. A: Why did you call the police?

   B: Because I _______________ a burglar!

7. A: Where did you go yesterday?

   B: I _______________ my son and daughter to the zoo.

8. A: What time did you get up this morning?
   B: 6:15.
   A: Why did you get up so early?
   B: The phone ________________.

9. A: Did you enjoy the party?
   B: Yes, I had a good time. We ________________ songs and danced. It was fun.

10. A: You look sleepy.
    B: I am. I ________________ up before dawn this morning and never went back to sleep.

11. A: Did you give the painter a check?
    B: No. I ________________ him in cash.

12. A: A bird ________________ into our apartment yesterday through an open window.
    B: Really? What did you do?
    A: I caught it and took it outside.

❑ Exercise 53. Let's talk: pairwork. (Chart 8-10)

Work with a partner. Take turns asking and answering simple past tense questions.

Example: fly
PARTNER A: Did you fly to Paris last week?
PARTNER B: Yes, I did. I flew to Paris last week. OR
No, I didn't. I didn't fly to Paris last week.

PARTNER A	PARTNER B
1. hear	1. fly
2. break	2. leave
3. take	3. speak
4. sing	4. wake up
5. ring	5. send
6. pay	6. meet

❑ **Exercise 54. Listening.** (Chart 8-10)

Listen to the story. Then read each sentence and choose the correct answer.

CD 1 Track 37

A doctor's appointment

1. The man was at the doctor's office.	yes	no
2. He took some medicine.	yes	no
3. He was in bed for a short time.	yes	no
4. The man spoke to the nurse.	yes	no
5. He is feeling okay now.	yes	no

❑ **Exercise 55. Warm-up.** (Chart 8-11)

Which sentences are true for you?

1. ____ I sometimes lose my keys.
2. ____ I lost my keys last week.
3. ____ I often wear jeans.
4. ____ I wore jeans yesterday.

8-11 Simple Past Tense: Irregular Verbs (Group 4)

begin – began	say – said	tell – told
find – found	sell – sold	tear – tore
lose – lost	steal – stole	wear – wore
hang – hung		

❑ **Exercise 56. Vocabulary and speaking.** (Chart 8-11)

Practice using irregular verbs. Close your book for this activity.

Example: ***begin–began***

TEACHER: begin–began. Our class begins at (9:00) every day. Class began at (9:00 this morning). When did class begin (this morning)?

STUDENTS: (*repeat*) begin–began. Class began at (9:00 this morning).

1. ***lose–lost*** Sometimes I lose things. Yesterday I lost my keys. What did I lose yesterday?
2. ***find–found*** Sometimes I lose things. And then I find them. Yesterday I lost my keys, but then I found them in my jacket pocket. What did I do yesterday?
3. ***tear–tore*** If I make a mistake when I write a check, I tear the check up. Yesterday, I made a mistake when I wrote a check, so I tore it up and wrote a new check. What did I do yesterday?
4. ***sell–sold*** People sell things that they don't need anymore. My friend has a new bike, so she sold her old bike. What did she do?

5. ***hang–hung*** I like to hang pictures on my walls. This morning I hung a new picture in my bedroom. What did I do this morning?
6. ***tell–told*** The kindergarten teacher likes to tell stories to her students. Yesterday she told a story about a little red train. What did the teacher do yesterday?
7. ***wear–wore*** I wear a sweater to class every evening. Last night I also wore a jacket. What did I wear last night?
8. ***steal–stole*** Thieves steal money and other things. Last month a thief stole my aunt's wallet. What did a thief do last month?
9. ***say–said*** People usually say "hello" when they answer a phone. When my friend answered his phone this morning, he said "hello." What did he do this morning?

❑ **Exercise 57. Looking at grammar.** (Chart 8-11)
Complete the sentences with the correct form of the verbs from the box.

begin	hang	say	steal	tell
find	lose	sell	tear	wear

1. A: Did you go to the park yesterday?
   B: No. We stayed home because it ________________ to rain.
   A: Oh, that's too bad.

2. A: Susie is in trouble.
   B: Why?
   A: She ________________ a lie. Her mom and dad are upset.
   B: I'm sure she's sorry.

3. A: Did you find your sunglasses?
   B: No. I ________________ them at the soccer game. I need to get some new ones.

4. A: Where's my coat?
   B: I ________________ it up in the closet for you.

5. A: Where did you get that pretty shell?
   B: I ________________ it on the beach.

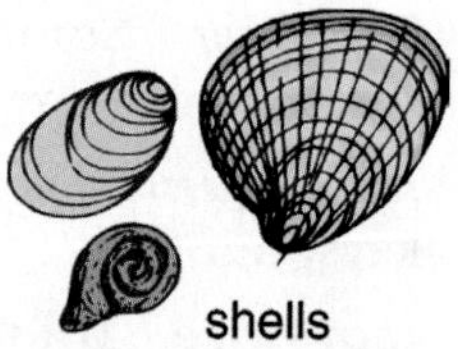
shells

6. A: Do you still have your bike?
   B: No. I ________________ it because I needed some extra money.

7. A: It's hot in here.
   B: Excuse me? What did you say?
   A: I _________________, "It's hot in here."

8. A: Why did you take the bus to work this morning? Why didn't you drive?
   B: Because somebody _________________ my car last night.
   A: Did you call the police?
   B: Of course I did.

9. A: Did you wear your blue jeans to the job interview?
   B: Of course not! I _________________ a suit.

10. A: I wrote the wrong amount on the check, so I had to write a new check.
    B: What did you do with the first check?
    A: I _________________ it into pieces.

❑ **Exercise 58. Let's talk: pairwork.** (Chart 8-11)

Work with a partner. Take turns asking and answering simple past tense questions.

Example: wear
PARTNER A: Did you wear slippers last night?
PARTNER B: Yes, I did. I wore slippers last night. OR
No, I didn't. I didn't wear slippers last night.

PARTNER A	PARTNER B
1. hang 2. steal 3. wear 4. say 5. begin	1. find 2. sell 3. lose 4. tell 5. tear

❑ Exercise 59. Listening. (Chart 8-11)

Listen to the story. Then read each sentence and choose the correct answer.

CD 1 Track 38

A wedding ring

1. The woman lost her mother's ring.	yes	no
2. Someone stole the ring.	yes	no
3. Her dog found the ring in the garden.	yes	no
4. Her mother wore the ring for a while.	yes	no
5. The woman was happy at the end of the story.	yes	no

❑ Exercise 60. Looking at grammar. (Chapter 8)

You went to a birthday party last night. A friend is asking you questions about it. Complete the sentences with ***did, was,*** or ***were***.

1. ____________ you go with a friend?
2. ____________ your friends at the party?
3. ____________ the party fun?
4. ____________ many people there?
5. ____________ you have a good time?
6. ____________ there a birthday cake?
7. ____________ you eat a piece of birthday cake?
8. ____________ everyone sing "Happy Birthday"?
9. ____________ you hungry?
10. ____________ you bring a present?

a present

❑ Exercise 61. Looking at grammar. (Chapter 8)

Complete the sentences with ***did, was,*** or ***were***.

1. I ____*did*____ not go to work yesterday. I ____*was*____ sick, so I stayed home.
2. Ray ____________ not in his office yesterday. He ____________ not go to work.
3. A: ____________ Mr. Chan in his office yesterday?

   B: Yes.

   A: ____________ you see him about your problem?

   B: Yes. He answered all my questions. He ____________ very helpful.

4. A: ___________ you at the meeting yesterday?

   B: Yes.

   A: ___________ I miss anything?

   B: No. It ___________ really short. The fire alarm went off right after it started.

   We ___________ outside for the rest of the hour.

5. A: Where ___________ you yesterday?

   B: I ___________ at the zoo.

   A: ___________ you enjoy it?

   B: Yes, but the weather ___________ very hot. I tried to stay out of the sun.

   Most of the animals ___________ in their houses or in the shade. The sun

   ___________ too hot for them too. They ___________ not want to be outside.

❑ Exercise 62. Looking at grammar. (Chapter 8)

Make questions.

A bad experience

1. A: *Do you live in an apartment?*

   B: Yes, I do. (I live in an apartment.)

2. A: *Do you have a roommate?*

   B: No, I don't. (I don't have a roommate.)

3. A: ____

   B: No, I don't. (I don't want a roommate.)

4. A: ____

   B: Yes, I did. (I had a roommate last year.)

5. A: ____

   B: No, it wasn't. (It wasn't a good experience.)

6. A: ____

   B: Yes, he was. (He was messy.)

   For example, he never picked up his dirty clothes. He never washed his dirty dishes. He was always late with his part of the rent.

7. A: ____

B: No, he didn't. (He didn't help me clean.)

8. A: ____

B: Yes, I was. (I was glad when he left.)

❑ Exercise 63. Let's talk. (Chapter 8)

Work in pairs or small groups. Read the facts about four people: Lara, Josh, Max, and Kira. They live in an apartment building on the same floor. Which apartment does each person live in? Use the clues to find out.

Clues:

1. Lara painted her door yellow.
2. Josh and Lara lived in the same neighborhood as children. Now they are next-door neighbors.
3. Max loves music. He works at a music store. His parents were musicians in a band.
4. Kira isn't very social. She didn't want neighbors on both sides, so she rented an end unit.
5. Lara moved into her apartment last year.
6. The first time Max played loud music, both Kira and Josh knocked on the walls. They told him to turn it down.

APARTMENT NUMBER	1	2	3	4
NAME				

❑ Exercise 64. Check your knowledge. (Chapter 8)

Correct the mistakes.

1. Someone ~~stealed~~ *stole* my bike two day*s* ago.
2. Did you went to the party yesterday weekend?
3. I hear an interesting story yesterday.
4. The teacher not ready for class yesterday.
5. Did came Dennis to work last week?
6. Yesterday night I staied home and work on my science project.
7. A few students wasn't on time for the final exam yesterday.
8. Your fax came before ten minutes. Did you got it?
9. Did you the movie watch?
10. The store no have yellow bananas. I get some green ones.
11. Did you nervous about your test last week?
12. I didn't saw you at the party. Did was you there?

❑ Exercise 65. Reading and writing. (Chapter 8)

Part I. Read the story.

An Embarrassing Week

Andy did some embarrassing things last week. For example, on Monday, he wore his slippers to work. He got on the bus and looked down at his feet. He felt very stupid and wanted to hide his feet.

That night, he typed an email to his girlfriend. He told her he loved her. But he hit the wrong button and he sent the message to his boss. His girlfriend and his boss have the same first name. He didn't know until the next morning when she greeted him at work. She didn't look very happy.

On Friday, he went to a nice restaurant with co-workers for lunch and ate a salad. After lunch he had a meeting. He talked a lot at the meeting. People gave him strange looks, but Andy didn't know why. Later he found out the reason. He had lettuce on his front teeth.

Andy is hoping for a better week this week. He hid his slippers under the bed and put a mirror in his desk drawer. But he didn't tell his girlfriend about the email because he is still very embarrassed.

Part II. Write about something embarrassing that you did or something embarrassing that happened to you. Your title can be "An Embarrassing Week," "An Embarrassing Day," "An Embarrassing Night," "An Embarrassing Experience," etc. If you can't think of things, write about a family member or a friend.

1. First, write single sentences about one or more embarrassing things you or someone else did. Use simple past tense verbs.
2. Add details to make the story interesting. Answer these questions:

   Where and/or when did it happen?

   What did you think?

   How did you feel?

   What did you do next?

   Did you need to find a solution?
3. Put this information into one or more paragraphs.

Part III. Editing check: Work individually or change papers with a partner. Check (✓) for the following:

1. ____ indented paragraph
2. ____ capital letter at the beginning of each sentence
3. ____ period at the end of each sentence
4. ____ correct use of the simple past for a completed activity
5. ____ correct use of ***didn't*** and ***wasn't*** for simple past negatives
6. ____ correct spelling (use a dictionary or computer spell-check)

Appendix 1
English Handwriting

English Handwriting					
PRINTING			CURSIVE		
Aa	Jj	Ss	Aa	Jj	Ss
Bb	Kk	Tt	Bb	Kk	Tt
Cc	Ll	Uu	Cc	Ll	Uu
Dd	Mm	Vv	Dd	Mm	Vv
Ee	Nn	Ww	Ee	Nn	Ww
Ff	Oo	Xx	Ff	Oo	Xx
Gg	Pp	Yy	Gg	Pp	Yy
Hh	Qq	Zz	Hh	Qq	Zz
Ii	Rr		Ii	Rr	

Vowels = *a, e, i, o, u*
Consonants = *b, c, d, f, g, h, j, k, l, m, n, p, q, r, s, t, v, w, x, y, z**

*The letter ***z*** is pronounced "zee" in American English and "zed" in British English.

Appendix 2
Numbers

CARDINAL NUMBERS

1	one
2	two
3	three
4	four
5	five
6	six
7	seven
8	eight
9	nine
10	ten
11	eleven
12	twelve
13	thirteen
14	fourteen
15	fifteen
16	sixteen
17	seventeen
18	eighteen
19	nineteen
20	twenty
21	twenty-one
22	twenty-two
23	twenty-three
24	twenty-four
25	twenty-five
26	twenty-six
27	twenty-seven
28	twenty-eight
29	twenty-nine
30	thirty
40	forty
50	fifty
60	sixty
70	seventy
80	eighty
90	ninety
100	one hundred
200	two hundred
1,000	one thousand
10,000	ten thousand
100,000	one hundred thousand
1,000,000	one million

ORDINAL NUMBERS

1st	first
2nd	second
3rd	third
4th	fourth
5th	fifth
6th	sixth
7th	seventh
8th	eighth
9th	ninth
10th	tenth
11th	eleventh
12th	twelfth
13th	thirteenth
14th	fourteenth
15th	fifteenth
16th	sixteenth
17th	seventeenth
18th	eighteenth
19th	nineteenth
20th	twentieth
21st	twenty-first
22nd	twenty-second
23rd	twenty-third
24th	twenty-fourth
25th	twenty-fifth
26th	twenty-sixth
27th	twenty-seventh
28th	twenty-eighth
29th	twenty-ninth
30th	thirtieth
40th	fortieth
50th	fiftieth
60th	sixtieth
70th	seventieth
80th	eightieth
90th	ninetieth
100th	one hundredth
200th	two hundredth
1,000th	one thousandth
10,000th	ten thousandth
100,000th	one hundred thousandth
1,000,000th	one millionth

Appendix 3
Ways of Saying Time

9:00	It's nine o'clock. It's nine.
9:05	It's nine-oh-five. It's five (minutes) after nine. It's five (minutes) past nine.
9:10	It's nine-ten. It's ten (minutes) after nine. It's ten (minutes) past nine.
9:15	It's nine-fifteen. It's a quarter after nine. It's a quarter past nine.
9:30	It's nine-thirty. It's half past nine.
9:45	It's nine-forty-five. It's a quarter to ten. It's a quarter of ten.
9:50	It's nine-fifty. It's ten (minutes) to ten. It's ten (minutes) of ten.
12:00	It's noon. It's midnight.

A.M. = morning: It's nine A.M.
P.M. = afternoon/evening/night: It's nine P.M.

Appendix 4

Days/Months/Seasons

DAYS	ABBREVIATION	MONTHS	ABBREVIATION	SEASONS*
Monday	Mon.	January	Jan.	winter
Tuesday	Tues.	February	Feb.	spring
Wednesday	Wed.	March	Mar.	summer
Thursday	Thurs.	April	Apr.	fall or autumn
Friday	Fri.	May	May	
Saturday	Sat.	June	Jun.	
Sunday	Sun.	July	Jul.	
		August	Aug.	
		September	Sept.	
		October	Oct.	
		November	Nov.	
		December	Dec.	

*Seasons of the year are only capitalized when they begin a sentence.

WRITING DATES:

Month/Day/Year

10/31/41 = October 31, 1941
4/15/98 = April 15, 1998
7/4/1906 = July 4, 1906
7/4/07 = July 4, 2007

SAYING DATES:

Usual Written Form	Usual Spoken Form
January 1	January first / the first of January
March 2	March second / the second of March
May 3	May third / the third of May
June 4	June fourth / the fourth of June
August 5	August fifth / the fifth of August
October 10	October tenth / the tenth of October
November 27	November twenty-seventh / the twenty-seventh of November

Appendix 5
Supplementary Charts

A5-1 Basic Capitalization Rules

	Use a capital letter for:
(a) Joan and I are friends.	the pronoun "I"
(b) They are late.	the first word of a sentence
(c) Sam Bond and Tom Adams are here.	names of people
(d) Mrs. Peterson Professor Jones Dr. Costa	titles of people*
(e) Monday, Tuesday, Wednesday	the days of the week
(f) April, May, June	the months of the year
(g) New Year's Day	holidays
(h) Los Angeles Florida, Ontario Germany Lake Baikal Amazon River Pacific Ocean Mount Everest Broadway, Fifth Avenue	names of places: cities, states and provinces, countries, lakes, rivers, oceans, mountains, streets
(i) German, Chinese, Swedish	languages and nationalities
(j) Pirates of the Caribbean Romeo and Juliet	the first word of a title, for example, in a book or movie. Capitalize the other words, but not: articles (***the, a, an***), short prepositions (***with, in, at,*** etc.), and these words: ***and, but, or.***
(k) Buddhism, Christianity, Hinduism, Islam, Judaism	religions

* *Mrs.* = woman: married
Ms. = woman: married or unmarried
Miss = woman: unmarried
Mr. = man: married or unmarried

A5-2 Voiceless and Voiced Sounds for *-s* Endings on Verbs

Voiceless	Voiced	
(a) /p/ *sleep* /t/ *write* /f/ *laugh*	(b) /b/ *rub* /d/ *ride* /v/ *drive*  	Some sounds are "voiceless." You don't use your voice box. You push air through your teeth and lips. For example, the sound /p/ comes from air through your lips. The final sounds in (a) are voiceless. Common voiceless sounds are ***f, k, p, t, sh, ch,*** and voiceless ***th.*** Some sounds are "voiced." You use your voice box to make voiced sounds. For example, the sound /b/ comes from your voice box. The final sounds in (b) are voiced. Common voiced sounds are ***b, d, g, j, l, m, n, r, v,*** and voiced ***th.***
(c) sleeps = *sleep*/s/ writes = *write*/s/ laughs = *laugh*/s/	(d) rubs = *rub*/z/ rides = *ride*/z/ drives = *drive*/z/	Final **-s** is pronounced /s/ after voiceless sounds, as in (c). Final **-s** is pronounced /z/ after voiced sounds, as in (d).

A5-3 Final *-ed* Pronunciation for Simple Past Verbs

Final ***-ed*** has three pronunciations: /t/, /d/, and /əd/.

End of Verb	Base Form	Simple Past	Pronunciation	
VOICELESS	(a) help laugh wash	helped laughed washed	*help/t/* *laugh/t/* *wash/t/*	Final ***-ed*** is pronounced /t/ if a verb ends in a voiceless sound, as in (a).
VOICED	(b) rub live smile	rubbed lived smiled	*rub/d/* *live/d/* *smile/d/*	Final ***-ed*** is pronounced /d/ if a verb ends in a voiced sound, as in (b).
-d OR ***-t***	(c) need want	needed wanted	*need/əd/* *want/əd/*	Final ***-ed*** is pronounced /əd/ if a verb ends in the letters ***d*** or ***t,*** as in (c).

Listening Script

NOTE: You may want to pause the audio after each item or in longer passages so that there is enough time to complete each task.

Chapter 1: Using *Be*

Exercise 20, p. 11.

A: Hi. My name is Mrs. Smith. I'm the substitute teacher.
B: Hi. I'm Franco.
C: Hi. I'm Lisa. We're in your class.
A: It's nice to meet you.
B: We're glad to meet you too.

Exercise 24, p. 12.

A: Hello. I'm Mrs. Brown. I'm the substitute teacher.
B: Hi. I'm Paulo, and this is Marie. We're in your class.
A: It's nice to meet you.
B: We're happy to meet you too.
A: It's time for class. Please take a seat.

Exercise 28, p. 14.

1. Andrew isn't a child.
2. Isabelle is an aunt.
3. Marie is a mom.
4. David isn't a dad.
5. Billy and Janey are brother and sister.
6. Marie and Andrew are adults.
7. Billy and Janey aren't parents.
8. David and Andrew aren't daughters.

Exercise 41, p. 23.

The First Day of Class

Paulo is a student from Brazil. Marie is a student from France. They're in the classroom. Today is an exciting day. It's the first day of school, but they aren't nervous. They're happy to be here. Mrs. Brown is the teacher. She isn't in the classroom right now. She's late today.

Exercise 44, p. 25.

1. Grammar's easy.
2. My name's Josh.
3. My books're on the table.
4. My brother's 21 years old.
5. The weather's cold today.
6. The windows're open.
7. My money's in my wallet.
8. Mr. Smith's a teacher.
9. My parents're at work now.
10. The food's good.
11. Tom's sick today.
12. My roommates're from Chicago.
13. My sister's a student in high school.

Chapter 2: Using *Be* and *Have*

Exercise 4, p. 29.

A: Elena's absent today.
B: Is she sick?
A: No.
B: Is her husband sick?
A: No.
B: Are her children sick?
A: No.
B: Is she homesick?
A: No.
B: So? What's the matter?
A: Her turtle is sick!
B: Are you serious? That's crazy!

Exercise 25, p. 43.

Anna's clothes

1. Her boots have zippers.
2. She has a raincoat.
3. Her raincoat has buttons.
4. They are small.
5. Her sweater has long sleeves.
6. She has earrings on her ears.
7. They are silver.
8. She has on jeans.
9. Her jeans have pockets.

Exercise 36, p. 52.

In the kitchen

1. That is my coffee cup.
2. This is your dessert.
3. Those are our plates.
4. Those sponges are wet.
5. These dishcloths are dry.
6. That frying pan is dirty.
7. This frying pan is clean.
8. That salt shaker is empty.

Chapter 3: Using the Simple Present

Exercise 4, p. 61.

1. I wake up early every day.
2. My brother wakes up late.
3. He gets up at 11:00.
4. I go to school at 8:00.
5. My mother does exercises every morning.
6. My little sister watches TV in the morning.
7. I take the bus to school.
8. My brother takes the bus to school.
9. My friends take the bus too.
10. We talk about our day.

Exercise 15, p. 66.

1. eat
2. eats
3. push
4. pushes
5. sleeps
6. fixes

Exercise 17, p. 68.

1. Mrs. Miller teaches English on Saturdays.
2. Mr. and Mrs. Hanson teach English in the evenings.
3. Chang fixes cars.
4. His son fixes cars too.
5. Carlos and Chris watch DVDs on weekends.
6. Their daughter watches TV shows on her computer.
7. I brush my hair every morning.
8. Jimmy seldom brushes his hair.
9. The Nelsons wash their car every weekend.
10. Jada rarely washes her car.

Exercise 24, p. 71.

Marco is a student. He has an unusual schedule. All of his classes are at night. His first class is at 6:00 P.M. every day. He takes a break from 7:30 to 8:00. Then he has classes from 8:00 to 10:00.

He leaves school and goes home at 10:00. After he has dinner, he watches TV. Then he does his homework from midnight to 3:00 or 4:00 in the morning.

Marco has his own computer at home. When he finishes his homework, he usually goes on the Internet. He often stays at his computer until the sun comes up. Then he does a few exercises, has breakfast, and goes to bed. He sleeps all day. Marco thinks his schedule is great, but his friends think it is strange.

Chapter 4: Using the Present Progressive

Exercise 7, p. 99.

1. Tony is sitting in the cafeteria.
2. He is sitting alone.
3. He is wearing a hat.
4. He is eating lunch.
5. He is reading his grammar book.
6. He is holding a cup.
7. He is studying hard.
8. He is smiling.
9. He is listening to the radio.
10. He is waving to his friends.

Exercise 24, p. 111.

1. I write in my grammar book . . .
2. I am writing in my grammar book . . .
3. It is raining outside . . .
4. It doesn't rain . . .
5. My cell phone rings . . .
6. My cell phone isn't ringing . . .
7. My friends and I listen to music in the car . . .
8. We're not listening to music . . .

Exercise 28, p. 114.

A: What are you doing? Are you working on your English paper?
B: No, I'm not. I'm writing an email to my sister.
A: Do you write to her often?
B: Yes, but I don't write a lot of emails to anyone else.
A: Does she write to you often?
B: No, but she texts me a lot.

Chapter 5: Talking About the Present

Exercise 6, p. 129.

1. I have class in the morning. I was born in July. I was born in 1990. Who am I?
2. My birthday is in June. I was born on June 24th. I have class every day at 1:00 o'clock. Who am I?
3. I was born in 1997. My birthday is July 7th. I go to class at night. Who am I?
4. I have class at 7:00 o'clock. I go to class in the morning. I was born in 1992. Who am I?

Exercise 16, p. 134.

1. There're ten students in the classroom.
2. There's a new teacher today.
3. There're two new math teachers this year.
4. There's a piece of gum on the floor.
5. There's some information on the bulletin board.
6. There're some spelling mistakes on this paper.
7. There's a grammar mistake in this sentence.
8. There're two writing assignments for tonight.

Exercise 32, p. 145.

1. There are trees behind the train.
2. A bird is under the picnic table.
3. There are butterflies near the flowers.
4. There is a knife on top of the table.
5. There is a fishing pole on the boat.
6. A boat is under the water.
7. The bridge is below the water.
8. There are clouds above the mountains.
9. There are flowers beside the river.
10. There are flowers next to the river.
11. A guitar is in back of the table.
12. Two bikes are under the tree.
13. A fish is in the water.
14. The table is between the tree and the river.
15. The boots are far from the picnic bench.

Exercise 41, p. 151.

1. I'd like a hamburger for dinner.
2. We like to eat at fast-food restaurants.
3. Bob'd like to go to the gym now.
4. He likes to exercise after work.
5. The teacher'd like to speak with you.
6. The teacher likes your work.
7. We like to ride our bikes on weekends.
8. We'd like to ride in a race.
9. Bill and Kay like jazz music.
10. They'd like to go to a concert next week.

Chapter 6: Nouns and Pronouns

Exercise 18, p. 168.

1. Renata knows Oscar. She knows him very well.
2. Where does Shelley live? Do you have her address?
3. There's Vince. Let's go talk to him.
4. There are Dave and Lois. Let's go talk to them.
5. I'm looking online for JoAnne's phone number. What's her last name again?
6. I need to see our airline tickets. Do you have them?

Exercise 19, p. 169.

1. A: Mika and I are going downtown this afternoon. Do you want to come with us?
   B: I don't think so, but thanks anyway. Chris and I are going to the library. We need to study for our test.
2. A: Hi, Abby. How do you like your new apartment?
   B: It's great. I have a new roommate too. She's very nice.
   A: What's her name?
   B: Rita Lopez. Do you know her?
   A: No, but I know her brother. He's in my math class.
3. A: Do you see Mike and George very much?
   B: Yes, I see them often. We play video games at my house.
   A: Who usually wins?
   B: Mike. We never beat him!

Exercise 22, p. 172.

1. toys
2. table
3. face
4. hats
5. offices
6. boxes
7. package
8. chairs
9. edge
10. tops

Exercise 23, p. 173.

1. The desks in the classroom are new.
2. I like to visit new places.
3. Luke wants a sandwich for lunch.
4. The teacher is correcting sentences with a red pen.
5. This apple is delicious.
6. The students are finishing a writing exercise in class.
7. I need two pieces of paper.
8. Roses are beautiful flowers.
9. Your rose bush is beautiful.
10. The college has many scholarships for students.

Exercise 40, p. 184.

1. Mack's parents live in Singapore.
2. Mack has two brothers and one sister.
3. My teacher's apartment is near mine.
4. My teacher is very funny.
5. What is your friend saying?
6. My friend's birthday is today.
7. The store manager's name is Dean.
8. My cousin studies engineering.

Exercise 45, p. 186.

1. Who's that?
2. Whose glasses are on the floor?
3. Who's coming?
4. Who's next?
5. Whose homework is this?
6. Whose car is outside?
7. Who's ready to begin?
8. Whose turn is it?
9. Whose work is ready?
10. Who's absent?

Chapter 7: Count and Noncount Nouns

Exercise 10, p. 197.

1. I live in an apartment.
2. It's a small apartment.
3. My biology class lasts an hour.
4. It's an interesting class.
5. We have a fun teacher.
6. My mother has an office downtown.
7. It's an insurance office.
8. My father is a nurse.
9. He works at a hospital.
10. He has a busy job.

Exercise 43, p. 216.

1. Vegetables have vitamins.
2. Cats make nice pets.
3. The teacher is absent.
4. I love bananas.
5. Cars are expensive.
6. I need the keys to the car.
7. Are the computers in your office working?
8. Let's take a walk in the park.

Exercise 45, p. 217.

1. A: Do you have a pen?
   B: There's one on the counter in the kitchen.
2. A: Where are the keys to the car?
   B: I'm not sure. You can use mine.
3. A: Shh. I hear a noise.
   B: It's just a bird outside, probably a woodpecker. Don't worry.
4. A: Henry Jackson teaches at the university.
   B: I know. He's an English professor.
   A: He's also the head of the department.
5. A: Hurry! We're late.
   B: No, we're not. It's five o'clock, and we have an hour.
   A: No, we don't. It's six! Look at the clock.
   B: Oops. I need a new battery for my watch.

Chapter 8: Expressing Past Time, Part 1

Exercise 8, p. 227.

1. I wasn't at home last night.
2. I was at the library.
3. Our teacher was sick yesterday.
4. He wasn't at school.
5. There was a substitute teacher.
6. She was friendly and funny.
7. Many students were absent.
8. They weren't at school for several days.
9. My friends and I were nervous on the first day of school.
10. You weren't nervous.

Exercise 19, p. 234.

A soccer coach

1. Jeremy works as a soccer coach.
2. His team plays many games.
3. His team played in a tournament.
4. Yesterday, they scored five goals.
5. Jeremy helped the players a lot.
6. They learned about the other team.
7. They watched movies of the other team.
8. The players like Jeremy.
9. All year, they worked very hard.
10. Every practice, each player works very hard.

Exercise 25, p. 238.

Part I.

1. What day was it two days ago?
2. What day was it five days ago?
3. What day was it yesterday?
4. What month was it last month?
5. What year was it ten years ago?
6. What year was it last year?
7. What year was it one year ago?

Part II.

1. What time was it one hour ago?
2. What time was it five minutes ago?
3. What time was it one minute ago?

Exercise 30, p. 242.

1. I ate . . .
2. We sat . . .
3. They came . . .
4. She had . . .
5. He got . . .
6. I stood . . .

Exercise 40, p. 248.

1. Did we do well on the test?
2. Did you finish the assignment?
3. Did it make sense?
4. Did I answer your question?
5. Did they need more help?
6. Did he understand the homework?
7. Did she explain the project?
8. Did they complete the project?
9. Did you do well?
10. Did she pass the class?

Exercise 42, p. 249.

Part I.

1. Did you see the news this morning?
2. A: Jim called.
   B: Did he leave a message?
3. A: Julia called.
   B: Did she leave a message?
4. Did it rain yesterday?
5. A: The kids are watching TV.
   B: Did they finish their homework?
6. My keys aren't here. Did I leave them in the car?

Part II.

1. Did you finish the homework assignment?
2. Did it take a long time?
3. Did you hear my question?
4. Did they hear my question?
5. Did I speak loud enough?
6. Did he understand the information?
7. Did she understand the information?
8. Did you want more help?
9. Did I explain it okay?
10. Did he do a good job?

Exercise 48, p. 253.

1. She caught . . .
2. They drove . . .
3. We read . . .
4. I rode . . .
5. He bought . . .
6. We ran . . .

Exercise 54, p. 257.

A doctor's appointment

I woke up with a headache this morning. I took some medicine and went back to bed. I slept all day. The phone rang. I heard it, but I was very tired. I didn't answer it. I listened to the answering machine. It was the doctor's office. The nurse said I missed my appointment. Now my headache is really bad!

Exercise 59, p. 260.

A wedding ring

My mother called me early this morning. She had wonderful news for me. She had my wedding ring. I lost it last year during a party at her house. She told me she was outside in her vegetable garden with her dog. The dog found my ring under some vegetables. My mom said she immediately put it on her finger and wore it. She didn't want to lose it. I was so happy. I hung up the phone and began to laugh and cry at the same time.

Let's Talk: Answers

Chapter 3, Exercise 33, p. 75.

1. No. [They like to look for food at night.]
2. Yes.
3. Yes.
4. Yes.
5. Yes.
6. No. [Only female mosquitoes bite.]
7. Yes.

Chapter 3, Exercise 53, p. 88.

Name	Where does she/he live?	What does he/she do?	Where does she/he work?	What pets does he/she have?
ANTONIO	(on a boat)	catches fish	on his boat	a turtle
LENA	in a cabin in the mountains	(teaches skiing)	at a ski school	ten fish
KANE	in an apartment in the city	makes jewelry	(at a jewelry store)	three cats
LISA	in a beach cabin on an island	surfs and swims	has no job	(a snake)
JACK	in a house in the country	designs web pages	at home	a horse

Chapter 4, Exercise 18, p. 106.

PARTNER B

1

2

3

4

5

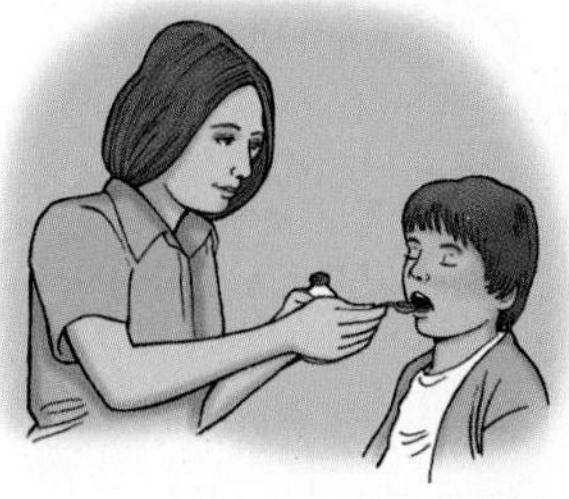

6

Chapter 5, Exercise 20, p. 136.

	a swimming pool	a beach	hiking trails	horses	ocean-view rooms
HOTEL 1	(yes)	yes	yes	no	yes
HOTEL 2	yes	(yes)	yes	yes	no
HOTEL 3	yes	yes	(yes)	yes	yes
HOTEL 4	yes	yes	no	(yes)	yes
HOTEL 5	no	yes	yes	yes	(yes)

Chapter 7, Exercise 17, p. 201.

Partner B

1. an apple
2. some apples
3. some childen
4. an old man
5. some men
6. a word
7. some music
8. some rice
9. an hour
10. an island

Partner A

11. an animal
12. some animals
13. some people
14. some fruit
15. an egg
16. a university
17. an uncle
18. some bananas
19. some bread
20. some vocabulary

Chapter 7, Exercise 26, p. 207.

Partner B's answers:

1. a. some food.
   b. an apple.
   c. a sandwich.
   d. a bowl of soup.
2. a. a glass of milk.
   b. some water.
   c. a cup of tea.
3. a. some medicine.
   b. an ambulance.
4. a. a coat.
   b. a hat.
   c. some warm clothes.
   d. some heat.
5. a. some sleep.
   b. a break.
   c. a relaxing vacation.

Partner A's answers:

6. a. a snack.
   b. some fruit.
   c. an orange.
   d. a piece of chicken.
7. a. some juice.
   b. a bottle of water.
   c. a glass of iced tea.
8. a. a doctor.
   b. some help.
9. a. some boots.
   b. a blanket.
   c. a hot bath.
   d. some gloves.
10. a. some strong coffee.
    b. a break.
    c. a vacation.
    d. a nap.

Index

A/an, 6, 8, 196 (*Look on pages 6, 8, and 196.*)	The numbers following the words listed in the index refer to page numbers in the text.
Capital letters, 159*fn.* (*Look at the footnote on page 159.*)	The letters *fn.* mean "footnote." Footnotes are at the bottom of a chart or the bottom of a page.

NOTES

NOTES

NOTES

NOTES

NOTES

NOTES

NOTES

AUDIO CD TRACKING LIST

CD 1	TRACK	EXERCISE
Introduction	1	
Chapter 1	2	Exercise 20, p. 11
	3	Exercise 24, p. 12
	4	Exercise 28, p. 14
	5	Exercise 41, p. 23
	6	Exercise 44, p. 25
Chapter 2	7	Exercise 4, p. 29
	8	Exercise 25, p. 43
	9	Exercise 36, p. 52
Chapter 3	10	Exercise 4, p. 61
	11	Exercise 15, p. 66
	12	Exercise 17, p. 68
	13	Exercise 24, p. 71
Chapter 4	14	Exercise 7, p. 99
	15	Exercise 24, p. 111
	16	Exercise 28, p. 114
Chapter 5	17	Exercise 6, p. 129
	18	Exercise 16, p. 134
	19	Exercise 32, p. 145
	20	Exercise 41, p. 151
Chapter 6	21	Exercise 18, p. 168
	22	Exercise 19, p. 169
	23	Exercise 22, p. 172
	24	Exercise 23, p. 173
	25	Exercise 40, p. 184
	26	Exercise 45, p. 186
Chapter 7	27	Exercise 10, p. 197
	28	Exercise 43, p. 216
	29	Exercise 45, p. 217
Chapter 8	30	Exercise 8, p. 227
	31	Exercise 19, p. 234
	32	Exercise 25, p. 238
	33	Exercise 30, p. 242
	34	Exercise 40, p. 248
	35	Exercise 42, p. 249
	36	Exercise 48, p. 253
	37	Exercise 54, p. 257
	38	Exercise 59, p. 260

CD 2	TRACK	EXERCISE
Chapter 9	1	Exercise 5, p. 267
	2	Exercise 7, p. 268
	3	Exercise 13, p. 271
	4	Exercise 19, p. 276
	5	Exercise 24, p. 279
	6	Exercise 28, p. 281
	7	Exercise 32, p. 283
	8	Exercise 51, p. 296
Chapter 10	9	Exercise 9, p. 308
	10	Exercise 11, p. 308
	11	Exercise 18, p. 312
	12	Exercise 25, p. 316
	13	Exercise 31, p. 319
	14	Exercise 35, p. 320
	15	Exercise 39, p. 323
	16	Exercise 40, p. 324
	17	Exercise 41, p. 324
	18	Exercise 43, p. 326
	19	Exercise 49, p. 330
Chapter 11	20	Exercise 10, p. 339
	21	Exercise 13, p. 341
	22	Exercise 26, p. 347
	23	Exercise 32, p. 351
	24	Exercise 39, p. 356
Chapter 12	25	Exercise 5, p. 363
	26	Exercise 6, p. 364
	27	Exercise 7, p. 364
	28	Exercise 11, p. 366
	29	Exercise 26, p. 375
	30	Exercise 32, p. 380
Chapter 13	31	Exercise 6, p. 387
	32	Exercise 12, p. 391
	33	Exercise 18, p. 395
	34	Exercise 36, p. 406
Chapter 14	35	Exercise 4, p. 414
	36	Exercise 15, p. 424
	37	Exercise 31, p. 434
	38	Exercise 40, p. 441
Chapter 15	39	Exercise 6, p. 448
	40	Exercise 14, p. 454
	41	Exercise 17, p. 459
	42	Exercise 27, p. 468
	43	Exercise 31, p. 471
	44	Exercise 40, p. 476
	45	Exercise 43, p. 478